8/8/87
96 84
3 75 in all

ECONOMIC GROWTH AND NEIGHBORHOOD DISCONTENT

SYSTEM BIAS IN THE URBAN RENEWAL PROGRAM OF ATLANTA

by CLARENCE N. STONE

The University of North Carolina Press
Chapel Hill

Copyright © 1976 by
The University of North Carolina Press
All rights reserved
Manufactured in the United States of America
Library of Congress Catalog Card Number 75-22274
ISBN 0-8078-1262-5

Library of Congress Cataloging in Publication Data

Stone, Clarence Nathan, 1935–
   Economic growth and neighborhood discontent.

   Bibliography: p.
   Includes index.
   1. Urban renewal—Atlanta.   I. Title.
HT177.A77S76   309.2'62'09758231   75-22274
ISBN 0-8078-1262-5

CONTENTS

MAPS

To the casual visitor Atlanta is Peachtree Center, the Omni, Regency Hyatt House, office buildings, restaurants, motels, Underground, and the Convention Center. This is the Atlanta of glamour and prosperity. It is the product of long-standing efforts, public and private, to promote economic growth. There is another Atlanta, the Atlanta of Buttermilk Bottom, Vine City, Lightning, Peoplestown, Cabbagetown, Mechanics-ville, and Blue Heaven. These are colorful names for neighborhoods whose history has been one of neglect and hardship. The present study is an analysis of the political relationship between these two Atlantas. It is concerned with power, group conflict, and the formation of public policy. Research was addressed to the question of how and why, in the urban renewal program of Atlanta, the neglect of poor neighborhoods occurred. The answer seems to lie within the city's politics, and the search for an explanation is an invitation to consider once again the subject of community power.

People with unmet social and economic needs can be expected to use the political process as one way of improving their life circumstances. But, as the residents of Atlanta's poor neighborhoods learned, efforts to use the political process are not necessarily successful—even if dissatisfaction is intense and discontent is widespread. The case of the two Atlantas offers a full opportunity to ponder the problems encountered by groups trying to shape policy in ways that accord with their strongly felt wants. The objectives of my analysis are first to show that community power can be studied in a way that allows the indirect and less overt aspects of group influence to be examined, and second to provide a set of interrelated propositions about how power is exercised that take into account increasingly evident shortcomings in pluralist theory.

The present study is not an attempt to determine whether or not the neglect of poor neighborhoods was a worthwhile and necessary price to pay for downtown prosperity. This is a question perhaps not completely answerable or, at least, not answerable on the basis of an analysis of the political aspects of urban renewal. The study that follows is therefore not an attempt to answer all questions that might be raised about urban renewal. But it is, without apology, a study that was undertaken in the belief that it should be possible for our cities to be renewed without engendering either neighborhood despair or discontent. Regrettably, Atlanta's politics has led the city to try only a restricted range of strategies of public action and resource deployment. The Atlanta experience has thus been a limited one. However, Atlanta has always been a community of change and forward vision, and so it continues to be. Perhaps, then, the future will not be a repeat of the past. I can only hope that my analysis of a portion of Atlanta's past will in some way contribute to a future in which the city's neighborhoods can enjoy an ample share of the prosperity, if not the glamour, now found in the central business district.

Writing a book is an enterprise that is peculiarly individual and collective at the same time. The author alone experiences the gratification and the frustration that come with putting a personal imprint on human knowledge. The completed work bears a mark that is unmistakably the author's. Yet from its inception as an idea to its completion, a book goes through a process that depends upon the help and guidance of many people. That I do not here mention individually all who have assisted me does not mean that they are unappreciated, nor does it mean that their assistance has been small in scale.

I am especially grateful to the people whom I interviewed during the field research for this volume. Assurances of anonymity prevent my naming them, but my debt to them is nonetheless great. It is remarkable that the vast majority of such a large number of people talked openly and gave freely of their time to a total stranger who came to them with what may have seemed an abstruse interest in research. That some of the most fruitful interviews bridged gaps of race, class, and age makes the experience all the more remarkable.

I wish also to express appreciation to a number of persons who read all or portions of the manuscript and offered many invaluable comments: Robert Alperin, Madelyn Bonsignore, Eleanor Feldbaum, Floyd Hunter, Hugh LeBlanc, Frank Munger, Joyce Munns, and Mancur Olson. They performed well that difficult task of constructive criticism. The shortcomings that remain are the fault of the author, not of the advice he received.

To the late Franklin L. Burdette, who was Director of the Bureau of Governmental Research at the University of Maryland, I am indebted in many ways. He generously made the resources of the bureau available to me, and provided words of encouragement. His suggestions about writing style and manuscript organization invariably proved helpful. Most of all I value the wise counsel he offered and the example of undeviating commitment to scholarship he provided.

My thanks are also due Malcolm M. MacDonald, Sandra Eisdorfer, and other members of the staff of The University of North Carolina Press. They have proven that efficiency and amiability can coexist, and I fully appreciate both.

Laura Poracsky merits my special gratitude for the patience as well as the skill with which she did the cartographic work.

I also most gratefully acknowledge financial assistance from the General Research Board of the University of Maryland.

Finally, my greatest appreciation is to my family. They have made the joys of writing more enriching and the anxieties more tolerable. My children, Mark and Valerie, have been helpful and understanding far beyond their years. My wife, Mary, has given selflessly of her time and talent at every step from the preliminary research to the compilation of the index. She has been a steadfast guardian of the English language through many readings of the manuscript. But most important of all, in authorship as in so many other experiences, she has been the mainstay of my spirits. To her, I dedicate this book.

CACUR	Citizens Advisory Committee for Urban Renewal
CAIA	Central Atlanta Improvement Association
CBD	Central Business District
CRP	Community Renewal Program
FHA	Federal Housing Administration
GNRP	General Neighborhood Renewal Program
HRC	Housing Resources Committee
HUD	U.S. Department of Housing and Urban Development
NAACP	National Association for the Advancement of Colored People
NDP	Neighborhood Development Program
PAC	Project Area Committee
SNCC	Student Nonviolent Coordinating Committee

PART 1

THEORY, METHOD, AND CONTEXT

During the 1960s, particularly under the leadership of Mayor Ivan Allen, Atlanta made a bid to become urban America's foremost success story. In "the city too busy to hate," the most spectacular accomplishments have been economic; the most visible signs of achievement are in the central business district. Here a profusion of new office buildings and luxury hotels attests to Atlanta's emergence as a modern metropolis.

Over the past two decades the commercial center of the city has expanded outward and upward. Much of the land and the impetus for the enlarged and rejuvenated central business district has come from the city's urban renewal program. Sites for civic facilities, expansion room for medical and educational institutions, and land for commercial redevelopment have all been provided under the aegis of urban renewal. Although some of the city's most imposing commercial structures have been built under purely private auspices, downtown revitalization was conceived and executed as a joint public-private venture. For example, the city constructed a new civic center and exhibition hall on land acquired through urban renewal. The civic center, in turn, encouraged the private development of nearby hotels. And, at a time when many communities built sports facilities in outlying areas, city officials in Atlanta promoted the construction of a new stadium on a renewal site just south of the central business district.

There is, however, another side to the story of Atlanta's economic success and another side to Atlanta's experiences with urban renewal. To some segments of the community, the new stadium and the civic center were a symbol of misplaced priorities. During the time that redevelopment activity was at its height, the city pursued a policy under which one-seventh of its population was displaced by government action.[1] Some neighborhoods were simply demolished to make way for commercial and other forms of nonresidential redevelopment. Relocation activities drastically affected other neighborhoods. Inaction as well as action by the city influenced the quality of residential life. Neglect, overcrowding, and unaverted racial tensions changed the character of many areas.

When Atlanta first initiated a redevelopment program in 1950, non-affluent neighborhoods lacked adequate facilities. Twenty years later, that lack had been studied, documented, and lamented, but not corrected. Moreover, housing conditions and neighborhood facilities were not merely items covered in planning reports. They were matters of urgent concern to many individuals and organizations.. Throughout the time that Atlanta was considering, designing, and executing a renewal program, blacks and some white neighborhood groups made known their unhappiness with city efforts. And, in the years between 1965 and 1970, low-income citizens voiced their interests with special insistency. They called on the city to correct past inequities by inaugurating programs to improve housing and neighborhood conditions. In response to the discontent of low-income neighborhoods, the news media gave a public airing to several important policy issues, and a variety of individuals raised questions about urban redevelopment and its overall impact on the city. The promotion of commercial prosperity was explicitly challenged as the prime objective of city policy.

Housing and neighborhood conditions thus became matters of wide concern during the 1960s just as business district vitality and economic growth had been earlier. The parallel can be extended: an initially reluctant city hall in the 1960s was brought to the point of acting to improve housing and neighborhood conditions for low-income families just as city hall in the 1950s had been drawn into broad-gauge action to promote commercial redevelopment in and around the central business district. The parallel carries no further, however. Unlike the effort that began in the 1950s, that of the 1960s faltered.

The mayor had publicly committed himself to the elimination of slums and the rehousing of slum dwellers in standard residences. He established a Housing Resources Committee to oversee a "crash program" of building new low- and moderate-income housing, he worked hard for Atlanta's inclusion in the Model Cities program, and he lent his strong support to newly specified renewal priorities that called for the improvement of substandard neighborhoods. However, despite his proven reputation for a willingness to act in the face of public opposition, the mayor failed to follow through with actions deemed necessary to carry his slum-elimination program forward. Some housing was built, but not in the numbers or in the locations desired by low-income citizens. Neighborhood renewal, including the new Model Cities program, failed to exemplify city concern for the welfare of its less-advantaged citizens. Instead, neighborhood renewal became a source of further disillusionment among the poor of Atlanta.[2] Atlanta's urban renewal program thus poses sharply the question of why the policy backed by business was sustained and substantially succeeded, while the neighborhood effort faded and fell far short of widely held expectations.

Possible Determinants of Policy Direction

The attempt to understand how public policies take shape can be made at various levels. Research, for example, might focus on the immediate circumstances surrounding a given policy. Attention could be fixed on the specific features of program administration, such as the complexity of the bureaucratic process,[3] or on the admixture of public and private efforts that characterize the policy.[4] A researcher might also concentrate on the personalities involved; the temptation is always strong to lend human interest to an otherwise abstract analysis by describing the dynamics of mayoral leadership[5] or the entrepreneurial skills of prominent administrative officials.[6] The quest to understand how policy is formed can, however, be conducted at a very different level. The researcher can try to penetrate the immediate circumstances of program administration and look beyond the particular political figures. He may look for broad and impersonal forces not fully evident in the surface flow of events, forces that constrain individual actions and give direction to the decisions of policymaking institutions.

The examination of Atlanta's urban renewal program that follows is such an attempt to penetrate the surface flow of events. There is strong evidence that, while personalities are important and administrative details have their impact, major questions of policy choice are resolved over time by underlying political, economic, and social forces. New leaders are easily made and old leaders undone as circumstances change. Administrative details are hardly more than bureaucratic shoals through which well-supported policies can readily be navigated.

The explanation of underlying forces might take one of several forms. Policy choices might, for example, be explained in terms of popular sentiment, that is, as a matter of prevailing public opinion or of dominant community values.[7] Economic growth, it could be argued, was successful in Atlanta because it was a policy that was consistent with the community belief system and had popular support. Neighborhood renewal, by contrast, conceivably could have been weakened by a lack of popular support and by a low level of legitimacy within the tenets of the community's system of beliefs. The matter is important enough to receive further discussion later, but for now, two observations might be made.

First of all, with specific reference to Atlanta, there is little concrete evidence to suggest that economic growth was a more popular policy than neighborhood renewal. Various attempts to survey opinion consistently indicated that Atlantans regarded housing, not economic growth, as the city's most serious problem. More importantly, the specific actions to promote economic growth were, as the case history of renewal in Atlanta shows, the targets of at least as much overt opposition as were the various proposals to renew neighborhoods and rehouse slum dwellers.

Second, belief systems tend to be vague and diffuse, and, because they are loosely structured, belief systems exert no well-defined pressures.[8] Even on specific actions, the intensity and stability of public sentiment is notoriously hard to measure and assess. As a consequence, officials exercise great latitude in interpreting public feeling. In a given community, officials very likely are predisposed more toward some readings of public opinion than toward others.

Nor should we overlook the fact that officials shape opinion as well as respond to it. With specific reference to Atlanta, there was no indication that popular opinion dictated renewal policy. Indeed, as we shall see later, officials often seemed to be maneuvering around rather than following public opinion.

The socioeconomic environment might also be analyzed as a determinant of policy direction. Some writers have argued that public policy is best explained by the level of economic development or the degree of social complexity that characterizes a given community.[9] The environment presumably generates pressures that must be responded to and accommodated in the policies of communities. As the environment varies, the pressures and the responses vary.[10] Yet the attempt to explain public policy choices (policy outputs, in systems terminology) through environmental factors alone has a serious shortcoming. Not all demands become policies. Some do, others do not, and still others are substantially modified when they are acted upon by governmental agencies.[11] Limited resources and conflicting objectives require that choices be made.

Policy results, not from the mere presence of demands, but from the decisions of public officials who choose variously to alter, reject, or assent to demands. Thus, while the socioeconomic environment is a generator of demands for public action, this environment does not necessarily generate consistent demands. Demands give rise to counter-demands, and choice making is intertwined with the forces of political struggle. The environmental explanation can account for the presence of demands; it cannot account for choices between competing sets of demands. Clearly, pressures emanating from the socioeconomic environment must in some way be transformed into policy responses, and that transformation involves choices between alternative courses of action. Predictably, some of the recent comparative community research suggests that political-structure and political-process variables are important as intervening factors in the chain of causation that leads from environment to policy.[12]

Although it is unquestionably important to study the socioeconomic environment as a source of demands for public action, it is necessary to look elsewhere for an explanation of how decision makers make choices between competing demands. Specifically, with regard to Atlanta's urban renewal program, why was economic growth fostered in the face of opposition, while neighborhood and housing improvements came eventually to falter despite a long history of vocal support? The answer lies in the conflicting interests of contending groups. Economic growth had the backing of a politically active and united business community; neighborhood renewal and rehousing efforts had strong if less consistent support from other groups. Almost certainly, urban renewal policy in Atlanta moved in response to the interplay among the city's various political forces. It is therefore a principal assumption of the present study that group influence and community power are major factors in the making of public policy. The socioeconomic environment may be a generator of demands. Community sentiment may set some vague boundaries of popular tolerance. But the formation of policy, in a context of competing group interests, is fully understandable only by analyzing the processes by which community power is exercised.

Purpose of This Study

In part the present study is a case analysis of group influence as it bears on the process of choosing between competing policy alternatives. The analysis focuses on one policy (urban renewal) in one city (Atlanta) over a twenty-year period (1950–70). It is hoped that the reader finds the case study worthwhile in itself. Atlanta is an important city. Urban renewal in the post-World War II period has been a major weapon in the attack on central city decay.

The principal aim, however, has been for something more than just a case analysis. Studies of single cities are academically useful mainly to the extent that they serve to increase our general understanding. Case analyses by their very nature cannot be conclusive and must therefore be tentative steps in the total research process. Nevertheless, they can and should attempt to mark out theoretically significant lines of inquiry. By taking a more intensive look at a single case, the researcher can help disentangle threads of inquiry and can contribute to the overall scholarly enterprise. After all, while comparative research is much needed, comparative studies themselves will be fruitful only if they have meaningful theoretical guidelines to follow.

In the instance of studies of local politics and public policy, the time would seem to be right for reformulating some of the basic propositions about power and its exercise. The need for revision is, in part, a matter of a continuing effort to refine our knowledge and bring it up to date. Revision is a constant process. Floyd Hunter's *Community Power Structure*[13] was a substantial departure in method and form of analysis from the earlier work of Robert and Helen Lynd.[14] Moreover, whereas the Lynds had found a business-control system culminating in a single family, Hunter, at a later time and in a different setting, found an interlocking network of individuals and institutions in which economic power was the dominant force. And, whereas the Lynds had found that men of wealth had little interest in the local political arena beyond a desire to keep politics innocuous, Hunter discovered that the community's business leadership was very much concerned with manipulating the governmental sector and enlisting the support of governmental officials in the pursuit of business objectives. Pluralists,[15] a school of political scientists eager to attack the notion that a modern community could be run by a single and covert elite,[16] argued on the basis of their research that elected officials occupy a prominent and autonomous place in the making of policy decisions. As if to prove that political theory is guided by a dialectical force, pluralism, in turn, has been followed by a new school of dissenters, also in the main political scientists. Building on some of Floyd Hunter's earlier ideas about "gaps in the power arc" and about the capacity of powerful groups to suppress issues, these critics of pluralism have called for the study of nondecision making— that is, the study of the processes by which issues are kept latent, stifled, or thwarted.[17] Nondecision making has, however, proved to be a difficult concept to work with, one that lends itself more easily to a critique of pluralism than to the development of a systematic alternative.

The move toward a revised theory of community power and public policy formation is more than simply another step in the orderly succession of ideas. Because the sixties were both intellectually and socially turbulent, the times have added a special impetus to the need for reformulation. New perspectives and new programs have emerged. The issue of how the interests of have-not groups are to be represented has moved to the forefront, and pluralism in particular has come in for sharp questioning. Protests and other political tactics available to nonpowerful groups have become an important subject for study and research.[18] Power has come to be viewed, as one writer expressed it, "from the bottom up."[19]

Though there is a substantial need to rethink problems of power, policy, and interest representation, few academicians appear willing to attempt to develop a thoroughgoing alternative to pluralism.[20] Pluralism is a broad-gauge theory, deeply embedded in the political science discipline. It is a theory that developed in stages and is likely to be replaced only through a succession of revisions, each adding to the one before.

This study offers one such revision in the form of an alternative theory of group influence. It is not a total rejection of pluralism. On the contrary, it takes pluralist theory as a point of departure for reformulating propositions about community power and group influence. The term "revisionist theory" should in fact serve as a reminder that pluralism is a useful starting point, not a point to be avoided, in working out for political science a more fully explanatory theory of community power.

There is a certain appropriateness in the fact that Atlanta, the "regional city" studied in Hunter's *Community Power Structure*, has been the site for the research on which this study is based. The revised theory offered here shares with Hunter's work the view that, although power relations are not static or fixed, they are structured and do not change in kaleidoscopic fashion with each new issue. Of course, relationships do vary from policy area to policy area. Nevertheless, as Hunter argued, the political and governmental aspects of community power are interwoven with the social and economic aspects, and their interrelationships provide a relatively stable context in which decisions are made and policy is shaped.

This study is not intended, however, to be an updating of Hunter's work. It employs a different methodology and, confining itself to one area of public policy, has a different scope of analysis. As is the case in the research of Robert Dahl and other pluralists, political and governmental institutions are treated as primary phenomena. Particular attention is given herein to public officials, the part they play in policy formation, and the question of how in their capacities as decision makers they respond to various segments of the community.

The next chapter represents my effort to bring together a coherent alternative to pluralist theory and methodology. While the effort is my own, it stems from the work of several other writers. And, while the effort is presented as an alternative to pluralism, it owes a special debt to those who are criticized. In a very real sense, the revisionist theory offered here is a synthesis—drawn together by my research on Atlanta's urban renewal program but derived in good measure from the labors of earlier students of community politics. Finally, none of the criticism leveled against the pluralist approach should obscure the fact that Robert Dahl joined the analysis of local politics with the study of political theory, to the benefit of both.

2. PLURALISM, REVISIONISM, AND THE POLICY PROCESS

The community power debate has been chronicled often enough without its having to be detailed here. But there is still a need to clarify theoretical alternatives. This chapter is an attempt to set forth the major elements in a revisionist approach to the study of group influence in public policy formation. It begins, however, with a brief look at pluralism so that the revised theory and research method offered here will be put into perspective. After that, various elements of revisionist theory are examined: electoral competition and the distribution of political resources, interest advocacy and conflict management by public officials, system bias as a concept, and positional advantage as a source of system bias. The chapter then contrasts pluralist and revisionist conceptions of power and concludes with a discussion of demand conversion as a revisionist focus of analysis.

Pluralism and the "Rule of Minority Satisfaction"

Although pluralism can be described and defined in many ways, there is a central core of ideas that relates specifically to group influence and policy formation. Robert Dahl and his students have developed a closely reasoned explanation of this process.[1] In the main, the pluralist argument is that influence is both dispersed and specialized, and the dispersion and specialization give rise to a process variously described as "mutual adjustment," "minorities rule," or the "rule of minority satisfaction." Let us first look at dispersion.

Influence, pluralists believe, is dispersed because there are many bases from which it can be exerted, and those groups lacking in one resource are likely to possess other means to make their will felt. Although pluralists acknowledge that there are inequalities, they maintain that tendencies toward inequality are counterbalanced by the ballot box. As they see it, competition for public office places leaders in the position of having to seek support. More than any other factor, then, universal suffrage is seen as an equalizing force. It gives officials a strong incentive to try to maximize their popular appeal, and popularity is a base of influence independent of other factors such as wealth and social standing. Therefore no group is without some strength and inequalities are noncumulative. In pluralist theory, electoral competition is thus the central force in shaping the representative role of public officials.

As pluralists see it, electoral competition makes public officials broadly representative of the people they govern. Officials, according to the pluralist view, are without "well-defined class interest"[2] and are accessible to a wide spectrum of groups. In the words of Robert Dahl, "elected leaders keep the real or imagined preferences of constituents in mind in deciding what policies to adopt or reject."[3] Although some officials are acknowledged to be more active and creative than others, all elected leaders are conceived of as performing mainly a brokerage role. They mediate differences between contending interests; they bargain and negotiate; but they always operate within the bounds of widely shared values and goals and with a great concern for the need to reach mutual accommodations among parties in disagreement.

Influence, pluralists believe, is not only dispersed, it is also specialized. Specialization follows the pattern of interest and activity. Groups become active on those issues in which they have a substantial stake. Thus, while most citizens are indifferent to public affairs and prefer to use their time and energy on other pursuits, they can, if provoked, become active and mobilize their resources for political purposes. Political leaders understand this phenomenon, "slack in the system" (in pluralist terminology), and govern accordingly. Top-level public officials, Edward Banfield observed, "believe that they ought to be responsive to the wishes of the public and especially to the wishes of that part of the public which has the most at stake in the particular matter."[4]

Dispersion of power and specialization of influence, pluralists thus believe, lead to a form of governance characterized by mutual adjustment and accommodation. Elected political leaders, in pluralist theory, promote policies that are acceptable to the groups that have the most substantial interests in them. Aaron Wildavsky coined the very apt phrase, "the rule of minority satisfaction," to describe the type of group influence he believed to characterize the pluralist systems. Wildavsky had in mind adjustments in public policy that take into account how strong group feelings are about the issues that arise. As he explained, it is minority influence in the sense that those who feel intensely about an issue, often less than a majority, "receive consideration and some satisfaction from the outcome."[5] Even in cases where the conflict lies between two minorities, there is still presumed to be a tendency toward compromise and mutual accommodation. Specialization of influence as represented by "the rule of minority satisfaction," Wildavsky argued, "serves the public interest in contributing to a political system which comes closer than others to meeting the widest range of preferences."[6]

The revisionist theory to be set forth here provides an alternative view about community governance. Specifically, it will be argued that electoral competition does not necessarily offset imbalances in the distribution of political resources and that some groups are better positioned than others to further their interests through the political system. The "rule of minority satisfaction" may therefore be thwarted. Equally affected and concerned groups are not always equally accommodated, and cumulative biases in policy formation may develop. To explain why pluralist patterns do not necessarily hold, it is essential to consider some revisionist thoughts on electoral competition and the distribution of political resources, the policy role of public officials, and the nature and origins of system bias.

Revisionism: Electoral Competition and the Distribution of Political Resources

Most political scientists would agree that democracy is a system of government in which leaders compete for public support in order to gain electoral office. On the consequences of that competition, there is much less agreement. The pluralist view, as we have seen, is that because public officials are caught up in a never-ending search for constituent support, they are responsive to active discontent and even anticipated discontent. Presumably, leaders can bring about policy innovation only if there is latent, and perhaps even active, support for the measures proposed. The pluralist view is therefore that officials are closely accountable for their actions. But if it turns out to be the case that electoral accountability is loose or uncertain, then a new perspective is called for with regard to power, its distribution, and its exercise. Revisionism thus rests on a view of electoral competition that differs in important ways from the pluralist view.

In one respect, it must be accepted as an article of common sense that, unless a major policy falls within the bounds of acceptability to a substantial segment of the community, city officials could not continue to be reelected. But this common sense view rests on the assumption that the policy, *as a policy*, is visible to the public. It may be visible, however, only if an *electorally* active group makes it so. Competition for public office does not guarantee that every major policy will be a point of open contention. Politicians are notoriously cautious about bringing up new issues. Moreover, a given policy question may go uncontested because electorally active groups are oriented toward other issues. It is simply not the case that contestants for public office are so detached in attitude that they will exploit any and every issue.

Elections do not appear, in fact, to be contests in which all sources of discontent are equally likely to find an outlet. Rather, elections—local ones especially—offer constituents highly structured and hence restricted alternatives.[7] This is not to say that the local electoral process is stagnant and unchanging, but it is to argue that in the short run electoral cleavage has great stability.[8] As a result, some issues may simply not thrive at election time.[9] E. E. Schattschneider has aptly observed that the presence of one cleavage may inhibit the development of another. Alliances become established and a pattern of contacts and procedures becomes fixed. Thus, Schattschneider argued, "a radical shift of alignment becomes possible only at the cost of a change in the relations and priorities of all the contestants." And he added, "The new conflict can become dominant only if the old one is subordinated, or obscured, or forgotten, or loses its capacity to excite the contestants or becomes irrelevant."[10]

Of course, any single issue may emerge as a point of electoral contention. A controversial decision can become a cause célèbre and can serve as a focal point for constituent dissatisfaction. Yet the impact of this discontent may be temporary, and electoral competition may revert to an earlier pattern of cleavage as soon as the controversial decision loses salience. It is easier to mobilize discontent for a given election campaign than it is to restructure electoral competition around a whole set of issues and candidates. Such restructuring requires a stable and organized means for recruiting candidates and for supporting their campaigns.

Popular discontent does not automatically convert into either the incentives to organize or the kinds of resources that are necessary to sustain an electoral thrust. Candidates are greatly dependent upon established organizations and traditional issue appeals. The former are often necessary to reach voters, the latter to activate them. If neither established organizations nor traditional appeals are to be used, then very substantial resources are required to put together an effective campaign mechanism.

Political realignment is most likely to occur over a long time span and in response to community-wide alterations in social composition, economic makeup, or value orientation. In short, although electoral competition is not fixed permanently around a single cleavage, change does not come about easily. Electoral cleavage alters more in response to long-range modifications in community structure than in response to popular dissatisfaction with policy directions (which are often ill defined and little discussed). The electoral process is therefore a cumbersome means by which to exert influence on policymaking, and it is cumbersome because the formation of policy is itself a complex process.

The pluralist theory of electoral accountability assumes that a few decisions of high salience serve as adequate indicators of policy direction. When a policy direction is being established or challenged, the outcome—pluralists believe—hinges on one or more key issues. Election contests, referenda, and spontaneous community controversies presumably center on a few basic policy questions, and these manifestations of "controversy and conflict" provide a means by which popular control is exercised over officials.[11]

Policies usually result, however, not from a few key decisions but rather from a series of decisions, many of which appear to be unimportant when viewed singly. Policies are complex phenomena, and the ways in which they come to take shape are intricate. Decisions at one stage may be negated by the absence of follow-through actions at a subsequent stage. Conversely, proposals rejected at one point may be revived, altered, or even replaced by substitute proposals that still enable objectives to be realized. Policy success, then, is rarely a matter of winning spectacular battles. Rather, it is more akin to prevailing in a war of attrition. Cumulative results give shape to policies. But the populace is seldom in a position to observe the full scope of official conduct and to weigh the cumulative results of governmental actions.

Information is scarce. Much policymaking is technical and, to the layman, obscure. Knowledge about priorities, alternative courses of action, and the details of policy implementation are not available on a mass basis. Only those intimately involved in official decision making are in a position to be well informed. While some policy questions appear in a highly dramatic and focused form, seemingly agreed-upon courses of action have a way of being transformed by subsequent events and circumstances. In the policy struggle, those groups fare best which are able to acquire detailed information and to maintain an unrelenting pressure on behalf of their interests. Constituents qua constituents do not operate from an extraordinarily strong power base. Consequently, inequalities in the distribution of other resources are not necessarily counterbalanced by numbers at the ballot box.

A revisionist view of official responsiveness to constituency pressures thus contains the following elements: (1) electoral competition tends to be structured around a single dominant cleavage (or possibly a few major cleavages); (2) particular controversies, not necessarily related to the dominant cleavage, may occasionally penetrate election campaigns; (3) however, the outcomes of particular controversies do not necessarily determine policy direction because public knowledge of the decision-making process is imperfect, and on many matters constituency pressure is not durable over time; (4) therefore, public officials may be able to promote a line of policy that does not have a broad base of public support and may even have substantial opposition.

Revisionism: Interest Advocacy and Conflict Management

Implicit in the revisionist argument above is the view that public officials are not necessarily neutral participants in the policy process. Indeed, the assumption is made that, under some conditions, officials may be strong partisans of one group or another. Of course, no one would argue that officials can be completely neutral in the process of decision making. Conflicting demands cannot be balanced with precision. Yet there are gradations of partisanship. As Oliver Williams and Charles Adrian have maintained:

. . . it is possible to conceive a scale along which governments can be plotted. On one end of the scale would be governments basically committed to a particular segment of the citizenry, and problems are solved according to the goals of that segment. On the other end of the scale government would approach neutrality. The machinery of government would remain basically uncommitted over the long run. Various segments of the citizenry would win occasional skirmishes, but no group would generally prevail.[12]

In contrast to the pluralist position that officials are relatively uncommitted to any one segment of the population, the argument here is that officials, even those who hold major elected posts, may not serve as impartial arbiters of group conflict. They may play a role other than that of neutral broker. In short, they may be consistent advocates of some interests at the expense of others. And, to the extent that public officials perform an interest-advocacy role, policymaking may not be a matter of bargaining, negotiation, and mutual accommodation. It may be a process in which the not-so-fine arts of deception and manipulation are practiced in order to manage conflict on behalf of certain favored groups and objectives. Conciliation and compromise are, after all, only one pair of tactics for confining conflict. Machiavelli did not earn his reputation as the first modern political scientist by ignoring the devious aspects of governorship. As the pluralists themselves have argued so persuasively, political skills are not broadly dispersed but are concentrated heavily among those whose livelihood is public affairs.[13]

No one is in a better position to develop and use the skills of conflict management than are public officials. They, more than any other group, can manipulate the timing and the scope of issues and give direction to conflict. To be sure, public officials do not necessarily act in concert, nor do they, even as a collectivity, necessarily act in alliance with only one or a few interests. Nevertheless, under given conditions they *may* act in concert, and they *may* act on behalf of some interests at the expense of others.

Viewed in the manner suggested above, conflict is not a means whereby officials are controlled and held accountable. Rather it is something that leaders shape, confine, and divert as they go about their business of policy formation. The outcome of a key issue is nothing more than a tactical point from which skilled leaders resume their efforts to achieve desired policy goals. Public office is thus a position of great strategic importance in contests among competing group interests.

Obviously public officials are more than partisans of a few favored groups. Office holding generates a perspective of its own and cannot be totally insulated from public pressures. Yet, when all of that is said, officials may have predispositions and preferences that make them stronger and more active proponents of some interests than of others. To the degree that these predispositions and preferences are not neutralized by external pressures, they constitute a potentially important element in the shaping of public policy, and contending interest groups understand this fact. While they are willing to generate external pressures, most groups much prefer to have friends and allies in public office. A basic fact of political life is that officeholders are not equally accessible to all groups, and some important political advantages and disadvantages flow from this fact of unequal accessibility.

Again, to clarify what is at issue in the present discussion, no one would maintain that public officials are purely neutral or that they are completely partisan. But tendencies in one direction or the other have a profound impact on the policy process. To argue, as has been the case here, that under some circumstances public officials may serve as interest advocates is to urge a theoretical view much at odds with the pluralist view. It is to suggest that competing interest groups may enjoy positional advantages and disadvantages in the form of the predispositions and the consequent behavior of public officials. Positional advantages may be cumulative for some interests, and, similarly, disadvantages may be cumulative for other interests. Under these circumstances, policy would not correspond to the "rule of minority satisfaction" but would move in the direction favored by advantaged groups. One interest may prevail consistently, although occasional skirmishes would still be won by competing groups.

Revisionism: The Concept of System Bias

The pluralist theory of community power is a plausible one, perhaps offering an apt explanation for some areas of policy formation. However, it should be evident by now that the "rule of minority satisfaction" does not explain all aspects of policy formation. Urban renewal policy in Atlanta, for example, was far more accommodating to the city's business interest than to the proponents of housing and neighborhood improvements—even though the latter groups were both vocal about their dissatisfactions and active in their attempts to change policy. Some groups are clearly more successful in gaining policy objectives than others. The revisionist theory offered here is an attempt to provide one explanation for these different rates of policy success.

To be sure, there are long-standing arguments that such attributes as wealth, esteem, and organizational superiority can be used to establish dominance and to perpetuate established power relationships. Community politics has become too complex, however, for power to be explained as a matter of dominance and subordination. Further, the elitist/pluralist dichotomy, we have come to realize, is an intellectual dead end. We need to get away from the question of whether power is exercised by one group or many. It is, of course, exercised by many groups. But to say that power is not monopolized by a single elite is not the same as saying that lines of influence are fluid or that communities are controlled by "shifting coalitions of participants drawn from all areas of community life."[14] It is this very fluidity and changeability of power relations that needs to be reconsidered.

Policy is made and power is exercised within a structured set of relationships. These relationships are neither neutral nor easily changed. They confer advantages and disadvantages on various groups in the local community in the form of the preferences and predispositions of leading local officials.

The major elements that give shape to a locality's political system—the political mores, the institutional structure, the decision-making procedures, and the electoral practices—help determine who is involved, on what basis, and with which salient concerns. To the degree that system characteristics work consistently to favor the selection of top level officials with predilections to facilitate actions on some policy measures and impede actions on others, then the system may be said to be biased. In that they confer strategic advantages and disadvantages, system characteristics are themselves elements in any community power equation.

The general notion of bias (that is, the notion that groups may enjoy strategic advantages or suffer disadvantages in their efforts to influence the course of public policy) has not escaped the attention of pluralist writers. However, these writers have argued that biases are crosscutting and, like political inequalities, noncumulative. Pluralists have specifically disputed the view that biases "operate systematically and consistently to the benefit of certain persons and groups at the expense of others."[15]

The idea of *system bias*, as it is used here, assumes some identifiable point of impartiality or neutrality from which the bias is a departure. Pluralist theory provides us with such a departure point. As argued above, pluralist writers depict politicians, who are selected in a competitive electoral process, as relatively neutral mediators of group conflict. According to pluralist theory, democratic politicians make their calculations, not just on the basis of numbers, but on the basis of numbers and *intensity of interest*.[16] Differences in the intensity of interests provide the foundation for the "rule of minority satisfaction."

The view set forth here is that, if officials disregard the "rule of minority satisfaction" and pursue policies that do not take into account the interests of immediately affected and concerned groups, then we may speak of a system bias; and such a departure from the "neutral" workings of democratic politics invites attention to the circumstances that give rise to it.

It is further argued here that "neutrality" may break down, first of all because official behavior is only sporadically visible and loosely accountable to the electorate, and secondly because some groups are better positioned than others to further their interests through the political system. In short, a city's governmental machinery may be influenced to operate *consistently* in favor of some interests at the expense of others—even if the other interests are a sizable and active political force.

Revisionism: Positional Advantage as the Source of System Bias

In the framework of the argument developed here, system bias comes about through positional advantages and disadvantages. A positional advantage is simply the predisposition on the part of public officials to favor the interests of a given group more strongly and actively than the interests of other groups.[17] A positional disadvantage is the absence of such a predisposition. A predisposition can be countered by external pressure, that is, by the opposition of some mobilized group. However, since it is difficult to maintain external pressure, policy in the long run is likely to reflect the predispositions of public officials about group interests. Moreover, because external pressure is costly to mobilize, difficult to maintain, and inadequate over the long run, groups with sufficient power attempt to gain positional advantages, that is, to encourage the selection and continuance in public office of persons who are favorably predisposed to their interests.

A favorable predisposition might come about in any of three ways (and there is no reason to assume that the three ways occur in isolation from one another). First and most obviously, a group could achieve a positional advantage through the selection of spokesmen to serve its interest in strategically vital offices. For example, throughout the twenty-year period covered in my Atlanta research, the Board of Commissioners of the Housing Authority (the city's redevelopment agency) was controlled by members of the business community, who were appointed as and acted as representatives of business interests.

Second, a group might enjoy a positional advantage by virtue of the fact that the occupants of important places in the governmental system share the group's perspective on leading policy questions. Redevelopment administrators, as has been the case in a variety of communities including Atlanta, might share with the business community the view that the revitalization of the downtown area is an objective of overriding importance. A shared perspective, if it appears as more than a random occurrence, presumably reflects influence in some manner. Recruitment might be based on ideological as well as technical criteria, or recruitment might be ideologically neutral but followed by enough indicators of approbation and disapprobation to bring to the top and keep at the top individuals of a given predilection.

Third, a group might possess an advantage in that their leaders have informal ties to and enjoy the respect of major officeholders. Since their views are expressed in a relationship of mutual trust, the group leaders can expect a sympathetic hearing. In Atlanta, members of the business community were early sponsors and long-standing political allies of Mayor Hartsfield. Because of this close relationship, business leaders were frequently sought out for advice; and they had ample opportunity to meet with the mayor informally at their own initiative.

A positional advantage thus might be structured into the process whereby public officials are selected, it might be a matter of ''ideological'' congruence, or it might rest on an informal basis. In any instance or combination of instances, it seems likely that if a bias is consistent and durable over time, then something other than happenstance has occurred. A positional advantage can be the result of the exercise of influence as well as a means by which influence can be exerted. This is to say that groups use their resources to gain and maintain positional advantages, and a positional advantage is itself a resource that can be used in exercising influence.[18]

Contrasting Conceptions of Power

The revisionist theory outlined here has disagreed with pluralism on some basic points about how power is distributed and exercised. Revisionism also presupposes a technique of studying power that diverges from the one emphasized by pluralists. The revisionist approach can perhaps be set forth best by showing first that pluralism and revisionism involve different conceptions of power, which in turn call for different ways of analyzing power.

Pluralists have tended to treat power as an interpersonal phenomenon that can be seen most clearly as the demonstrated ability to overcome the opposition and resistance of others. Thus *Who Governs?* uses as a principal measure of power the actions of individuals in initiating and vetoing decisional alternatives. But pluralists have not attempted to look at all decisional alternatives, only those involved in key issues.

A key issue can be identified in any of several ways: size of budget, number of people affected, or scope of impact, for example.[19] However, pluralists have tended to center their attention on conflict. From the early Dahl rejection of the "indifference versus preference" test of power[20] to Richard Merelman's call for studying "the pattern of actual, observable, past and present force applications,"[21] pluralists have looked primarily at who prevails in major community controversies.

Critics of pluralism have argued, however, that conflict constitutes only one face of power, a highly visible but nevertheless atypical aspect of power. Much more important, the antipluralists believe, are the forces that confine and prevent conflict. The absence of conflict may mean that power has been exercised to suppress opposition or to exclude some issues from being considered.[22] Conflict outcomes or participation in key decisions may therefore be only a partial guide to community power. Attention needs to be given to those elements in a political system that influence the issue agenda and thereby limit the amount of conflict that occurs or shape the form that it takes.

Power, as antipluralists see it, is more than the ability to overcome opposition in specific decisions. Power also involves the capacity to affect the context within which decisions are made, that is, the capacity to secure positional advantages; and it involves the ability to exploit the positional advantages that have been secured. To consider only the amount of resistance overcome in decision making is to ignore the fact that resources can also be used to alter the amount of resistance encountered. Thus the present study treats power as a systemic phenomenon, which involves opportunities for groups to further their interests without necessarily encountering opposition.

The conception of power employed here shifts attention from the question of who governs (who individually initiates and vetoes) to the issue of how governance occurs and with what effects (which group interests are served and by what means). What the researcher most needs to know is not the level of political participation by various segments of the community, but the predispositions of official decision makers. It is therefore necessary to look at decision making, but to do so in a way that will broaden the scope of official behavior examined and enable us to analyze this behavior in a light appropriate for a consideration of positional advantages and disadvantages.

Demand Conversion

As the preceding discussion suggests, pluralism and revisionism differ not only over how power is distributed and exercised but also over how power should be studied and analyzed. What is needed, in accordance with the revisionist perspective, is a focus of inquiry that will bring attention to the less direct aspects of community power (that is, less direct than the power revealed in overt conflict). In the present section, demand conversion will be suggested as such a focus. In short, one way to highlight a broad scope of behavior by official decision makers is to study the full process by which they act—or do not act—upon demands associated with various group interests, in making public policy. The researcher thus need not be dependent upon controversy or the presence of key issues as a guide to decisional analysis. Instead, the researcher can look at all of the relevant demands and see that some are neglected, that others receive quite different treatments as they move from one policy stage to another, and that some issues never become salient to the public at large. As a focus, this "conversion" process takes into account the less visible but nonetheless observable forms of official behavior. It thus expands decisional analysis in a way that meets some, but perhaps not all, of the objections of the critics of the pluralist approach who call for an examination of nondecision making.

The approach suggested here, which was employed in the study of Atlanta's urban renewal experience, does not attempt to explain how demands originate (demand generation), but concentrates on the action that transforms articulated demands into policy outputs. Schematically, the policy process might be represented as in figure I below.[23] Demand conversion is thus only a part of the total process, but it is the phase of policy formation that most immediately involves group influence. Actions (or inactions) on articulated demands can be grouped into three stages: (1) mobilization—the stage at which proposals may or may not receive enough support to be brought up for formal consideration by local authorities; (2) official disposition—the stage at which officials formally decide to approve, either fully or in substantially modified form, or disapprove proposals; and (3) implementation—the stage at

Figure 1

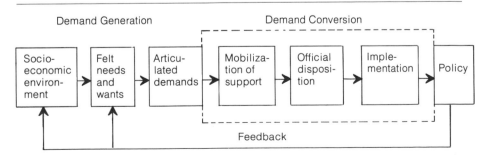

which it can be determined whether or not after gaining official approval proposals have been put into effect and if so, to what extent.

At each step, a demand can fail to move forward toward becoming a policy output. Failure to move forward is, of course, as observable as success is. Observable demands, that is, concrete suggestions, requests, proposals for action (or inaction) can then be used as the starting point to see what happens to the policy interests of various elements in the community.[24] The capacity to bring about or prevent change in policy is measurable in this way and can be treated as an indicator of community power. While the relevant behavior is observable, observation is not confined to decisional conflict nor is it tied to that elusive term, "key issues."

Influence whether direct or indirect and from whatever base can be taken into account so long as it bears on either the ability to move a proposal through the steps of making policy or the ability to block a proposal with a counterproposal. Equally important, "the capacity to bring about or prevent change" encompasses the implementation of policy as a dimension of power analyses. The concept of demand conversion is inclusive enough, then, to cover (1) the atrophying of proposals that never receive official consideration or otherwise remain in an undeveloped state, (2) the quiet rejection of policy alternatives that are considered officially but that are not part of a major community controversy or issue, and (3) low visibility or uncontested actions that occur during the implementation of decisions made earlier and that may alter the earlier outcome.[25]

Like initiations and vetoes, status and position, reputational rankings, and other measures, demand conversion is, of course, only an indicator of power and involves assumptions that may be questioned. Demand conversion does seem, however, to provide a measure that is especially appropriate for inquiry into indirect aspects of community power in the form of positional advantages and disadvantages.

The heart of the matter is not the question of who takes part in the disposition of specific issues; there is little doubt that public officials are the major actors. Rather than the number or proportion of proposals successfully initiated by public officials, we most need to know how policy choices are made, whose interests are served by these choices, and why officials come to formulate and advance some proposals while resisting or neglecting others.

To relate demand conversion to the policymaking process, the terms "decision" and "policy" should be distinguished from one another. As used herein, *decision* refers to a particular act. *Policy* refers to a course of action, flowing from a series of decisions, which allocates benefits in a definable way.[26] Official decisions or decisions made on points at issue are not treated as key decisions, but as individual actions that may be grouped with other actions and may contribute to some cumulative policy result or may be negated by subsequent actions.

Decisions affecting individual proposals are therefore examined in order to gain some understanding of when and under what conditions various groups encounter resistance. As a cumulative pattern, demand conversion should cast some light on the ways in which public officials interact with various community groups. Overt conflict can be placed in the broader context of policymaking,[27] and at least some tentative judgments can be made about its impact on policy choices. In this way policy can be seen as something that may in fact follow a path charted by various outcroppings of community conflict, or policy may be shaped by other forces less visible to the general public.

Although this study is concerned with the conversion rather than the generation of demands, it should be recognized that the distinction is somewhat artificial. Policy demands do not emanate from an apolitical "environment" to be acted upon by public officials. Rather, as the discussion below suggests, proposals are initiated and shaped in many instances by governmental officials themselves. Indeed, system bias comes about by virtue of the fact that, in personnel and outlook, some community groups and institutions are strongly represented in official governmental circles and involved directly in the process of making official decisions.

The analysis presented later is concerned with one policy area in one city. The purpose of that analysis is obviously not to offer the reader a definitive statement on how policy is formed in contemporary American communities. Instead the objectives are twofold: (1) to show that the pluralist method of study can be modified in a way that allows indirect and less overt aspects of power to be examined, and (2) to suggest that policy formation can be explained by theoretical propositions quite different from those put forth by various pluralist writers. The narrative account of urban renewal policy formation in Atlanta should provide the reader with a basis for assessing the worth of demand conversion as a focus of analysis.

The approach taken here is based on the view that we should ignore neither the context in which policy is formed nor the actions (and inactions) of officials as they make policy decisions. In the next chapter we shall consider the Atlanta political context and how it has afforded the business community a positional advantage. Subsequently, we shall examine urban renewal demands and the treatment they have received from public officials. At that stage we can then determine to what extent there is an observable bias in Atlanta's urban renewal program; we can also see (1) how, in concrete fashion, positional advantage and disadvantage manifest themselves in the actual process of policy formation and (2) to what extent a bias can be maintained in the face of opposition by actively discontented groups. This study perhaps differs from many others in that it is not an analysis of context with inferences about how demands were converted into policy, but rather an analysis of how demands were converted into policy with inferences about how context and group influence were intertwined.

Atlanta is a community of polarities and contradictions.[1] The capital city of a Deep South state, Atlanta has witnessed more than its share of racial demagoguery and violence. Yet it earned a reputation for racial moderation while many other southern communities were in the throes of massive resistance to racial desegregation. Moreover, verbal conflict between state capitol and city hall has borne testimony to a clash of cultures. Atlanta is in but not of the South, at least not of the Old South of familied white aristocrats and submissive blacks. Atlanta is New South.

Long a transportation and distribution center, Atlanta has emerged recently as the economic capital of the Southeast. It is, as former Mayor Ivan Allen once described it, "a businessman's town." It is also a home of civil rights organizations, esteemed black institutions of higher education, and a large black middle class.

Atlanta is a community of economic boom and cosmopolitan life-style. It is also a community of poverty and traditionalism. Poor blacks and whites continue to migrate into the city from rural and small-town communities. But the benefits of central-city economic growth have fallen largely to upper- and middle-income workers in white-collar and skilled occupations. As evidence of the extent to which professional, managerial, and service activities have flourished, downtown office space increased by 76 percent in the years between 1960 and 1970. The city's recent economic upsurge has also brought into being a booming convention and tourist trade; hotel and motel rooms more than doubled in the decade of the 1960s.[2] Unemployment has remained at a low level,[3] but rural migrants have been unable to take much advantage of the general prosperity that has characterized the metropolitan area.

As of the 1970 census, blacks accounted for just over one-half of Atlanta's population.[4] This fact can be misleading, however, if the diversity among Atlanta blacks is not taken into account. Black poverty coexists with black affluence. Even in the Jim Crow era of pervasive segregation, Atlanta had a sizable black middle class. Some black-owned commercial and financial institutions date back several generations. Today, a wide array of business, professional, and governmental positions are filled by blacks, but unemployment and underemployment remain as problems.

Stable black neighborhoods with residents who represent several generations of attachment to a particular place sometimes adjoin areas that are no more than stopover places for a rootless subcommunity of migrants. Among blacks, variations in ideology, life-style, and militance crosscut differences in education, transiency, and economic position.

In the white community of Atlanta, affluence and cosmopolitanism may also be found together with differing degrees of nonaffluence and traditionalism. Although it lacks the ethnic variety that characterizes some northern cities, Atlanta's white population nevertheless represents considerable diversity in income level, outlook, and style of life.

A Socioeconomic Comparison of Atlanta with Other Large Cities

With 1960 as a base year—1960 falls at the midpoint of the twenty-year period covered by the research reported here—some useful comparisons may be made between Atlanta and other American cities over 100,000 in population. In 1960, due in part to a successful annexation effort during the 1950s, Atlanta's population had reached 487,455. In general economic character, Atlanta was categorized as Diversified-Manufacturing, and thus was in a classification fairly typical of other large cities.[5] One-third of all cities over 100,000 fell into this same category.

Table 3.1 provides a summary of more specific social and economic characteristics for comparative purposes. White-collar occupations represented 44 percent of the city's work force, a proportion that ranked Atlanta 73rd among 130 cities over 100,000. The median educational level of 10.5 years again placed Atlanta near but below the average of other cities, with a ranking of 80th. In proportion of population in-migrating within the previous five years, Atlanta's 16 percent was 58th of 130 cities.[6]

In other characteristics, Atlanta deviated more sharply from the national norm. Even in 1960, the 38 percent nonwhite population gave Atlanta the 8th ranking in proportion of minority-group population. The city also showed signs of considerably greater than average poverty. With only 46 percent of its dwelling units owner-occupied and only 75 percent of its residences in standard repair (complete with all plumbing facilities), Atlanta rated 101st on the former and 102nd on the latter.[7] Perhaps the most thought-provoking figures concern income distribution. With 27 percent of its families earning annual incomes under $3,000, Atlanta ranked 14th out of 130 cities on this measure of poverty. However, the 16 percent of the city's families earning more than $10,000 annually constituted a sizable proportion of affluent residents and placed Atlanta 58th among the nation's large cities in this regard.[8] The proportions of Atlanta families at the extremes of poverty and affluence left the city with an unusually small share of its population in the moderate-income category. Of the 130 cities ranked, only 4 had a smaller proportion of moderate-income population. Overall, Atlanta was thus distinguished by the extent to which its population was sharply divided along racial and economic lines.

Table 3.1. Socioeconomic Comparison of Atlanta with Other Cities over 100,000 in Population, 1960

Socioeconomic Characteristic	Atlanta	Rank Order of Atlanta among 130 Cities
Percent in white-collar occupations (professional, managerial, clerical, and sales)	44%	73rd
Median school years completed (among population 25 years old and over)	10.5	80th
Percent of recent migrants (that is, persons 5 years old and over who came from a different county during the 5-year period preceding the census)	16%	58th
Percent of nonwhite population	38%	8th
Percent of owner-occupied housing units	46%	101st
Percent of standard housing units (sound with all plumbing facilities)	75%	102nd
Percent of families with incomes under $3,000	27%	14th
Percent of families with moderate incomes ($3,000–$9,999)	58%	126th
Percent of families with incomes $10,000 and over	16%	58th

Source: U.S. Department of Commerce, Bureau of the Census, *City and County Data Book, 1962*, 1962.

Government and Politics in Atlanta: A Reform Orientation

Socioeconomic data cannot tell the whole Atlanta story. They cannot by themselves give the entire framework within which urban renewal policy was made. Atlanta's government and politics have played a major part. And these in turn need to be set in a broader context, the context of general trends in urban government and politics.

In the early 1960s, Edward Banfield and James Q. Wilson completed a highly useful examination of urban politics in America.[9] Much of their analysis was concerned with a long-range decline in traditional politics and with the spread of a reform or "good government" ethos. Traditional politics, as the term is used here, refers to the politics of patronage and personal favors, ward-based organizations, and geographically and ethnically segmented loyalties. It is, of course, the politics practiced by the bosses and the infamous machines of a bygone era. But it is also a style of politics that has proved to have considerable staying power. Nevertheless, Banfield and Wilson predicted that the continuing growth of the middle class would lead to ever-increasing pressures for reform.

In the context of local government, reform has a very specific meaning. Reform politics is oriented toward expertise and professional management, civic-mindedness, a community-wide perspective, and a cooperative search for the common good. Advocates of reform have favored such devices as nonpartisan and at-large elections, professional administration, wide civil service coverage, and a strengthened chief executive. Less tangibly, reform advocates have called for leadership by those who are "best qualified" and for policies and programs that reflect a concern with the good of the community "as a whole." Reformers have sometimes suggested that running a city is more a matter of good management than of astute politics.

While many large cities have resisted the "modernization" of their electoral and governmental practices,[10] Atlanta has been a willing participant in the move toward "good government."[11] Certainly in the post-World War II era, Atlanta has had a reform style of politics. Municipal elections have been nonpartisan, patronage has been unimportant, and the merit system has been well entrenched. For the time period covered here, the seventeen-member Board of Aldermen consisted of a vice-mayor and sixteen aldermen elected at large.[12] Aldermen ran from the wards in which they resided, but they were voted on city-wide.

Reform government in Atlanta has been more, however, than a matter of structure. It has involved a style of political conduct in which the general well-being of the community was supposed to prevail over the interests of any segment of the community. Personal gain or favors bestowed on friends, neighbors, or fellow loyalists ran counter to the city's reform ethos. Even before the 1950s, Atlanta was beginning to emerge from the politically unreformed past and assume a place in the reformed and forward-looking present. "Ward courtesy," that is, the system of mutual deference and favor-granting among the representatives of the city's various districts, was a potent force in earlier political times; however, with some strategic encouragement by the mayor, it had virtually disappeared by the 1950s—at least from the urban renewal program. Instead of "ward courtesy," "committee courtesy" and other manifestations of deference to specialization and expertise have come to play an important part in legislative deliberations.

The reform style in Atlanta has involved a major role for executive leadership. City Hall observers have been fond of saying that Atlanta has "a weak mayor form of government with a strong mayor." The observation refers to a system in which the mayor did not have full authority over or even direct control of the administration of city programs. Administrative supervision for most departments was formally vested in the Board of Aldermen, and some departments were established as independent agencies. The School Department, for example, was headed by an elected school board. However, for most departments, the mayor's control was, in fact, substantial. He possessed the all-important authority to appoint aldermanic committee chairmen and other aldermanic committee members, and he has had the power to appoint department heads. In recent years, the mayor's potential for exerting executive leadership was increased by expansions in the staff assistance available to him—in the Planning Department and Budget Office and by the addition of a chief administrative officer to assist the mayor.

Mayoral strength thus has been partly a matter of exercising the formal authority that was available. Partly, however, mayoral strength has rested on less tangible factors. Both incumbents for the 1950 to 1970 time period were men of considerable leadership ability, men who knew how to combine formal authority with informal influence. Yet, the formal "weakness" of the office from time to time has offered a convenient cover for mayoral inaction. Nevertheless, the prominence of the office, the mayor's headship of an electoral majority, and the unavoidably central part a chief executive must play in coordinating and activating city programs have in the hands of skilled politicians added up to considerable strength even in a so-called weak mayor system.

One of the mayor's roles has been that of counterbalancing the various centrifugal forces at work. The particular interests of a ward or an administrative department could be and often have been checked by exertions of mayoral leadership. The formal powers of the mayor (particularly his appointment power) combined with his informal influence have made the city's elected chief executive into a centralizing force of considerable magnitude.

The impact of segmented interests on the city government has been checked in other ways. For example, the Atlanta Housing Authority—the agency charged with administering both urban renewal and public housing programs—was established as an "independent" body. The agency has been governed by five commissioners, appointed by the mayor for staggered, ten-year terms of office. The top administrative personnel in the Housing Authority, as in most agencies, have always enjoyed long tenure in office. Continuity and expertise rather than responsiveness and accessibility have thus been emphasized in the administration of urban redevelopment and other programs.

Atlanta's version of reform politics has had another important characteristic. Appointments to boards, commissions (including the Housing Authority), and advisory committees have been based more on "respectability'' than on representativeness. Most appointees have been high-status individuals regarded as uninterested in personal gain and free of self-serving motives. Further, they have not been inclined to engage in public controversy. Open conflict, while not completely avoidable, has certainly been discouraged. In a city often beset by racial and other tensions, officials have attempted to minimize public debate and to avoid confrontation. Open conflict, officials have feared, would make issues more difficult to resolve. Before the protest activities of the mid-sixties, at any rate, policy innovation was typically undertaken as a ''nonpolitical,'' preferably noncontroversial venture actively supported by prestigious individuals and organizations.

The reform ethos has involved a rhetoric of serving the public good. That rhetoric, like any other, can be used to hide coarse motives. Nonetheless, Atlanta's reform rhetoric corresponds to a style of politics in which political leaders, technical experts, and prominent citizens have joined together to produce what they considered the ''best'' remedies for the community's ills. Moreover, the major participants have acted as if they were charged with the responsibility of protecting a unified set of general interests against the intrusions of partial interests. Official decision making has thus been somewhat insulated from the more open forms of interest-group activity.

Political Cleavage in Atlanta

While a reform orientation tends to mute some forms of conflict, it does not altogether eliminate cleavages, especially in electoral politics. Banfield and Wilson found, in fact, a form of cleavage that they believed was characteristic of many communities—both those with and without a strong reform orientation. On the basis of studies of a large number of cities, Banfield and Wilson concluded that local elections frequently involve a conflict between the supporters of a high level of governmental activity on the one side and the proponents of a low level of governmental activity on the other side. But, Banfield and Wilson noted, this cleavage is not the classic one of ''have's'' versus ''have-not's.'' Rather, they pointed out, the backers of an active city government tend to be a coalition of economic opposites: the prosperous upper-middle class and the completely unprosperous lower class. The opposing force—the supporters of a low level of governmental activity— Banfield and Wilson found to be made up, typically, of the not-so-affluent members of the middle and working class.[10]

Atlanta has embodied the national pattern, with the modification that blacks, who, in Atlanta, are by no means all poor, have filled the coalition role of the lower class. City elections in Atlanta have revolved around three groups.[14] Two of these groups, blacks (of all classes) and the more affluent whites, formed a winning coalition in most city elections and referenda throughout the twenty-year period under consideration. Spokesmen for this coalition have been racially moderate, and they have been willing to use local governmental authority to promote change and encourage "progress." In their voting preferences, members of the dominant coalition have been proexpenditure and somewhat cosmopolitan. On the losing side of most referenda and contests for local office have been the city's less affluent whites. They have been antiexpenditure and largely provincial in voting preference; and their occasional spokesmen have displayed a cultural conservatism that mixed religious fundamentalism with strains of racism. While some officeholders have quietly shared this group's provincialism and conservatism, no elected official has been willing to put himself forward as a champion of the city's unaffluent whites. Thus, in the case narrative to be recounted later, all of the top-level public officials have been active participants in the city's "progressive" coalition.

William B. Hartsfield, whose election as mayor preceded the large-scale enfranchisement of blacks, was the principal architect of the voting coalition that dominated city elections for two decades. In the late 1940s when blacks began to register to vote in substantial numbers, Hartsfield was the central figure in putting together an alliance between this newly enfranchised group and upper-status whites, who had long been influential in city affairs. Hartsfield was reelected by this coalition throughout the 1950s. He sometimes had vigorous opposition, as in 1957 when he was opposed by Lester Maddox. Maddox, a die-hard segregationist, was the proprietor of the Pickrick Restaurant—an establishment that specialized in southern fried chicken and far-right political propaganda. Maddox had no ongoing political organization, but his flamboyant political style gave him a mass appeal. In his 1957 race against Hartsfield, Maddox captured large majorities in nonaffluent white precincts, but he was defeated by the overwhelming opposition of blacks and affluent whites. In the fall of 1961, when Hartsfield decided not to run again for mayor, businessman Ivan Allen became the coalition candidate. He too was strongly opposed by Maddox, who again ran well among nonaffluent whites and again lost the election because of the huge majorities against him in black and affluent white precincts.[15]

Allen assumed office in January 1962 and by the fall of 1965, when he ran for reelection, the "stand-pat" forces could no longer muster an effective campaign. They were never well organized; and, as the city approached a black majority, the "stand-pat" forces lost their political will to fight. Allen's only opponent in 1965 was another white moderate, who lost in a one-sided and low-keyed campaign.

As the 1960s closed, the "progressive" coalition itself was in some disarray. In the mayoral election that came at the end of the decade, the four candidates—one black and three white—had all been identified earlier with the coalition in some way, but they engaged in a bitter and divisive campaign. Sam Massell, a liberal white who temporarily broke with and was opposed by the city's business leadership,[16] was the ultimate victor. He proved, however, to be a one-term chief executive. In the fall of 1973, the population balance had shifted sufficiently for a black candidate, Maynard Jackson, to be elected mayor. Jackson assumed office in January 1974.

The period 1950 to 1970 thus coincides roughly with the life span of the "progressive" coalition.[17] It was a time of rapid change, but over the two-decade period there were some important constants in the city's politics: blacks did not have an electoral majority during this time, but they were a significant element in the dominant electoral coalition; throughout the twenty years whites were sharply divided between a more affluent, racially moderate and "progress-minded" element on one side and a less affluent, segregationist, and "stand-pat-minded" element on the other side. Affluent whites generally followed the lead of the city's business community; and businessmen were especially important, though not always highly visible, participants in the dominant coalition. Blacks were successful in keeping overtly racist candidates out of city office, but a black alderman was not elected until 1965. And not until the election in the fall of 1969 did blacks receive more than token representation in city government. Thus, throughout the time period covered in the case narrative, the city's top officials were racially moderate whites. Their leadership of the coalition included an unswerving public adherence to the view that amicable race relations were essential for the city's growth and well-being.

Overall, Atlanta was part and parcel of the national pattern of political cleavages. While race was perhaps a more salient factor in Atlanta than was the case for most cities in the fifties and early sixties, Atlanta's "progress" versus "stand-pat" cleavage conformed to the pattern found by Banfield and Wilson.

Constancy in electoral cleavage did not, of course, preclude some fundamental changes in the city's politics. The changes that occurred can be taken into account by dividing the twenty-year period into two phases, each under the incumbency of a different mayor. At the risk of some oversimplification, each stage can be characterized by a distinct type of leadership and race relations. The first round of renewal activity took place during the mayoralty of William B. Hartsfield, whose forte was brokerage politics.

The Hartsfield administration covers the period in which the "progressive'' coalition was formed, and it was a period in which leaders were able to operate largely by quiet negotiations and bargaining. The Allen mayoralty extended for two terms, and covered the somewhat turbulent years between 1962 and 1970. During the Hartsfield administration, negotiations within the dominant coalition were conducted by a few leaders and followed well-established channels of communication. On particularly delicate issues, Hartsfield dealt directly with A. T. Walden, head of the Atlanta Negro Voters League. The Negro Voters League had been formed as a bipartisan organization in the late 1940s as a way of maximizing the influence of newly registered black voters. It screened candidates and conducted get-out-the-vote campaigns, and Walden remained in close touch with Mayor Hartsfield. The Urban League was another important link between the black and white communities. Headed by a biracial board and funded in part through the Community Chest, the Urban League staff was keenly aware of sentiment among white civic leaders. At the same time, the Urban League maintained continuing contact with educational and business leaders in the black community.

During the Allen administration, an era of protests came eventually to penetrate and alter the city's politics. Old leaders and organizations gradually lost standing; blacks especially relied less and less on established channels of communication; and new, diversely based leaders emerged as spokesmen for various low-income and neighborhood groups. Although protest demonstrations related to public accommodations occurred as early as 1960, the period from 1965 to the end of the decade was a particularly volatile one in the city's politics.

Inevitably, some policy issues from the Allen administration spilled over into the administration of Sam Massell, but the detailed analysis of renewal policy ends with 1970 and is only peripherally concerned with the Massell mayoralty.

Positional Advantages and Disadvantages in Relation to Atlanta's Urban Renewal Program

For the period under consideration here, 1950 to 1970, two political facts are of overriding importance. The reform style of politics described above is one; that the business community was a cohesive and unified political force is the other.[18] These two facts are related, but the nature of the relationship cannot be fully uncovered from a single-city study. Was reform politics a precondition for business unity, or was business unity a precondition for the establishment of reform politics? The question is not really answerable because the two conditions are historically intertwined. Nevertheless, they can be separated somewhat for purposes of discussion. To see how the two conditions are related, it is necessary first to consider how the city's reform style of politics has enhanced the political influence of business. The City Hall/Main Street ties that have developed over the years should enable us to see that business influence may be both a cause and a result of political unity in the business community.

A major element in the revisionist theory presented here is the possibility that influence can produce positional advantage, and positional advantage can then be a factor in the group's ability to influence policy. Certainly in Atlanta, it seems that the business community played a significant role in the city's transformation from old style ward and patronage politics to a new, more centralized, and essentially reform style of politics. Business influence was used, first, during the late 1930s, to support the candidacy and administration of Mayor Hartsfield, and subsequently to promote a combined scheme of annexation and governmental reorganization.

Business leaders had originally formed an alliance with Mayor Hartsfield in the 1930s, providing the depression-hit city with badly needed credit during the mayor's first term and over the years furnishing financial and organizational support at election time. Hartsfield was a pragmatic politician, but he also genuinely felt that Atlanta's business leaders were a responsible and constructive force in the community. His frequent espousal of business causes was partly traceable to his belief that Atlanta's leading businessmen, as practitioners of enlightened self-interest, shared his concern for the city's well-being. The municipal tax base and the economic health of the central business district (CBD) were closely enough related to encourage a City Hall/Main Street alliance. Hartsfield recognized other advantages in the alliance as well. Highly sensitive to newspaper coverage and editorial commentary, the mayor regarded business support as an essential buffer against press criticism.

Hartsfield's success in asserting his leadership at city hall and in establishing an electoral appeal not based on patronage provided the initial break from the old pattern of ward politics. However, the upsurge of black-voter registration after World War II caused some concern among business leaders about the city's political future.[19] Moreover, there was growing interest in using a redevelopment program to combat central-city decay. In order to assure that "responsible" elements remained in control of the situation, business and city hall joined forces behind a "plan of improvement" (as the proposal was called in Atlanta) whereby the city's middle-class composition would be increased by annexation, and the city's governmental structure would be somewhat simplified.

Older styles of politics did not vanish overnight, but by the early

1950s ward courtesy, personal favoritism, and other types of particular-istic political connections had been sufficiently weakened so that they stood as no barrier to a redevelopment program. To guarantee that there would be no reversion to ward courtesy, Mayor Hartsfield (and Mayor Allen after him) always appointed as chairman of the aldermanic committee on urban renewal one of the representatives from Atlanta's "silk stocking" Northside, someone committed to "good government" who had close connections with the business community and who did not have a "parochial" view of the community's well-being. Further, since the Northside was an unlikely location for renewal projects, an alderman from that area would be unaffected by direct personal pressure from project residents. And, of course, in the Allen era as well as in the Hartsfield era, all Northside aldermen were white and thereby separated somewhat by race from the vast majority of renewal area residents.

Administratively, urban renewal was given a reform imprint by being placed with the Atlanta Housing Authority. Since the Housing Authority's five commissioners are appointed for staggered ten-year terms, it is therefore an agency thoroughly insulated from the immediate pressures of electoral discontent. As we have seen with the aldermanic urban renewal committee, Hartsfield was not one to rely strictly on formal structure as a way of achieving reform objectives. His appointments to the Housing Authority Commission were calculated to achieve maximum political autonomy for the agency. He believed that by appointing bankers and realtors as commissioners of the authority, the business community in general and the real estate association in particular would be inhibited from attacking the agency and its management.[20] Again he regarded prestige appointments as a buffer against criticism in the press.

The business community, from its side, lent support to the view that "politics" (meaning influence by groups who relied mainly on voting power) should be kept out of important policy areas. Combining philanthropy with influence, businessmen were able to have the Community Council (the city's social-planning agency) and the Citizens Advisory Committee for Urban Renewal (CACUR) jointly financed by public funds and direct business contributions. The latter were expressly intended as reminders that staff were to handle potentially controversial issues in a "responsible" rather than a political manner. The CACUR, moreover, was placed under the direction of chairmen who met criteria of high status and civic responsibility. For the twenty years covered in this study, CACUR chairmen were, without exception, white and upper-middle class (an architect, a banker, a transit executive, and the president of Georgia State University), with close ties to the business community.[21]

In line with Hartsfield's style of political leadership, he stayed in the background during the drawing up of the urban renewal plans. During his administration, the Urban Renewal Policy Committee—a specially created body consisting of the Housing Authority commissioners and members of the aldermanic urban renewal committee—presided over the formulation of redevelopment policy. Business leaders were given easy and direct access to the early stages of renewal policymaking, while other groups, in particular those with a neighborhood base, had only the opportunity to react to plans that were already fully developed.

Once Ivan Allen became mayor in 1962, City Hall was in the hands of an activist, who was firmly committed to the idea that Atlanta should become a national city. Allen himself was the personal embodiment of business prestige in public affairs. He came to the mayoralty from the presidency of the Chamber of Commerce.[22] Describing himself and his close associates in civic life, Allen said:

We were white, Anglo-Saxon, Protestant, Atlantan, business-oriented, non-political, moderate, well-bred, well-educated, pragmatic, and dedicated to the betterment of Atlanta as much as a Boy Scout troop is dedicated to fresh milk and clean air. That sounds corny to a lot of people, especially to those in other cities whose "white-power structure," as we were later to be called in a not-so-flattering way, tended to be divided and not so interested in the progress of their city as they were in their own personal progress—but it was true about the business leadership, the new civic leadership, in Atlanta at that time.[23]

Under Allen's leadership, the Urban Renewal Policy Committee gradually declined in importance as the mayor's office became the center of urban renewal activity. The Planning Department, which came to serve as a staff arm of the mayor, was expanded, was made more professional, and assumed a major role in formulating policy. However, neighborhood groups were still frozen out of the early stages of policy formulation. Moreover, under Allen, as under Hartsfield, the Housing Authority and other boards and commissions indirectly related to urban renewal were in the hands of businessmen. Because business was a cohesive force and because Ivan Allen added a dimension of personal dynamism, projects such as civic center and stadium construction could be and were coordinated with urban renewal activity. "Independent" agencies and authorities, especially in the Allen era, functioned relatively smoothly as units in a comprehensive effort to upgrade areas around the CBD. The smooth functioning was, however, due largely to the unifying influence of the business community and to the near absence of particularistic and "political" pressures on the agencies involved.

Reform structures in Atlanta have thus been used to provide business leaders with opportunities to participate extensively in public affairs.

This participation has been encouraged by top local officials. Both mayors Hartsfield and Allen pursued a policy (unsuccessful in Allen's case) of expanding the city's boundaries in part with the unconcealed motive of retaining the active participation of a group that they deemed progressive and responsible. Conversely, they openly feared the consequences of either a black or a low-income majority. In short, both mayors seemed to believe (as did the newspapers) that business participation in governmental affairs is more community-minded than is participation by other groups.

Atlanta's nonpartisan and at-large elections appear also to have served the political interests of the business community well.[24] Business leaders were an important source of campaign funds, and newspaper support was highly prized. Throughout much of the period under consideration, leaders in the black community seemed to feel that their alliance with white business leaders was a necessary protection against the extremes of white racism. White officeholders such as Hartsfield and Allen used their influence to bolster this coalition in which the business community was a major element. Allen, especially, made efforts to reinforce the cleavage between the "progressives" and the "stand-patters." For example, Allen's 1961 election strategy was to convert the mayoralty contest into a showdown between himself as the spokesman for moderation and understanding and Lester Maddox as an unreconstructed segregationist.[25] The "moderate versus segregationist" battle thus tended to preempt electoral conflict in the city.[26]

In summary, for the entire twenty-year period under consideration, Atlanta had what has been termed a reformed and centralized type of politics. "Reformed" refers to more than the absence of partisan and district elections; "centralized" refers to more than executive structure (and indeed by textbook standards the structure was of the so-called weak mayor type). The system had three major characteristics: (1) executive leadership was of overwhelming importance, and legislative bargaining ("ward courtesy" and related practices) was of minimal importance; (2) administrative agencies were insulated from constituency pressures and protected from "self-regarding" interests but accessible to "blue-ribbon" and presumably public-minded elements in the community; and (3) citizen pressures were confined mainly to the city's at-large elections—elections that enhanced universalistic appeals (campaign slogans tended to center on such words as "responsibility," "moderation," and "progress"), which gave the news media a crucial role to play, and which revolved around the cleavage between the progressive coalition and stand-pat whites. (Significantly, urban renewal was never a major campaign issue.) These conditions gave the business community positional advantages in shaping the city's renewal program.

Undoubtedly Atlanta's reform style of politics was in part a result of long-term forces that began to show themselves in the 1930s and that gained momentum in the 1940s. Among them were a shift in public attitudes,[27] the inability of ward politicians to cope with a general economic depression, and the latent consequences of the New Deal.[28] Still it seems reasonably clear that the business community made a concerted effort to shape the city's political and governmental structure. Business influence in Atlanta's urban renewal program has thus been a two-stage process, that first of obtaining a favorable position in the community's politics and then, by means of an advantaged position, of helping to determine the direction of policy.

In Atlanta, business influence clearly was used to encourage a re-formed and centralized style of politics, and within this style of politics business did enjoy a positional advantage. Later analysis will return to the uses and results of this advantage. First, we need to consider the possible interrelationship between positional advantage and another factor in the influence of Atlanta businessmen, namely, their unity as a force in the city's politics.

Community Influence and Group Cohesion

Despite the fact that urban renewal impinged on the collective inter-ests of all three major groups in the city's politics, these groups differed substantially in the degree of unity they brought to bear on the politics of the renewal process. The business community maintained a high level of cohesion. Less solidarity prevailed among blacks and among nonaf-fluent whites. Conceivably, the presence of reform politics has had little bearing on the fact that competing groups varied in their capacity to exert a unified pressure. The characteristics of the city's major political groupings were certainly important factors in their own right. Moreover, the pattern of solidarity and disunity within groups rested partially on what might be considered nonpolitical factors. Business unity might not have been forthcoming, for example, if Atlanta had been an older, more mature city.[29] Possibly a "growth" mentality, fed by steadily expand-ing economic opportunities, has been the glue that has held the Atlanta business community together as a political force. Similarly, lapses in black unity could have arisen for reasons unrelated to the city's reform politics. Black solidarity might have weakened on a number of occa-sions simply because Atlanta's black community is economically di-verse. While the point may be a touchy one to speculate about, the possibility nevertheless exists that black political unity in Atlanta was fundamentally hampered by a class division.

Finally, it could be that the political ineffectiveness of the city's nonaffluent whites stemmed less from governmental structure and political style than from the fact that the group was tradition-minded and largely isolated from the forces of change. The city, indeed the region, has a weak labor movement, and the state Democratic party has historically been controlled by leaders who were not oriented toward the urban working class.

One line of argument might therefore credit group cohesion strictly to the intrinsic traits of groups themselves and not to the political context in which they operate. However, there is another line of argument that at least warrants consideration, namely, the argument that group solidarity or disunity is in part a product of political and governmental activity. Political influence can be used to bring together or maintain a unified force, or it can be used to divide and weaken an opposing force. Both processes were evident in Atlanta's urban renewal program, and they worked to promote business unity, but not unity within or between the other two major elements.

In a sense, Atlanta's business community was as economically diverse as its black community. Size, location, and function all stood as elements that could have prompted business disunity. And, in fact, there were particular business interests—specifically, the Atlanta Hotel Association and the Atlanta Real Estate Board—that were strongly opposed to portions of the city's redevelopment program. Their opposition proved short-lived, however. Even between the city's two major business organizations, the Chamber of Commerce and the Central Atlanta Improvement Association (CAIA),[30] there was some friction and a potentially wide rift. As a comprehensive business association containing many smaller businesses, the Chamber of Commerce began the 1950s as an ideologically conservative and staunchly "minimum taxation" organization not much enamored of federally funded programs, especially those that involved the use of eminent domain. The CAIA, founded in 1941 as an association of businesses with major stakes in the CBD, was a much smaller organization, and one that had a pragmatic interest in protecting central area property values and in fostering economic growth in the heart of the city.

Although the community's economic elite was most directly represented in the CAIA, it felt constrained to work closely with the Chamber of Commerce. City officials, as will be seen later, were persuaded to pursue those policies that would promote economic growth, but to do so in a way that would maintain maximum business unity.

In the case of blacks, city actions not only failed to encourage solidarity, they explicitly discouraged it. Reform politics or not, policy measures and administrative practices (which will be detailed later) were used to afford *particular benefits* to segments of the black community in order to fragment opposition to the city's renewal program. Thus, for the 1950 to 1970 period, the city's reformed and centralized politics in practice worked against black solidarity and in many ways lessened the collective influence of blacks on urban renewal.

Until 1970, blacks were, of course, disadvantaged by the fact that they were a numerical minority in the city; but then no single element in the city's politics was a majority faction. However, it might be argued that blacks confronted an unsympathetic white majority and therefore could not reasonably expect their material welfare to be promoted in any visible manner. Such an argument overlooks two important facts: (1) the status aims of blacks were advanced considerably during this time—and at a pace faster than in many other southern cities, and (2) whites were neither active nor united as a hostile force against the material welfare aims of blacks.[31] Overt white resistance to black housing aims took the form of opposition to particular sites (much of that opposition was overridden, anyway), not to the providing of subsidized housing. Indeed, interracial friction over residential patterns was by no means confined to subsidized housing. At any rate, to argue that the housing and renewal aims of blacks were blocked by a general backlash effect is to ignore the considerable extent to which the status aims of blacks were advanced against the same supposed force. Significantly, most status aims of blacks did not conflict with the economic interests of the business community, but came instead at the psychological expense of nonaffluent whites.

Two things about Atlanta's nonaffluent whites merit specific mention. First, as a political force in the city, nonaffluent whites were too ineffective to hold a veto by themselves over the objectives of blacks. Indeed, there is no evidence that they actively attempted to wield such a veto over the welfare goals of blacks *as welfare goals*. Second, on a number of specific points, neighborhood leaders among nonaffluent whites articulated policy interests that were quite compatible with the policy interests of black neighborhood groups. Yet while there were some ad hoc cases of political cooperation between blacks and nonaffluent whites, the tradition-mindedness of neighborhood whites stood as an obstacle to coalition-building. The obstacle, of course, might have been overcome by a concerted city hall effort. As it was, mayoralty campaigns and official city actions tended to reinforce rather than weaken barriers to biracial cooperation between neighborhood groups. Obviously, the barriers had social and historical foundations separate from the city's political institutions and their impact, but city actions, at least as they related to urban renewal, almost certainly served to increase racial tensions at the neighborhood level.

In sum, political structure seems to have been a cause and not just an effect of the business community's power in Atlanta. Other factors contributed to that power, notably the cohesiveness that derived from the shared incentive of economic growth and the contrasting inability of have-nots to unite politically across racial lines. But the benefits that the business community derived from the politics of reform, of which it was a major proponent, cannot be denied.

The ironies are many. New biases benefitting the business community replaced old forms of favoritism. New advantages of access and influence replaced the old "ward courtesy" system. And nowhere are these generalizations more readily documented than in the land-use decisions of Atlanta's post-World War II urban renewal experience.

Political resources can be, and in Atlanta were, used to promote some conflicts and to discourage others. In the shaping of conflict, no resource has greater value than official allies. Atlanta's centralized and reform politics lent itself well to a City Hall/Main Street alliance, and that alliance worked hard at deflecting and dividing the opposition forces. The pattern of group unity and disunity thus seemed in part to grow out of the prevailing power relations and the ability of business interests to exploit their positional advantages in the community's politics. Contrary to conventional social science wisdom, solidarity seems to have been as much a consequence of as a foundation for influence in Atlanta's politics.

PART 2

URBAN RENEWAL DEMANDS IN ATLANTA, 1950–1970

priorities of a major war. The capital improvements and, more seriously, the kind of upkeep that would have been considered normal in times of peace, had been deferred for years. The business district was aging—portions were shabby. Residential neighborhoods were also aging, and adequate housing was in short supply. Some housing units even in their better days had been hardly more than wooden shacks. During those same years, the stimulus of a war-fueled industrial boom had stepped up the country-to-city migration.

But in addition to these problems, which it shared with other urban centers, Atlanta was undergoing some growing pains of its own. Currents of change were at work—economic change both in Atlanta itself and throughout the Southeast, changes in housing patterns, and political change. These changes were destined not to flow smoothly.

Because of Atlanta's long-established position as a transportation and distribution center, many of its boosters believed that the city could become the business and financial hub of the entire Southeast. Indeed, they believed that Atlanta could become a city of national prominence and importance. They saw Atlanta as an economic dynamo, of which its CBD was the essential core. Their top priority was to have that vital center activated.

Others focused their conception of Atlanta's future around patterns of community living. They saw Atlanta as an aggregation of neighborhoods, each with a certain tradition and esprit. Without these long-standing neighborhoods—black and white—they felt that Atlanta would not be a genuine community. But strong migratory forces were at work and they made neighborhood preservation a difficult-to-achieve goal. The postwar boom, which accelerated the pace of change, belonged initially to the suburbs, in Atlanta as elsewhere in the country. Housing, jobs, and even retail sales expanded rapidly in the suburban portions of the metropolitan area. The now-familiar population pressures were at work: the affluent whites who led the suburban exodus were replaced by inmigrating, poor blacks who came to Atlanta's inner city in increasing numbers, as work opportunities in southern agriculture declined. Even though Atlanta greatly expanded its borders with a 1952 annexation, the outward flow of people and commerce quickly overran these new boundaries.

The two views of Atlanta and its future were not incompatible in principle. A community could seek to rejuvenate its business district and at the same time strive to conserve existing neighborhoods. In practical application, however, some conflict was inevitable. Resources were limited. Moreover, business-minded boosters wanted expansion room for the CBD. To extend the CBD to the south or east would mean the displacement of inner-city residents in large numbers. The upgrading of the business district through expansion in these directions could only be achieved at considerable social cost: the breakup of low-income neighborhoods, upheaval for families who would have to search for low-cost housing elsewhere, and disruption for those areas into which displacees would crowd.

Had this inner-city population been mainly white, it would have been difficult enough to resolve the issues of displacement versus economic growth. But it was mostly blacks who were concentrated in the areas around the business district.[1]

There were also scattered pockets of black residences throughout the city, and some blacks lived in "alley" or "rear" dwellings, which had originated as servants' quarters. Black residential expansion seemed inevitable, but there were attempts to exclude and even displace blacks from some areas. Although the city's traditional residential pattern had not been one of complete separation, whites—of all classes—were urging the elimination of scattered black residences in predominantly white neighborhoods. (In 1954, the Board of Aldermen enacted an alley-and-rear-dwelling clearance program through which many substandard dwellings for blacks were removed. Public-works projects were also occasionally used to remove pockets of black residents.)[2] For their part, blacks wanted to remain in the areas they then occupied *and* to expand into new areas. And with good cause: although they were one-third of the city's population, they lived on one-sixth of the residential land.

The press for expansion of black residential space thus was on a collision course with the goals of most white Atlantans. White residents were eager to contain black expansion and even to get blacks out of many outlying neighborhoods that they had long occupied. To complicate matters further, the white business community wished to move blacks out of the deteriorated areas nestled around the city's commercial core.

But the planners, businessmen, government officials, and civic leaders of Atlanta would have to work out these conflicts in a political context in which portents of change were plainly visible. Federal courts, by declaring the white primary unconstitutional, were in the process of ending the white monopoly of political power. No longer could officials count on "stable" race relations, that is, on a passive black population. Although no one could predict how far the course of change would run, it seemed certain that the traditional patterns would undergo some alteration.

Blacks, never totally without a political voice in Atlanta, began registering to vote in substantial numbers. Combined with the out-migration of the white middle class, the large-scale enfranchisement of blacks in the late 1940s convinced some old-line leaders that "responsible" city government was an unsure prospect in the years ahead.

Conditions appeared to be favorable for previously dispossessed groups to make their political voices heard. The annexation that became effective in 1952 augmented the city's middle-class constituency and temporarily tilted the balance of electoral power away from the growing black population. Yet established leaders realized that blacks were likely to become increasingly assertive politically.

To complicate matters, community sentiment was divided over the question of how active a part the city government should play in shaping the future of Atlanta. Should the city engage in minimal planning and make few attempts to direct its own development, or should it make serious efforts to plan and guide development? In 1950, city officials, including Mayor Hartsfield, had one foot in the past and had no great sympathy for the idea of government planning. Neighborhood leaders, owners of small businesses, and various other parochially minded people were also suspicious of extensive government intervention in community life.

But city officials also had one foot in the present. They were allied with the moderate-"progressive" coalition that was composed of those members of the white middle class who were business-led and cosmopolitan-minded and of blacks who were becoming increasingly active in political affairs. These two groups generally supported the principles of planning and controlled development.

This dominant coalition, however, reflected the sharply competing priorities and conflicting interests just described. The business community was concerned primarily with ways to revitalize the CDD. Blacks were keenly interested in improved housing opportunities. Circumstances were bound to arise in which the issues would be, Who has first claim on public resources and which land use would have precedence in cases of conflict?

In 1952, the Metropolitan Planning Commission came up with a general guide for future development. Although the commission's report, *Up Ahead*, called for the conservation of existing neighborhoods and improved housing for all groups, it gave particular attention to the CBD, which it divided into an upper and a lower portion. The report stated: "If these central districts are allowed to decline, the future health of the entire metropolitan area is in danger. The central districts are the core of Metropolitan Atlanta's regional activity. They contain huge public and private property investments and account for at least one-fourth of the total taxable wealth of the two [metropolitan] counties."[3]

The report also gave explicit attention to the need for what it termed "Negro expansion areas." Some possible areas were pinpointed, and a general policy was outlined. The report observed (but did not elaborate on the reasons for its conclusion), "From the viewpoint of planning, the

LOWEST LEVEL
LOWER-MIDDLE LEVEL
UPPER-MIDDLE LEVEL
HIGHEST LEVEL
CBD

NORTHSIDE

WESTSIDE

CENTRAL

EAST
ATLANTA

SECTOR

SOUTHWEST
ATLANTA

SOUTHSIDE

Map 4.1. Socioeconomic Levels in Atlanta

ward from an existing black neighborhood, a rapid white-to-black expansion engulfed large portions of this section of the city during the
1960s. This racial changeover, in part a consequence of population
pressures generated by central-sector displacement, was apparently
quietly encouraged by city officials. East Atlanta lies partly in DeKalb
County (most of Atlanta is in Fulton County), and the process of racial
transition spilled over into the non-Atlanta portions of DeKalb County.

wise thing is to find outlying areas to be developed for ne
housing.''[4] At other points the commission recommended a ''
tration'' of low-income families around the CBD, and in one
report called for "public policies to reduce existing densities,
blighted areas, improve the racial pattern of population distribu
make the best possible use of central land areas.''[5]

To Atlanta planners in the early 1950s, an improved racial dist.
did not mean integrated housing. It meant the selective decentral
of blacks in a pattern that preserved segregated housing. And it
conflict. The business community did not want blacks comp
around the CBD, but blacks and whites would oppose any resettlen

While the newly annexed portions of Atlanta (the 1952 annex
increased the city's size from 35 to 118 square miles) provided ai
room for new housing, the area was not so unpopulated as to prec
intense struggles over the racial composition of any area of apprecia
size. Land use was thus a matter of vital and unavoidable commun
concern. Disagreement over how much or how little planning and pu
lic intervention was necessary was only the first layer of conflict-
underneath was a vast interplay of competing interests and objectives.

The Social Geography of Atlanta in Brief

To understand the interplay of various interests and objectives and to
understand the role of urban renewal in Atlanta's development, it is
helpful to know something about the city's shifting social geography.
Residentially, Atlanta can be divided into six broad areas: Northside,
Westside, East Atlanta, Southside, Southwest Atlanta, and the central
sector. Map 4.1, based on a neighborhood analysis in the 1960s, shows
the various socioeconomic levels of different parts of the city. Northside
Atlanta is the highest socioeconomic status area. Much of this area was
added to the city by the 1952 annexation, as was much of Westside,
Southside, and Southwest Atlanta. Though there have been a few long-
standing pockets of black residences, the area has been overwhelmingly
white and racially stable. A Metropolitan Planning Commission report
identified four small neighborhoods in Northside as potential core areas
of black residences, but, significantly, stopped short of making a specific
recommendation. Twenty years later, no new housing for blacks has been
built in this section of the city.

Westside Atlanta, which, by 1960, was largely black, falls into the
middle socioeconomic levels. This section of Atlanta has been the scene
both of extensive new developments of housing for blacks and of massive racial transition in existing neighborhoods.

East Atlanta has been another racially volatile area. Spreading east-

The heartland of white provincialism in Atlanta is the Southside. Although at the mid-socioeconomic level, Southside Atlanta contains and is adjacent to some poor white sections. It also contains a federal prison. (A leading official is alleged to have discounted Southside opposition to housing projects with the comment, "No one lives there but a bunch of prison guards.") Southside has long had a scattering of black neighborhoods, and it has been the site of some rehousing programs for displaced blacks. However, it has not undergone the kind of wholesale racial changeover experienced by Westside and East Atlanta.

Southwest Atlanta is something of an anomaly. It is relatively affluent and mostly white but has recently undergone some racial transition along the northern perimeter. Though separated physically and psychologically from the prestigious Northside, Southwest has produced some public officials who have been prominent in the city's politics. They have used their influence in efforts to stop black expansion into the area, and they have prevented subsidized housing from being built in the area. The recent racial transition has involved affluent residential neighborhoods.

The central sector of Atlanta is mostly poor and black. Many of the whites who lived in the central sector when the 1950s began were subsequently displaced by urban renewal and highway construction or they moved out as displaced blacks moved in. In 1950, the northernmost part of the central sector was white (and remains so today); black and white neighborhoods were intermingled in the area south of the CBD. The two major concentrations of blacks were in (1) the area to the west of the CBD and separated from it by the sizable "railroad gulch"—the Atlanta University district, and (2) the area to the east of and immediately adjacent to the CBD—the Auburn Avenue district. The eastern area has been particularly important—through its heart runs Auburn Avenue, the traditional center of commercial and organizational life for Atlanta blacks. To the north of Auburn Avenue was a large slum area variously known as Black Bottom or Buttermilk Bottom. As the later narrative will indicate, because Buttermilk Bottom adjoined the CBD, it was especially coveted.

Some Land-Use Activities Immediately Preceding Urban Renewal

In the narrative account that follows, attention will be concentrated on urban renewal as a device through which land use was changed, the revitalization of the CBD was promoted, and the pattern and quality of residential life were shaped. But urban renewal was not the only public activity that helped to recast Atlanta in the period after World War II. Several decisions that were not formally connected with urban renewal are noteworthy because they form part of the context in which redevelopment occurred.

The city's white political and business leaders played an active part in transactions through which Atlanta's Westside was opened up for black housing.[6] Blacks took the initiative. They had owned some land in the area for a long time. They bought enough additional land and commanded enough financial resources to show that black expansion to the west was feasible. In 1952, with white financial institutions providing some of the needed financing, agreements were worked out under city hall auspices. White business leaders also facilitated some private-housing construction in the Southside. Black expansion to the south and west was further encouraged by the construction of two large public-housing projects: Carver Community (990 units) on the Southside was completed in 1953, and Perry Homes (1,000 units) on the Westside was opened for occupancy in 1955 (see map 4.2). These two projects preceded urban renewal displacement but were part of a general effort, as noted by one set of observers, "to guide and concentrate the distribution" of blacks.[7] Table 4.1 shows that the location pattern of new public housing has

Table 4.1. The Location of Public-Housing Units

Number of Units by Time Period and Type		Percentage of Units Located by Sector					
		Central Sector	Westside	Southwest Atlanta	Southside	East Atlanta	Northside
1930s and 1940s (Pre-World War II)							
All units	5,014	100	—	—	—	—	—
Family units*	3,053	100	—	—	—	—	—
1950s (Prerenewal)							
All units	2,500	20.4†	40.0	—	39.6	—	—
Family units	2,082	20.8	49.9	—	38.2	—	—
1960 to 1970 (Units built for renewal relocation)							
All units	5,382	31.8	27.7	—	25.6	14.9	—
Family units	3,483	10.9	37.5	—	35.2	16.5	—

*Family units are those with two or more bedrooms.

†These units were developed as a white public-housing project, Joel Chandler Harris Homes. The project is located on the border between the central sector and Southwest Atlanta; it was built as a buffer against black residential movement.

changed drastically since World War II. In the years before and after renewal displacement began, some public housing was built in the central sector, but family units in particular were located in outlying areas.

Freeway location provided another force in reshaping the city. At the city's instigation, the north/south freeway was shifted from a proposed route on the west of the CBD (which would have been elevated over the "railroad gulch" area) to a route that looped around the eastern periphery of the CBD. The east/west freeway was located just south of the CBD; and, like the north/south freeway, served to displace a large number of close-in, low-income families. (Both freeways are shown on map 4.2.) Before an urban renewal program was officially launched (no project entered the execution phase until mid-1959), the major outlines of a resettlement policy were thus evident: low-income black families in the central sector would be moved to selected outlying districts. Westside, Southside, and later East Atlanta would absorb displacees and inmigrants. The Southwest was more complicated—some buffer zones were created; but there were black residential areas in the most outlying regions; and large areas were completely undeveloped. Northside would remain white. Governmental actions, "gentlemen's agreements," and white business backing converged behind this policy. As the urban renewal program reached fruition, it became a major arena in which this still-emerging policy was tested.

Urban Renewal

The early rationale of urban renewal was appealingly simple. By assembling suitable land tracts and offering them at written-down prices, a process made possible by federal subsidy, a local government could encourage redevelopment of former slums. It has, from the start, been an object of wide community interest and concern, and its use has been at the core of many attempts to improve the urban condition. Federal officials and others believed in the beginning that the land made available in this way would be inexpensive enough to make housing on it financially feasible for families of modest means. In fact, urban renewal was enacted as part of the nation's housing program, but redevelopment objectives were vague. Beyond the elimination of blighted areas, Congress established no well-defined program goals. Although Workable Program requirements were enacted in 1954 to set comprehensive standards of eligibility for federal aid, federal legislation has allowed widely differing objectives to coexist under the redevelopment umbrella.[8] By and large, local governments have been free to use their own condemnation authority and federal financial assistance to assemble

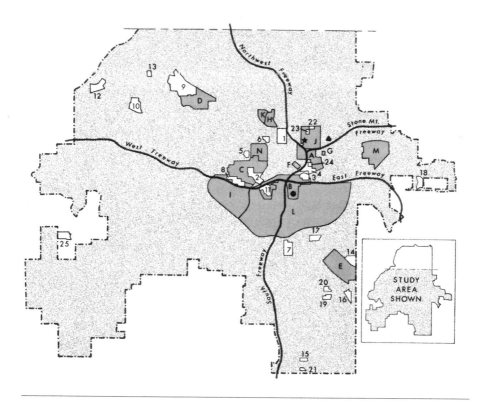

Map 4.2. Urban Renewal and Public-Housing Projects, 1970

LOW-RENT PUBLIC HOUSING [   ]

EXISTING PROJECTS

1. TECHWOOD (1936)
   CLARK HOWELL (1940)
   PALMER HOUSE (1966)*
   NORTH AVE.-TECHWOOD
   (in planning)
2. UNIVERSITY (1937)
   JOHN HOPE (1940)
3. CAPITOL (1941)
4. GRADY (1942)
   ANTOINE GRAVES (1965)*
5. EAGAN (1941)
6. HERNDON (1941)
7. CARVER (1953)

UNDER CONSTRUCTION

18. EAST LAKE
19. JONESBORO ROAD I
20. JONESBORO ROAD II
21. GILBERT GARDENS ANNEX
22. NORTH AVE.-LINDEN**

8. HARRIS (1956)
   JOHN O. CHILES (1965)*
9. PERRY (1955, 1969)
10. BOWEN (1964)
    (FIELD ROAD SITE)
11. McDANIEL-GLENN (1968)
12. BANKHEAD (1969)
13. HOLLYWOOD (1969)
14. THOMASVILLE HEIGHTS (1970)
15. GILBERT GARDENS (1970)
16. LEILA VALLEY (1970)
17. WELLSWOOD (1970)

IN PLANNING

23. BEDFORD PLACE-LINDEN
24. PITTMAN-HILLIARD ST.*
25. KIMBERLY
CAMPBELL DRIVE (FULTON
  COUNTY, NOT SHOWN)
BOAT ROCK ROAD (FULTON
  COUNTY, NOT SHOWN)

URBAN [   ] RENEWAL PROJECTS

A. BUTLER STREET
B. RAWSON-WASHINGTON
C. UNIVERSITY CENTER
D. ROCKDALE
E. THOMASVILLE
F. GEORGIA STATE
G. HOWARD HIGH
H. GEORGIA TECH
I. WEST END
J. BEDFORD-PINE
K. GEORGIA TECH II
L. MODEL CITIES
M. EDGEWOOD
N. VINE CITY

● STADIUM SITE
★ CIVIC CENTER
▲ EGLESTON SITE

( ) Date Opened for Occupancy   * Housing for the Elderly

**Housing Predominantly for the Elderly

URBAN RENEWAL DEMANDS IN ATLANTA, 1950-1970

tracts of property and change land uses in accordance with their own priorities. Once this fact was appreciated, urban renewal was subject to an array of demands. The urban renewal program has been used to attract affluent taxpayers and shoppers back to the city, to redevelop and revitalize business districts, to construct civic facilities, to expand medical and educational institutions, and to reverse neighborhood decline, as well as to rehouse the nonaffluent.

Although it is federally assisted, urban renewal is basically a local program, one in which local officials have had wide latitude in making choices. Hence, a study of a city's urban renewal program meshes well with the study of community power. The exercise of local authority to shape and control land use by means of urban renewal is an especially inviting focus for such a study. Of the various aspects of urban renewal, land use is the matter of widest community interest and the matter that most directly concerns the scope and direction of the program. Land use is also a topic manageable enough to be considered over a long time span. Last, but by no means least important, land use is a matter that lends itself to a determination of what did and did not occur by way of tangible policy outputs.

For purposes of the present research, the land-use-related aspects of urban renewal include the selection of areas for renewal, land-use designation and designation of the type of renewal treatment (that is, clearance or rehabilitation) that these areas would receive, the allocation of resources for renewal and for particular types of redevelopment, and the placement of relocation facilities.

Purpose and Scope of the Case Narrative

A comment should be offered about the amount of time covered in the research presented here. Obviously, interviewing, even when as here conducted over a period of two years and supplemented by access to a number of excellent documentary sources, cannot yield an exhaustive account of how and why major policy choices were made during two decades of experience with a program.[9] But the advantages of a longitudinal study appear to outweigh the advantages of confining the analysis to recent events that permit detailed reconstruction.[10] As argued earlier, if policy formation is to be studied effectively, policy choices emanating from indirect exertions of power (that is, from positional advantages) need to be compared with those that emerge from "forceful conflict." The long time perspective not only supplies sufficient instances to make comparisons fruitful, it also enables the researcher to analyze policy outcomes in more than their immediate circumstances, that is, as returns on the investment of power resources in obtaining positional advantages.

A lengthy period of policymaking also makes it possible to examine the follow-through to controversies in order to determine whether or not decisions were effectively implemented. Most researchers into community politics and policymaking can attest that current decisions are almost always importantly intertwined with those of the past—hence, one reason for beginning the case study with a brief look at land use in Atlanta in the years immediately after World War II. A justification, then, for studying urban renewal rather than some other areas of policy is that the renewal program has been in operation long enough for the durable aspects of power to be fully distinguishable from the transitory ones.

The case narrative that follows is not a general political history of Atlanta for a twenty-year period. Neither is it an exhaustive effort to consider and weigh every single factor that affected urban renewal policy in Atlanta. Federal programs, for example, are treated as ingredients in but not determinants of local policy.

While the presentation is not an attempt to deny the importance of such factors as the federal impact, the principal objective is to highlight the influence of local groups in policy formation. As a consequence, the analysis is narrowly focused on the process of demand conversion described earlier. The case narrative is centered squarely on the concrete proposals for city action in the land-use-related aspects of urban renewal. The main concerns are to identify the various demands, to examine the efforts to influence officials in connection with these demands, to see what strategies officials employed in responding to various demands, and to determine how demands were ultimately treated by official decision makers. While the narrative account should be useful in its own right, one of its purposes is to serve as a background for a later effort to analyze demand conversion in a more systematic and abstract manner.

During the mayoralty of William B. Hartsfield, whose tenure spanned a period of extraordinary social change, Atlanta acquired a reputation for racial moderation and civic progress. Hartsfield's political style was well suited to accommodation, if not to leadership, on racial issues. By the late 1940s, when blacks in large numbers began to register and vote, Hartsfield had already been in office for a number of years. Never one to be complacent about constituent support, he courted the new voters along with the old. Because he proved himself to be a master of the fine art of adding black support without giving up his close ties with business leaders and other upper-status whites, he was the central figure in the "progressive" coalition that dominated city elections throughout much of the post-World War II era.

Though Hartsfield's background did not predispose him to be a racial liberal, he did bring certain assets to the changing political scene. He was personally very accessible to constituents, black as well as white. He never forgot that constituents were individuals, with particular needs. But he also had a knack for making gestures that reassured groups of constituents of his concern for their welfare. He was a pioneer among southern white politicians in showing social courtesies to blacks. While Hartsfield was discreet about his contacts with black leaders, he nevertheless campaigned openly for black support and established a good working relationship with the leaders of the Atlanta Negro Voters League.

One other personal quality served him well. Although he had a flair for public relations, Hartsfield's political genius lay in conducting quiet negotiations. Whenever possible, he preferred to defuse tense situations by behind-the-scenes bargaining. It was a preference that was shared by most of the established black leaders, few of whom were inclined to pursue an uncompromising course in negotiations. This modus operandi was equally satisfactory to Hartsfield's white business allies. They were prepared to maintain an atmosphere of cordial interracial cooperation by making concessions to blacks, one to one and one by one, out of the glare of publicity. It was a strategy that worked for more than a decade.

The Hartsfield mayoralty was thus a time in which many of the city's racial questions were handled by mediation and by quiet accommodations worked out between a few individuals. While protests were resorted to on occasion, by all accounts the preferred method for settling disputes was closed, nonpublic negotiations, or as one observer explained, "the manipulative adjustment of interests."[1] As we shall see, this system of politics inevitably neglected some interests. After all, in the 1950s, Atlanta's black community was large, it was socially, economically, and geographically diverse, and it had many particular interests as well as important collective interests. Behind-the-scenes negotiations between leaders may have taken care of individual wants fairly well, but that kind of transaction was ill suited to solving the complex problems of a disadvantaged group. Not the least of these problems—and one especially significant for this account—was the lack of adequate housing for blacks. Such needs were often voiced without being acted upon. Thus, in this chapter and in others that follow, major demands will be mentioned even when there was no follow-through on them.

During the Hartsfield years, the major channels of black representation were the Atlanta Negro Voters League and the Urban League, but other agencies and organizations had views about housing and renewal, which they expressed with varying degrees of urgency and determination.

Early Conflicts

Despite the skills of Hartsfield and others in the arts of political bargaining, the early attempts to plan and launch urban renewal in Atlanta were marked by a series of major community controversies. The program was strongly supported by business groups, by some prominent leaders in the black community, and by a number of white leaders and organizations regarded as racially moderate. At the same time, renewal policy was widely opposed in the black community. Other groups, particularly white neighborhood organizations, also vehemently resisted parts of the city's program. While planning officials and other proponents of redevelopment regarded business backing as essential to the undertaking of a renewal program, the business community was not powerful enough to prevent conflict or even to prevail consistently when conflict occurred. Issue outcomes seemed to depend greatly on what alignment of allies and opponents a particular controversy evoked. Moreover, the quest for allies and the efforts at coalition building were themselves evidence that no single group had the power to resolve conflicts entirely on its own terms.

Despite the shifting lines of conflict and despite its uneven won/lost record, the business community was clearly the winner when all of the city's actions and inactions are placed in perspective. Renewal policy, as it was actually put into effect, corresponded closely to the expressed interests of the major business groups in Atlanta. Furthermore, the business community was intimately involved in all phases of renewal planning.

While Hartsfield was the central figure in the city's electoral politics and a man who negotiated many delicate issues with the political leaders of the black community, he seldom assumed the role of innovator in policy matters. Outside of a few pet projects such as airport expansion, he relied on others to formulate proposals. He often consulted with an informal cadre of young professionals (planners, administrators in civic organizations, lawyers, and the like), most of whom were not even on the city payroll, and made use of their talents in promoting new programs. However, Hartsfield expected major proposals to have business backing before they were unveiled publicly.

Urban redevelopment as a concrete policy proposal took shape initially among the young professionals who advised Hartsfield. They, in turn, engaged in early consultation with leading businessmen, particularly those who were represented in the CAIA.[2] Hartsfield and his informal staff shared the view that the CAIA was not only responsible but influential. As one civic activist described it, the CAIA was "the closest thing in town to the organized 'power structure.'"[3]

Because Atlanta's government and business leaders shared a common concern in maintaining the city as a thriving center for the metropolitan region, consultation came about easily. Even before the passage of the 1949 Federal Housing Act, plans for rejuvenating the CBD were being considered. It was not difficult, then, for staff members of the Metropolitan Planning Commission (an "independent" public body, but one that remained in close consultation with the mayor's office) and the CAIA to spark interest in slum clearance. The CAIA and the Georgia Institute of Technology were enlisted as publicly visible supporters of a proposal to redevelop a predominantly white neighborhood, the Hemphill Avenue area, close to the CBD and also adjacent to the Georgia Tech campus (see map 5.1).

A 1950 attempt to handle the Hemphill Avenue project quietly was unsuccessful. At the minimally publicized but legally required public hearing, neighborhood businessmen and residents began their determined resistance to the proposal. Their opposition, in turn, made salient some ideological questions about public subsidies over which the larger business community was divided. Moreover, relocation from the proposed redevelopment area was to be accomplished by building public housing in another neighborhood, a neighborhood that added its own disapproval to the city's plan. Public housing itself was also the object of strong disapproval by real estate interests.

Proponents quietly shelved the project, fearing that ideologically conservative neighborhood businessmen and nonaffluent white residents, worried over the future of their neighborhoods, might coalesce into a permanent opposition to redevelopment. They decided, instead, to find a test case through which to settle some of the legal questions that had been raised about redevelopment. Because

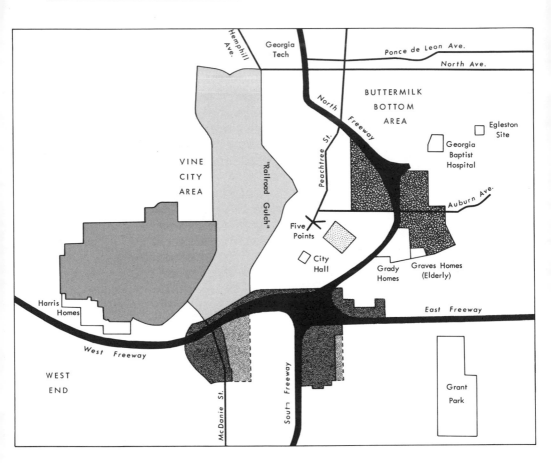

Map 5.1. Central Atlanta in the Hartsfield Era

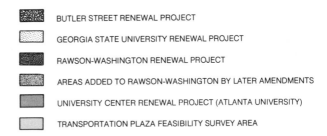

BUTLER STREET RENEWAL PROJECT

GEORGIA STATE UNIVERSITY RENEWAL PROJECT

RAWSON-WASHINGTON RENEWAL PROJECT

AREAS ADDED TO RAWSON-WASHINGTON BY LATER AMENDMENTS

UNIVERSITY CENTER RENEWAL PROJECT (ATLANTA UNIVERSITY)

TRANSPORTATION PLAZA FEASIBILITY SURVEY AREA

the black community viewed any renewal program with great apprehension, the selection of an appropriate site proved difficult. The city's initial interest in redevelopment had been greeted editorially by the *Atlanta Daily World*, a black newspaper, with the warning to its readers that urban redevelopment "could mean 'Negro clearance.'" The *Daily World* made it apparent that clearance in or around Auburn Avenue, the traditional center of black business and civic activity, would be resisted "by whatever influence" blacks could "bring to bear, politically, legally or otherwise."[4]

McDaniel Street, a small black area away from Auburn Avenue, was finally selected for redevelopment as an industrial site (see map 5.1). Again opposition developed. White property owners and black residents fought the proposal together. Meanwhile, ideological issues reemerged and temporarily produced divisions within both the City Council and the business community. Some opposition was based on the fear that the program would be expensive, and some concern was expressed that "the free enterprise system" was being threatened by a "socialistic" scheme.

The CAIA was the principal supporter of redevelopment for McDaniel Street. Urban League officials, eager to see housing conditions improved, were enlisted to counterbalance the opposition of black residents. Although this redevelopment alliance was able to generate majority support on the Board of Aldermen, it lost the subsequent court battle. In 1953, the Georgia Supreme Court ruled that the state enabling legislation was contrary to the constitution of Georgia.

Three years had been expended testing first the political feasibility and then the legality of urban redevelopment. Two more years were required to put redevelopment on a new legal basis by amending the state constitution and enacting new enabling legislation. Once the legal barriers were cleared, renewal proponents faced again the intricate task of making the program politically viable. Starting the program on a quiet, piecemeal basis had proved impossible, but the early experience had served to identify the major points of resistance.

Coalition Building

Even with a new legal foundation for redevelopment, the program did not have the mayor's enthusiastic support. In the task of building a coalition in support of urban renewal, the activists were again planners and other professionals who were tied closely to the CAIA. Strongly committed to two ideas, that Atlanta should be the economic capital of the Southeast and a community with a progressive racial policy, they presented urban renewal as a program that could simultaneously enhance the economic potential of Atlanta, especially its CBD, and improve housing conditions for blacks. Support was mobilized mainly within the electoral alliance of which Hartsfield was the leader—though Hartsfield himself did little leading in this phase of Atlanta's urban renewal history.

The CAIA, the Metropolitan Planning Commission, and the white newspapers (the major media of local news), had from the beginning supported urban renewal. The Metropolitan Planning Commission had prepared two major reports delineating areas in need of redevelopment. The newspapers had lent their support by running articles on blight around the CBD, articles that implied that opposition to redevelopment came mainly from slum landlords more intent on making profits than on serving the community. For its part, the CAIA had, over the years, presented a business-oriented rationale for the program.

In 1955, this nucleus of support was reactivated. A committee of the CAIA, staffed by the Metropolitan Planning Commission, drafted the Central Atlanta Plan, a program of CBD revitalization in which slum clearance and redevelopment were important elements. Protecting downtown property values by pushing back blighted areas, expanding the commercial core of the city, and solving the city's traffic and parking problems were linked together and used as a package to enlist further support.

Renewal proponents made an effort to appeal directly to both upper and lower CBD business interests. Two areas for urban renewal were pinpointed, one to the east (the Butler Street project of special concern to upper CBD interests) and the other to the south of the business district (the Rawson-Washington project of special concern to lower CBD interests). Although much of the emphasis was on slum *clearance* rather than on *reuse*, expansion of the business district to the east was given particular attention.

Advocates of urban renewal took special care to obtain the backing of the Chamber of Commerce because the chamber was the most broadly representative business organization. The Real Estate Board was also a highly desirable ally because of its direct concern with housing and land use. The Central Atlanta Plan called, in general terms, for "full utilization of private enterprise," in the urban renewal program,[5] but general terms were not sufficient to reassure some of the realtors and ideological conservatives. Because there was concern that urban renewal was just another way to build public housing, the chairman of the Atlanta Housing Authority took a further step. He discreetly gave assurance that urban renewal land would not be used for public housing and that the Housing Authority itself would initiate no requests for additional public housing. In short order, endorsements of the Central Atlanta Plan were forthcoming from the Chamber of Commerce, the Real Estate Board, and other business and professional organizations.

While business support was being solidified, an effort was made to enlist allies in the black community. Coalition-building hopes rested upon the Urban League, financially supported by the Community Chest, with white members on its board, and with a long-standing and active interest in housing for blacks. Moreover, the Urban League had two strategically important constituents, the Atlanta University complex and the Empire Real Estate Board (the black real estate association). The Urban League was interested in a general upgrading of the neighborhood around the university, and the colleges that made up the university system were particularly eager to obtain land for expansion. Renewal and relocation activities were also laden with business opportunities for real estate companies. A third area for renewal was thus added to the two identified in the Central Atlanta Plan.

A logroll was well on the way toward execution, but one critical issue still remained—that of relocation. The housing problem, always serious because of the shortage of land available to blacks and because of the continuing inmigration of low-income families, was being worsened by freeway displacement and code enforcement. The Atlanta Baptist Ministers' Union, an organization of black ministers, had already requested that public housing be increased by one thousand units. However, reliance upon public housing could weaken white business support. The FHA 221 program, by contrast, could satisfy the various coalition interests.

At that time, the mid-1950s, the 221 program consisted of single-family housing without direct subsidy. Under this program, houses could be built in outlying areas on small lots and under relaxed FHA standards. Persons displaced by government action would be eligible for no-down-payment, long-term FHA-insured mortgages. Inexpensive land and small monthly payments, it was hoped, would make home ownership feasible for many families of modest means. The recent annexation had provided undeveloped land in outlying areas of the city. Thus the program was feasible for Atlanta, and it was politically palatable to the urban renewal coalition. Real estate companies and developers could realize profits, conservative businessmen would be undisturbed ideologically by the program, and the CAIA would receive an added dividend in that low-income families would be moved away from the business district. Urban renewal proponents at one time suggested that the city meet a portion of the development costs for 221 housing, but the city did not act on the idea.

One further attraction was devised for the black community. The Urban League and the Empire Real Estate Board had for years worked to secure land for black housing developments. So, in addition to a commitment to use the 221 program, some barriers to the expansion of black residential areas were removed. Two remote areas of substandard but low-density housing occupied by blacks were also earmarked for future renewal and redevelopment. This ploy brought the number of areas designated for renewal to five.

As the initial package of projects was moved into the final planning stage, the funds available from the 1957 bond issue proved to be inadequate for all that had been proposed. The three inner-city projects were trimmed in size and in amount of clearance, but in such a way as to maintain support from the CAIA and selected black leaders. For instance, when planners deleted a clearance area of high-cost land bordering the CBD, CAIA officials were able to have the area reinstated as a clearance section of the project. The Housing Authority explained its decision to federal regional officials by stating that this action was "endorsed by the Central Atlanta Improvement Association which, as you know, represents the top downtown business leadership in this community. It thus became a 'must' not only on the basis of planning desirability, but also because it has become the key to continuing civic and business support for the entire Atlanta program."[6] Instead, a clearance section intended to permit redevelopment of a black shopping center was deleted.

In the paring process, a large rehabilitation area was dropped from the project encompassing the Atlanta University system; later a small industrial area marked for clearance was also excluded. In justifying these actions, as well as its decision to retain for future clearance another area adjacent to Morris Brown College (of the Atlanta University system), the Housing Authority explained that it was necessary "to provide for the expansion needs of Morris Brown College. . . . This is a particularly vital element since failure to provide in our planning for the needs of Morris Brown College might jeopardize support of the Urban Renewal Program by much of the Negro civic and church leadership."[7]

One other suggestion got short shrift: a proposal by one of the prestigious businessmen members of the CACUR who wanted to drop completely one of the outlying projects scheduled for 221 redevelopment. The support of black real estate men was tied too closely to the 221 housing program to risk conflict on that issue.

More than two years of planning and negotiation were required to put together an urban renewal coalition. Several member groups in the coalition had strong and immediate interest in the success of the program.

Proponents of urban renewal abandoned the quiet approach in favor of the "hard sell." They saw to it that urban renewal was discussed extensively, especially within the business community, and they promoted renewal as a program absolutely essential to the future well-being of Atlanta. A large enough renewal and relocation package was undertaken to make possible the formation of a sizable group of supporters, who were brought together as a coalition in support of economic growth and racial justice. Opponents of redevelopment were vulnerable to the charge that they were against urban renewal because they had vested interests in the economic and racial status quo. The coalition used this argument aggressively, singling out owners of slum property for extensive publicity, and they gave every indication that opposition to redevelopment would be met with still more unfavorable publicity. Concessions had been made to some potential opponents within the business community. The city's commercial interests were to be the major beneficiaries of redevelopment. Selected black interests were also offered opportunities to attain their goals, but the involvement of blacks was restricted both in the aspects of the program on which they were consulted and in the number of groups represented. As had been the case earlier, in this period of planning and coalition building (roughly 1953 to 1957), Mayor Hartsfield played a relatively passive role, but the young professionals around him were in the thick of all the important activities.

Urban Renewal Implementation and Community Conflict

Once capital bonds for redevelopment and other community improvements became available in 1957,[8] general planning gave way to specific steps toward implementation. Moving urban renewal from the drawing board, the coalition building, and the early promotion stages to actual execution was not an easily accomplished task. In the first place, maintaining an aura of broad support for urban renewal proved difficult. Overt conflict was impossible to prevent. Several interest groups were involved, each of whom possessed resources that had to be reckoned with. As conflict emerged, the questions became, Would stalemate occur, and whose interest would be served if the program survived?

Relocation precipitated the first challenge to the urban renewal coalition. When housing under the 221 program was started to accommodate freeway displacees, most of them black, opposition in the middle- and working-class white neighborhoods was aroused. Noncooperation by the aldermanic board and city departments ensued, and it extended across a range of activities. Zoning was used to obstruct 221 housing, and at one point the aldermen with the mayor's concurrence were on the verge of suspending all building permits for 221 housing. Construction standards (and therefore costs) were raised to offset some criticism. Resistance spread from relocation to other phases of the Workable Program, with finances proving to be the most critical area of noncooperation. The Parks

Department and the Public Works Department refused to earmark funds for urban renewal areas, and without these expenditures the city would not meet its share of the full five-project urban renewal program. Retrenchment to a smaller program was not feasible because the urban renewal coalition would be endangered.

Rescuing the embattled urban renewal program from a recalcitrant city government required the forceful intervention of key members of the CAIA. The confrontation was with the mayor, for he was regarded as the major link between the business community and City Hall. In one private meeting, the mayor defended himself by asserting that if urban renewal had been delayed it was due not to his opposition but to resistance by the aldermen, to his own lack of power, and to the "sniping" of the press. The newspaper followed with an editorial attacking the mayor for his passivity in the face of a floundering program of urban renewal. The editorial expressed the view that the mayor could provide much-needed leadership if he wanted to, and concluded, "the only question is, does he want to marshal city fathers behind the urban renewal program?"[9]

Shortly thereafter the mayor acceded to business pressure for more active support of redevelopment. He passed the warning around City Hall that "our downtown citizens, together with the newspapers" would "go to the extent of rooting the entire government out if they feel we have been remiss in the face of federal opportunities to make progress."[10] It could not be said that the various city agencies subsequently gave their full and enthusiastic cooperation, but the urban renewal program survived intact.

In contrast with this quiet and complete accession to business pressure, Mayor Hartsfield chose to respond to continuing neighborhood attacks on the program with a public counterassault. Once City Hall was more or less brought into line behind the redevelopment program, Hartsfield proved highly resistant to further constituency pressures. Forsaking the role of mediator, he sought no compromises. Instead he placed the spotlight of publicity on critics of the program by openly questioning their motives. The Hartsfield strategy was obviously that of isolating program opponents by treating them as a noisy group who enjoyed no official support and who cared little for the welfare of the whole community.

A white neighborhood organization from the Southside, the Fourth Ward Zoning Committee, was an especially vocal and persistent critic of the city's renewal program. Spokesmen for this organization argued that outlying land should be used for middle-class residences, and close-in land, such as that included in renewal projects, should be redeveloped as public housing and other types of multifamily projects. The mayor was finally provoked into a public rebuttal, in which he charged "certain synthetic organizations" with trying to make Atlanta "the only city in the nation where a poor man cannot build a home."[11]

Concurrently with other challenges to urban renewal, discontent built up within the black community. As early as 1955, black leaders along with a few white neighborhood leaders had indicated their preference for City Hall over the Housing Authority as the local redevelopment agency.[12] Fears that access to the renewal planning process would be restricted to white business organizations were reinforced by Mayor Hartsfield's delay in appointing a citizens' advisory committee. By the time a committee of six whites and three blacks was appointed in January 1958, project plans were fairly complete. No representation was provided for the residents of the areas to be renewed. While there had been consultation with the Urban League, Atlanta University officials, and some members of the Empire Real Estate Board, white neighborhood opposition to relocation efforts threatened to undermine even that limited base of support among blacks. If white resistance had extinguished the building of 221 housing, probably no blacks would have defended urban renewal—at least not publicly. As it was, apprehension ran high in the black community.

In a mass meeting sponsored by an organization of church and business leaders within the black community, a twelve-page document detailing grievances was read and later transmitted to various white leaders and officials. This organization, which named itself the Localities Committee, made efforts to have federal approval of renewal funds withheld on the grounds that Atlanta's citizen participation and relocation actions did not meet federal standards. Specific attention was given to the provision that required that

there be a feasible method for the temporary relocation of families displaced from the urban renewal area, and that there are or are being provided in the urban renewal area, or in other areas not generally less desirable in regard to public utilities and public and commercial facilities and at rents or prices within the financial means of the families displaced from the urban renewal area, decent, safe, and sanitary dwellings equal in number to the number of and available to such displaced families and reasonably accessible to their places of employment.[13]

The legal position of black leaders seemed also to be strengthened by federal administrative regulations. Clearance other than for housing called for a showing that "representative local leadership among Negro and other racial minority groups in the community had indicated that there is no substantial objection thereto."[14] There were objections, however. Existing project boundaries, drawn to include areas of maximum appeal to potential redevelopers, were considered unsatisfactory because they did not envelop the areas of greatest dilapidation. Black leaders preferred that clearance be confined to what they termed "the worst areas," and that redevelopment not decrease the amount of close-in land devoted to housing for their constituents.[15] At the heart of the Localities Committee's concern was the fear that renewal as well as other forms of government action might displace the population served by centrally located black businesses and churches. Inner-city residents themselves made it clear that they wanted to remain in their existing neighborhoods.

Although the backing of a large number of business, religious, political, and service organizations was obtained by the Localities Committee, the committee's position was attacked as self-serving and its tactics were labeled irresponsible. Mayor Hartsfield fixed his fire publicly on the Localities Committee's close working ally, the local branch of the NAACP. The mayor openly questioned the motives of NAACP officials, charging them with "an arrogant effort to break up what they cannot control."[16] He maintained that blacks had been consulted, that they were represented on the citizens' advisory committee, and that plans under consideration would provide rehousing opportunities for thousands of blacks displaced by freeways as well as those displaced by urban renewal. Hartsfield concluded his public attack thus: "It is ironic that an effort to improve Atlanta and give Negroes a better place to live should be attacked by an organization pretending to work in their interest. Time is now an all-important factor, and our plans will go forward unless the local president of the NAACP has more power in Washington than in Atlanta."[17]

Federal officials did take an active interest in the Atlanta situation, but the actual federal role was that of mediation. A race relations officer from the Washington office brought representatives of the city and the black community together without much initial success. But with gentle pressure on the city some concessions were eventually made to the Localities Committee's position. Project boundaries remained essentially unchanged, but the 221 program was unblocked. While federal authorities would require only that the city provide relocation housing for urban renewal displacees, not for all displacees,[18] the city did agree to conduct an additional study of relocation-housing needs.

Before 1958 had ended, white business leaders further confirmed and consolidated their support, principally for urban renewal but also for relocation housing for blacks. CACUR was expanded and included several prominent businessmen. This expanded committee established a number of subcommittees, one of which was concerned with the relocation program and assisted for a time in the finding of land for 221 housing.

The large amount of clearance around the business district made relocation a continuing concern. A housing study conducted in 1958 had shown that by 1963 government action would displace more than ten thousand families, many with extremely low incomes. Not everyone worried, however. One Housing Authority commissioner blithely dismissed the relocation problem with the statement that ''experience in other cities shows that some, especially those who are renting slum dwellings, will just fade away as the deadline for moving nears. In many cases this group lives on a day-to-day basis and prefers to quietly get out of the picture.''[19]

Gradually, however, black leaders, working through the CACUR and joined by whites from health and welfare professions, persuaded city officials that additional public housing was needed. During hearings held in November 1958, little adverse testimony was given, and the Board of Aldermen authorized the planning and construction of one thousand new units of public housing. Still, as no sites had been agreed upon, aldermanic support of public housing was not severely tested at that time.

A year was spent considering possible locations for public housing. In an effort to gain a concession to the desire of blacks to have some close-in housing, the Urban League proposed that low-rent housing be built in the Buttermilk Bottom section, an area of slum housing immediately east of the CBD (see map 5.1). The CAIA voiced objections on the ground that the land was too valuable for low-cost housing. Other sites not so close to the CBD were considered and dropped because of objections either by aldermen or by white members of the CACUR. Public-housing placement was constrained by an earlier ''gentleman's agreement'' between white business and political leaders and black real estate men that housing for blacks would not be built or acquired outside agreed-on corridors in the city. Finally two sites, both requiring a rezoning action, were agreed upon. One—the Field Road site that was eventually to become Bowen Homes (see map 4.2)—was for 650 units in an outlying area, and the other—the Egleston site (see map 5.1)—was for 350 units (210 of which were to be for the elderly) in a somewhat close-in area.

Neighborhood resistance developed, as anticipated, but the close-in location, the recently abandoned Egleston Hospital site, aroused opposition far beyond the residences immediately affected.[20] The site was near the Georgia Baptist Hospital, a white institution once fringed but later encircled by black residences, as whites left the neighborhood. Some of the hospital board members believed that public housing would accelerate racial transition and leave a white hospital deep in the midst of a black ghetto. As the controversy waxed, several white neighborhood organizations and churches became involved. Wide-ranging white fears over the expansion of the black community thus came to be focused on the Egleston site.

The issue also assumed symbolic importance for the coalition of black and white moderates. Significantly, in early 1960, at the very time that the attempt to have the Egleston site rezoned was reaching a conclusion, the student sit-in movement was beginning. One white civic leader foresaw a crisis in Atlanta's race relations, and voiced the fear that if the Egleston site were lost, then "moderate and responsible Negroes" would lose leadership or become more militant. He cautioned, "We must restore their leadership and keep their cooperation if Atlanta is going to have stable housing."[21]

Among the backers of urban renewal there was some general concern that the program might be endangered by the displacement of moderate leaders in the black community. Apprehension extended to the possibility that blacks would bring suit for public-housing desegregation and that blacks might disregard existing racial agreements and expand into several white residential areas. In other words, blacks had considerable capacity to rock the boat of Atlanta's white leaders, and those leaders depended on a few strategically placed individuals to restrain the actions of the black community. Much was therefore at stake in the handling of the Egleston issue.

The coalition between blacks and white business and civic leaders mobilized support for the rezoning of the Egleston site. Mayor Hartsfield took an open stand on the matter and argued publicly that the issue was one of whether the rehousing of displaced blacks would be controlled or uncontrolled. He endorsed rezoning with the warning that the alternative to approval of the Egleston site was "uncontrolled infiltration all over the city and very largely to the detriment of the people who are fighting this site."[22] Breaking with a tradition of not taking public stands on controversial issues, the Chamber of Commerce added its endorsement of rezoning. Other upper-status white civic and professional organizations made public their support for rezoning, as did a number of white business leaders individually. The newspapers spelled out possible consequences of aldermanic rejection of rezoning and added a not very subtle political warning:

It appears inevitable that the question of urban renewal and redevelopment will be a major issue in the city's next political campaign. The program has been kicked around so much by selfish and greedy interests that to have a public expression on it would indeed be welcomed. We firmly believe that the majority want the slums cleared out and that those obstructing the programs will pay the penalty at the polls.[23]

Despite the full mobilization of support, the moderate coalition was defeated. While the outlying and thus symbolically less important site was approved by a decisive eleven-to-five vote, Egleston rezoning was defeated by a one-vote margin. The vice-mayor was in the unhappy position of casting the tie-breaking vote, and the following year he paid the political consequences and was voted out of office. Blacks singled him out for retribution, as one who had in the past received their solid backing but who had failed to support the moderate position when so much was "on the line."[24]

Blacks regarded the Egleston defeat as a rejection of the basic principle that blacks should be able "to develop in their own areas." A large, open meeting was held to protest the aldermanic decision. However, despite earlier threats, A. T. Walden, head of the Atlanta Negro Voters League and long-standing political leader of the black community, sought to maintain an air of moderation. He remarked that blacks "do not like what has happened," but he urged that they "not be thrown off . . . balance" so as to "lose liaison" with "the people who have the best interests of Atlanta at heart."[25] Despite dissatisfaction expressed earlier through the Localities Committee and despite defeat on the Egleston rezoning issue, the black alliance with upper-status whites remained intact. The following year, Hartsfield decided not to run again for mayor, and blacks gave overwhelming electoral support to Ivan Allen, the candidate backed by the business community.

Latent Conflicts

When Hartsfield—a man already in his seventies—decided not to run for reelection, his twenty-three years as the city's chief executive ended in 1962. The Egleston rezoning issue was the last and most intense public controversy over urban renewal during Hartsfield's lengthy administration. The Hartsfield mayoralty was more, however, than a series of major controversies. Some important issues remained latent, but they surfaced in enough uncontested actions and inactions to be observable. Because they were largely latent, these issues are not clearly focused as to time and place; they are nevertheless identifiable and certainly important in Atlanta's renewal program. Four such issues from the Hartsfield era—some even extending into the early Allen years—provide further insight into policy formation.

The overt struggle over the survival of the 221 housing program was only the publicly visible tip of a much larger issue involving the community's residential pattern and the question of how a growing black population's needs would be accommodated. Real estate transactions in the 1950s and into the 1960s were constrained by what one group of observers termed a set of "semiofficial and 'understood' boundaries and 'buffers' separating Negro and white neighborhoods."[26] While blacks acquiesced in these boundaries and in some instances were active parties to the so-called gentlemen's agreements, there is no question that they would have preferred an open and unsegregated housing market. Bargaining from what they regarded as an unequal position, blacks received limited amounts of expansion land and the transition of some neighborhoods from white to black in exchange for acceptance of a pattern of residential segregation.

Sites for 221 and public housing were chosen within the limits of these understandings: formal as well as informal planning activities designated certain areas as "Negro expansion areas." Yet blacks were highly dissatisfied with the arrangements. Although the housing director of the Urban League was a staunch spokesman for coalition politics and for the strategy of negotiated settlements, he did not hesitate to testify before the United States Civil Rights Commission on the "'artificial' shortage of land" facing Atlanta blacks. He observed, "When the amount of land that can be developed for residential purposes is 're-served' for a racial group at the exclusion of all other groups because of race or religion, an 'artificial' land shortage for the excluded group of individuals is created."[27] The president of the Empire Real Estate Board stated in the same hearings that blacks were compelled to live "in tightly contained less desirable parts of our cities" and that in Atlanta segregated housing "is hallowed by the long and continuing support it has had from government [local and federal]."[28]

Although white neighborhood resistance did prevent the full quota of 221 housing from being built (3,008 of a proposed 5,500 units had been built when the program was closed out in early 1964) and did delay the construction of public housing, the massive displacement of blacks from urban renewal and other forms of government action was not curtailed. As a result, much of the relocation process took place by the transition of neighborhoods from white to black.

City officials, with the support of the CAIA, insisted that the density of close-in renewal areas had to be decreased and therefore some residential transition was necessary. While the mayor on occasion argued that expansion of the black community was inevitable and that the choices were only whether this expansion would be controlled or uncontrolled, he turned aside all moves to get an official body to work on the land-acquisition aspect of relocation. His strategy was apparently to play down official involvement in the racial transition of residential areas. An official or quasi-official commission would highlight housing and relocation as a public issue and perhaps draw even greater attention to the number of families affected by the Egleston rezoning controversy. Hartsfield did come out against "uncontrolled" expansion by blacks, but his general stance was one of official uninvolvement. The mayor did employ a community relations staff member to hear neighborhood grievances, but refused to do more.

Nor would he support the use of the expanded CACUR subcommittee on "Residential Expansion" (later named the "Panel on Housing Needs") to explore this problem. Initially, this subcommittee was described as one to "deal with the problems of Atlanta's expanding and shifting population . . . , aid in the solution of specific area problems," and attempt "to organize mutual development associations enabling Atlanta to grow in an orderly manner."[29] But Hartsfield blocked its work, declaring that the CACUR should not become involved in the racial aspects of housing.

Some CACUR members and City Hall staff, acting with what they regarded as indirect but strong support from blacks and whites concerned over the rapid changeover of older neighborhoods, proposed that the mayor create a committee of leading citizens to deal with the problems generated by relocation. Acutely aware that residential transition and the resulting community tension were being increased by the shortage of housing sites for blacks, the staff saw a blue-ribbon citizens' committee as a way of lending legitimacy and respectability to the efforts to provide new sites for relocation housing. The committee would oversee not only research and analysis of housing patterns and housing needs but also the coordination of public and private activities related to the acquisition and development of sites.

Mayor Hartsfield rejected this proposal, contending that leading businessmen would be unwilling to become involved in racial and other controversial matters. In practice, however, white business leaders were involved and influential, but not publicly so. Through the CACUR and other channels, they raised objections to proposed sites for 221 and public housing. Locations in Northside Atlanta and locations adjacent to the CBD were vetoed quietly and informally. White business interests were therefore able to support but not be held accountable for efforts to lessen the concentration of inner-city blacks through relocation into selected corridors of the city.

In the end, most of the relocation was accomplished by racial transition in existing housing. Neither racial group mounted a challenge to the use of "turnover" housing for relocation purposes, even though transition often occurred at such a pace and in such a manner as to lead to panic selling by whites and overcrowding by blacks. Relocation by means of turnover housing took place family-by-family, through individual transactions, with no large public expenditure, no rezoning, no official announcements, and no major-site acquisitions. In contrast, proposals for *new* housing sites might mean all these things. As a result, racial fears centered on the few proposals for new housing projects that did emerge, and white neighborhoods focused their attention on specific disputes such as Egleston rezoning, as did black city-wide leaders.

As a consequence, new housing sites for blacks had to survive not only the covert veto of upper-status whites but also the overt opposition of lower- and middle-status whites. Blacks were confronted with inadequate as well as segregated space for their housing needs. Yet the problem was handled in such a way as to make it difficult for dissatisfied blacks to affix responsibility except in a few instances such as the Egleston rezoning. Blacks thus failed to include among the targets of their dissatisfaction the wielders of covert vetoes.

A shortage of money as well as of land hampered blacks in their quest for adequate housing. Although there were various proposals to reduce housing costs and encourage rehabilitation, resources were not forthcoming for these purposes. Attempts to persuade the city to ameliorate relocation and rehabilitation hardships eventuated in a proposal to establish a revolving fund, but the plan ran counter to the declaration of economy and frugality by the mayor and was shelved by the aldermanic Finance Committee. The shelving went uncontested, as energies of black leaders and sympathetic whites were directed into an effort to establish a nonprofit corporation that would make high-risk loans. The chairman of the CACUR sought support for a rehabilitation assistance program and revolving fund modeled after a Baltimore program. An intensive promotional campaign culminated in a meeting with nearly fifty white financial and real estate firms, whose spokesmen rejected the proposal as impractical. In its stead they suggested and eventually promoted a "Clean Up—Paint Up—Fix Up" drive. Subsequently black members of the CACUR initiated a proposal for lending institutions to establish a credit pool for "substandard risks" who are forced to make home repairs. Although the banks' response was that they could not make loans unless the risks were good, the matter was kept as a subject for further study. No effort was made to press the issue.

An attempt to promote rehabilitation in a black business section adjacent to the CBD also came to nothing. The redevelopment agency provided a staff of one to work in the area, but no planning or financial resources were made available although the area was part of a renewal project and was affected by nearby residential clearance and expressway construction. The Housing Authority, as the redevelopment agency, took the position that rehabilitation was a private responsibility and that they could do no more than provide some coordination of private efforts. The Housing Authority staff man assigned to the area eventually resigned because of the lack of agency support. Again no overt conflict occurred.

The white Atlanta Real Estate Board also proved to be disinclined to engage in controversy. Although the realtors made known their dislike for "socialized public housing subsidized by taxpayers,"[30] they did not challenge city approval of a thousand new units of public housing, in part because they felt vulnerable to attack by the news media. At various times, in some instances to counter opposition to renewal and in other instances to forestall such opposition, newspapers ran articles and series on "slumlords" and on "profits from poverty."[31] In 1958, when some independent white real estate companies challenged the constitutionality of the city's newly enacted housing code, they were greeted editorially with: "Are Atlanta real estate developers opposed to urban renewal? Is the motive behind this move an attempt to block and delay a program which is vital to the city's future? Are some property owners who make money on incredibly filthy slums so greedy they would perpetuate blight which threatens to destroy all property values in the downtown area?"[32]

To be sure, the Real Estate Board's public neutrality grew out of more than a fear of adverse publicity. There had been earlier concessions to their viewpoint as a precondition of their joining the renewal coalition. Even the figure of a thousand units was itself a compromise, falling short of expectations by some of the staff involved in the relocation survey. In the face of a restudy of relocation that showed that existing resources could not accommodate all low-income displacees, to insist that there be no additional public housing would have been to assume a position regarded as irresponsible. Atlanta businessmen expected one another to be sufficiently flexible to allow business solidarity to be maintained and to allow the alliance with black leaders to be continued.

A second instance in which the Real Estate Board was unwilling to break business solidarity occurred after the Egleston rezoning had been defeated. With white neighborhoods aroused in opposition to public housing (a second site, one in south Atlanta was rejected), the search for a new site proved a difficult one. After an alderman suggested that the authorized 350 units of public housing be divided among existing black public housing sites, the Housing Authority proposed to add the 140 family units to an already existing project in an outlying area (Perry Homes) and to build the 210 elderly units in a single high-rise structure adjacent to a close-in project.[33] (The existing project was Grady Homes; the elderly housing became Antoine Graves Homes.) However, the proposed close-in site lay within the boundaries of a renewal area (Butler Street—see map 5.1), and would therefore be in violation of the understanding with the business community that no renewal land be used for public housing. Consequently, the Housing Authority was unwilling to proceed until the exception was "cleared." The chairman of the CACUR, a bank official himself, contacted leading businessmen serving on the CACUR to get their written support for the proposition that "this high rise facility will be considered an 'exception' and it is not contemplated that any garden-type general public housing be located in existing Urban Renewal Areas "[34] The matter was then discussed informally with other businessmen to gain their acquiescence. In the absence of opposition, the Board of Aldermen provided speedy approval.

A final area of latent conflict concerned the establishment of renewal priorities and the designation of additional areas for renewal. Even before the original urban renewal package was moved into the implementation phase, planning and lobbying began for a second round of projects. The disposition of these proposals cast further light on the constraints surrounding and imposed by the urban renewal coalition. The following actions took place:

1. Georgia State College was provided with expansion land through the clearance of a blighted commercial area in the southern portion of the CBD. No city funds were involved because the local share was met by state expenditures. Georgia State expansion had firm and active CAIA support.

2. A bank executive and a member of the CACUR suggested a renewal project near the heart of the CBD, but withdrew the suggestion after a preliminary cost estimate showed that the proposal would be an extraordinarily expensive one.

3. A feasibility study was conducted of a renewal area on the western fringe of the CBD (the Transportation Plaza Feasibility Survey Area—see map 5.1), but was not carried further because it failed to generate wide enough business support. The project would have been expensive and would have involved a public-housing project.

4. The Board of Aldermen designated for further study the Buttermilk Bottom area immediately east of the CBD. The understanding was that the area had high priority for renewal once additional funds became available through a new bond election; the project had strong CAIA support.

5. The Board of Aldermen also designated for further study a renewal area to provide expansion land for the Georgia Institute of Technology once the school had completed its own planning. The project would involve no city funds because the local share would be met by state expenditures; Georgia Tech expansion had firm and active CAIA support.

6. The Board of Aldermen designated for further study an older white neighborhood, West End, close to but not adjacent to the CBD. The project had strong support from some proprietors of small businesses on the CACUR who had long been active in civic affairs. It was understood that the project would be advanced once new funds became available.

7. The Board of Aldermen approved preliminary planning for an area considerably away from the CBD, Edgewood in East Atlanta. The project was backed by a white alderman from the area, who was believed to be promoting the clearance of a blighted section for the purpose of establishing a barrier to the residential expansion of blacks into the eastern corridor of the city. The proposal was placed in the "inactive file" by the Housing Authority.
8. An Urban League proposal for renewal action in a severely blighted area (Vine City—see map 5.1) close to Atlanta University but not immediately adjacent to the CBD was turned aside on the ground that money was not and would not be available for renewal of the area. The Urban League was encouraged to seek foundation support for a self-help program in the area. The effort to obtain such support proved unsuccessful.
9. Requests for neighborhood renewal assistance for a black neighborhood south of the CBD and for a black neighborhood east of the CBD, both of which were experiencing transition and overcrowding due to displacement activities in adjoining areas, were ignored. City officials would suggest only that neighborhood spokesmen look into the possibility of a federally funded Demonstration Grant.

Even though important policy choices were being made, none of the above steps in project selection generated overt conflict. Officials proceeded under the assumption that CAIA support was essential to a viable renewal program. Other interests were put aside, albeit in some cases inconspicuously as when the East Atlanta proposal was placed in bureaucratic limbo rather than rejected outright.

The business community itself contained differing policy leanings that had to be reconciled in order to generate a broad base of business support. On the one hand, there were businessmen who were economy-minded and would support renewal only if no large demands were made on the city budget. The CAIA and the Chamber of Commerce both made it clear that they expected the city to retain its traditionally low tax rate. On the other hand, there were individual businessmen who were concerned primarily with boosting and expanding the city's economic base. To them, even very large expenditures would be justified if the economy of the city were enlarged and the volume of downtown commerce increased. Two types of projects permitted reconciliation of the differing business viewpoints. Expansion of college campuses was favored because no city funds were required and, as the CAIA argued, a downtown campus "is one of the big and important dollar generators in Central Atlanta."[35] Both segments of the business community could also agree on the expansion of the CBD by clearing adjacent low-income neighborhoods. Residential clearance was not only much less expensive than commercial clearance, but it also offered the further attraction of moving from the center of the city a population regarded as undesirable.

The inclusion of West End for future action involved a pattern of influence different from that with which other project areas advanced. The CAIA and the general business community were largely indifferent toward the project. Since the area was under consideration as a predominantly rehabilitation project, costs would be limited. The West End neighborhood leaders were strategically placed by virtue of representation on the CACUR and were favorably viewed because of past support given the city's political and civic leadership. They were able to persist until their demands were acceded to—though not in full until Atlanta moved into the Ivan Allen era of renewal policymaking and a new round of coalition building began.

Conflict, Collective Business Influence, and Policy: An Overview

In the midst of a given controversy, conflict appears to be multifaceted and ever-changing. Over a longer time period, cleavages of interest have a chance to recur and display their stability. A brief overview of Atlanta's urban renewal experience under Hartsfield may, therefore, be useful.

Business influence and renewal policy in Atlanta have been associated in a complex way that warrants discussion and explanation. Businessmen, as pluralists have long argued, do not have homogeneous interests. In Atlanta, for instance, the holders of slum property around the CBD at one time were determined (but unsuccessful) opponents of redevelopment. Hotel owners also engaged in a futile and short-lived fight with the Chamber of Commerce and the CAIA over the building of new motel and hotel facilities on renewal land. In addition, it might be noted that during the late 1950s and early 1960s the Atlanta Real Estate Board was a vocal critic of federally subsidized low-rent housing. While important concessions were made to the realtors,[36] the city did request additional public-housing allocations whenever it seemed necessary to the continuance of the redevelopment program. Particular business groups thus had little impact on city policy. Atlanta's reformed and centralized style of politics had been relatively impenetrable to the so-called special interests.

While segmented business interests have had little standing with city officials, the business community as a whole has enjoyed a close and cooperative relationship with City Hall. Consequently, the collective, unsegmented interest of the business community in the upgrading of the CBD was from its inception a prime concern of the officials involved in renewal decision making. But, while rejuvenating the business core and augmenting property values therein were generally desired goals, they were not widely desired at the cost of increased city taxes. For a community with an activist reputation, Atlanta has maintained a notably low property tax rate.[37] Renewal policy has thus been shaped by the collective interest of businessmen in low taxation as well as by their collective interest in CBD rejuvenation. Those proposals for revitalizing the CBD that departed substantially from the minimum expenditure/low taxation outlook of the business community as a whole have thus tended to falter. Two observations can thus be offered. The business community as a whole is not to be confused with some special segment of the business community. Second, while there was a collective business interest in CBD renewal (and that is what the analysis of demand conversion is centered on), any specific measure that was incautiously designed was subject to official rejection. Indeed, two proposals that would have required very large outlays of city money failed before they ever reached the official decision-making stage.

In short, renewal policy was shaped by two related forces: (1) the influence of the business community *as a whole* and (2) the desire by city officials to maintain a unified business community. Redevelopment therefore took the form of extending the CBD into surrounding residential areas and providing land for the expansion of educational institutions in the center of the city. These renewal activities could be conducted at a minimum expense to the city, and were not divisive within the business community.

Relocation and rehousing policies did not affect the collective interests of the business community as directly and immediately as CBD redevelopment did. Business influence was not as dominant a force in the first two as in the last. Yet the business community had a perceived collective interest in the former, especially in relocation policy. The business community deliberately promoted a policy of moving low-income blacks away from the center of the city into selected outlying areas away from the CBD. This policy of selective decentralization involved placing relocation facilities in areas that were already black or in areas adjacent to black residences; but, by long-standing "agreement," relocation facilities were not placed in the prestigious Northside area—not even in or adjacent to the scattered pockets of black residences in that section of the city.

Overt opposition to the business-backed relocation policy was intense at times, and business incurred significant defeats at all stages of policy-making. Nevertheless, in the long run, most of the residential displacement from urban renewal and other forms of government action occurred in the central sector of the city, and most of the relocation units were built in outlying areas.

Although demands that the supply of standard housing for blacks be expanded were made and were partially met, housing expansion was linked in important ways with the redevelopment and relocation policy favored by the business community. Throughout the Hartsfield era, the city planned rehousing programs only as a way of meeting relocation needs, never as an effort to improve housing per se; even the building of relocation facilities was always limited by the availability of "acceptable" sites.

CBD renewal was not reciprocally limited by the availability of relocation facilities. In fact, public-housing units requested and allocated in 1958 did not become available for occupancy until 1964, and then only in part. During that lapse of time more than two thousand families eligible for public housing were displaced by urban renewal alone. In the meantime, the supply of private low- and moderate-income rentals was drastically reduced. Central-sector displacement thus did not await new housing construction; and, when new units were built, most were constructed in outlying areas.

Federal regulations and the maintenance of black allies required city leaders to give some attention to rehousing needs, but the city's consistent policy was to locate new units in selected areas away from the CBD. If neighborhood opposition occasionally blocked the development of a particular site, then new housing was delayed and was therefore unavailable for relocation purposes. Overcrowding and racial transition in older neighborhoods served to meet most of the city's relocation needs. And this policy, *as a policy*, was unchallenged throughout the 1950s and early 1960s.

The present chapter draws on the various episodes in the Hartsfield era of urban renewal to derive some generalizations about how policy, influence, and conflict management were interrelated. Because the Hartsfield years were the prime years of the "progressive" coalition, the analysis here is particularly concerned with how the business community was able to exert a strong and unified influence on the renewal process, while blacks were unable to make anything more than fragmented and short-lived efforts to shape renewal policy. It is important to remember, however, that the CAIA incurred significant defeats in some of the particular episodes in Atlanta's unfolding urban renewal experience. But the form that the city's redevelopment policy took owed more to the way in which conflict was managed than to the outcomes of specific controversies. For example, the early failure to launch a redevelopment program did not signal the end of urban renewal as a way of altering land use. Instead, this unsuccessful trial run served as a learning experience for the City Hall/business community alliance. Learning from the past, members of the alliance subsequently tried new and more effective strategies of diverting and withstanding opposition.

Policy Direction

When attention is focused on major policy questions rather than on isolated events or conflicts, the overriding influence of the CAIA on renewal policy is evident. During the Hartsfield mayoralty, there were five major policy questions at issue. As table 6.1 indicates, two were questions on which business interests were furthered in the face of substantial community resistance. Significantly, both were issues in which the black community failed to provide effective opposition. In the case of CBD renewal, black opposition developed but waned with the passage of time. Relocation of blacks into segregated, outlying areas failed to generate any active opposition from blacks, even though they were opposed to residential segregation in principle and they were specifically concerned over displacement from the center of the city. As noted in chapter 5, though many blacks sporadically opposed various aspects of the city's renewal policy, their sense of frustration coalesced and peaked during the Egleston controversy, with the somewhat ironic result that their resentments thus came to be focused on spokesmen for nonaffluent whites rather than on the business community that was behind the effort to move blacks away from the center of the city. The established cleavage along "progressive"-"stand-pat" lines continued in the 1961 city election, and blacks came out of the Hartsfield era still a part of the coalition that stood behind the renewal program.

On two issues business interests prevailed without any community conflict. The only policy question on which there was substantial compromise and on which other groups gained a significant portion of their objectives was an issue that the CAIA had little direct interest in: the development of low-income housing. In the Hartsfield era, blacks, despite the fact that they were a supporting force in the city's governing coalition, thus succeeded only partially in gaining one policy objective. Even that came at the cost of giving up convenient and close-in locations for less convenient but still segregated sites in outlying areas. White neighborhood groups had a partial success in that the building of low-

Table 6.1. Major Policy Questions during the Hartsfield Mayoralty

Policy Issue	Stance of Various Groups	State of Group Conflict	Issue Outcome
CBD expansion and upgrading	Business—active and united support; blacks—divided with some overt opposition; white neighborhoods—active opposition	Overt	Business success
Relocation of blacks into outlying and segregated areas	Business—active and united support; blacks—divided with some active support; white neighborhoods—active opposition	Overt	Business success
Development of low-income housing	Business—selective support and no active opposition; blacks—active and united support; white neighborhoods—active opposition	Overt	Mixed
Priority in new project selection to low-expenditure proposals for CBD upgrading	Business—active and united support; blacks—indirect opposition in that they supported neighborhood renewal; white neighborhoods—indirect opposition in that they supported neighborhood renewal	Latent	Business success
Rehabilitation assistance	Business—indirect opposition in that they favored minimum public expenditures; blacks—active and united support; white neighborhoods—no stance	Latent	Business success

income housing units for blacks was restricted in scope and delayed in time. Some units were built, however, in areas adjacent to white neighborhoods and contributed to the general pattern of racial transition in older and less affluent residential areas. Overall, then, CAIA policy objectives were realized in four out of four issues in which collective business interests were in substantial conflict with the interests of other major community groups. Defeats in specific controversies thus proved no deterrent to policy success for the business community. Conversely, blacks and white neighborhood groups prevailed on particular items at issue but scored only very limited policy success.

Alliance building took place in support of the upgrading of the CBD and the relocation of blacks into outlying areas; no such efforts were made on behalf of neighborhood renewal and rehabilitation. The city did make some efforts to meet the housing needs of urban renewal displacees, and, indeed, some of the early proponents of urban renewal had believed that relocation activities would improve housing conditions for blacks. However, in the face of community resistance, relocation housing goals were substantially compromised; CBD upgrading was not.

The inability of white neighborhoods to have a substantial impact on renewal policy is not difficult to explain. They were not a part of the city's governing coalition, and occasional victories as in the Egleston rezoning issue were followed by electoral failures. Blacks, by contrast, were a part of the dominant coalition. Still, while black leaders were part of a working alliance with Mayor Hartsfield and business leaders, they received few policy concessions. The Localities Committee's opposition to CBD expansion was strong evidence that the black community was divided over, and perhaps predominantly opposed to, the city's renewal program. Yet, as time proceeded and the gravest concerns of the black community proved to be well founded, opposition lessened rather than increased.

How could this come to be? The chief explanation lies in the fact that City Hall's major strategy in managing conflict was the disaggregation of black opposition. City officials offered some concessions to blacks, concessions as in the case of Auburn Avenue rehabilitation that proved to have no substance; and officials raised some diversionary issues, such as the suggestions that neighborhood renewal be attempted under a foundation or Federal Demonstration grant. These, however, were tactical moves that had little lasting impact by themselves. No substantive or apparent changes in policy direction were made. Instead, carefully orchestrated offerings of particular rewards were made to strategically placed black interests.[1]

Overall, renewal policy coincided with business interests because policy alternatives were structured and program goals pursued in such a way as to unite the business community, to isolate white neighborhood opposition, and to subject black leaders to cross-pressures. Conflict was thus managed on terms that reflected business influence.

Business Influence

Renewal policy coincided with the collective interests of the business community because business influence was effectively used to protect and promote those interests. In its most dramatic appearance, business influence took the form of an ultimatum to City Hall to move forward with the renewal program or face the prospect of a major challenge in the next municipal election. The threat was fully credible. Money, prestige, organization, and the support of the news media were readily available for a business-backed campaign.

While the ultimatum was dramatic, other forms of business influence were probably more important. A complex web of relationships served on most occasions to give City Hall and Main Street a shared perspective on what should be done and how. The mayor's personal and political ties to the business community formed the foundation on which other connections were built. The Housing Authority, thanks to the mayor's appointments, was firmly under the guidance of business leadership.[2] The chairman of the aldermanic urban renewal committee, also a mayoral appointee, regarded his mandate to be that of furthering a program of CBD rejuvenation. Legislative leadership fell to him, and he served as the liaison between the various planning agencies and the Board of Aldermen. The formal responsibility for devising urban renewal policy was exercised by the Urban Renewal Policy Committee, a specially created body of Housing Authority commissioners and members of the aldermanic committee on urban renewal.

The official structure of policy formulation was a reflection of business influence. Renewal planning rested with bodies whose principal claim to legitimacy was expertise, not representativeness. Indeed, the 1955 decision to designate the Housing Authority as the local redevelopment agency was a decision to insulate renewal planning from constituency pressure. Anticipating their exclusion from the formation of renewal policy, black and white neighborhood spokesmen had unsuccessfully opposed the decision. With good reason, they were fearful that business influence would be dominant and other groups would be excluded. The mayor, however, supported the placement of renewal administration with the Housing Authority.

Because of the administrative arrangements, the mayor was able to avoid publicly any direct responsibility for renewal policy. Moreover, he was free to assume the stance of a disinterested defender of the public welfare. Thus he challenged program critics as "obstructionists," who were "playing politics" and disregarding the good of the community.

Given the city's formal arrangements for drawing up and executing renewal plans and given the predilections of the key officials involved, the CAIA in particular had easy and direct access to the early stages of policymaking. The business community thus was able to combine its objectives with widely approved goals: the elimination of slums, the enhancement of the city's economic base, a visually attractive down-town, new housing opportunities for the nonaffluent, and expansion room for educational institutions. Support for urban renewal was mobi-lized on a basis that would not be injurious to CAIA interests but that would intertwine its interests with broader, community-related objec-tives.

Other groups, in particular those with a neighborhood base, could only react to plans that were already fully developed. Opposition to such plans could be and, as we have seen, was met with charges of obstruc-tionism. Even though some of the planning staff were sympathetic to an effort, as one planner phrased it, "to relate city-wide needs to particular needs of the hundred-odd neighborhoods which make up Atlanta," there was no effective channel through which to press such a policy considera-tion. As a token response to demands from the Localities Committee, project area committees were created; but they were deliberately ig-nored even by the city-wide CACUR. Although a renewal program oriented toward neighborhood conservation and improvement had po-tential support, both inside and outside City Hall, many requests for neighborhood planning were never officially considered by the alder-men.

The CAIA was able to use its resources not only to gain a favorable position for shaping public policy but also to undermine and disag-gregate opposition forces. Because Mayor Hartsfield was reluctant to move on major proposals without business support, the CAIA was regarded as an ally essential in any effort to activate City Hall. Further, the mayor was not the only one to recognize the close tie between the CAIA and the news media. No one was eager to antagonize the CAIA, and many groups such as those concerned with housing improvements, were quick to seek CAIA support for their ventures. Moreover, the major business firms were central to the success of any effort requiring voluntary contributions. Organizations, such as the Urban League, were attuned to the necessity of both financial and political support from white business leaders.[3] Atlanta's white business leaders did not depend upon the power implicit in their prestige and wealth. Instead, they actively exploited these resources in order to further the well-being of individuals and groups within the black community that they regarded as "responsible." One channel through which "responsible" attitudes were encouraged was the set of financial ties that many blacks had to the white business community. Jack Walker in his post-1960 study of Atlanta observed:

The conservatives [among the blacks] feel that their position bars them from taking an active part in protest demonstrations because these public displays of discontent naturally cause bitterness and rancor and tend to destroy the cordial, settled atmosphere which they feel is a necessary precondition to effective negotiations. They also worked hard to build institutions such as the Y.M.C.A., the Urban League and many churches which depend heavily on contributions from influential whites. . . . The businessmen among the conservatives have frequent dealing with influential whites in the city; both the bank and the savings and loan association operated by Negroes in Atlanta have very sizeable deposits from white customers. In fact, to a large extent, the power of the conservatives depends on their influence with the white community. They are spokesmen for the Negro community primarily because they have gained white recognition and favor, although their own achievements placed them in a position to be chosen for this role.[4]

With City Hall and Housing Authority cooperation, urban renewal and relocation offered additional opportunities to provide blacks with financial incentives to continue in alliance with white business interests. The 221 program in particular and the relocation process generally were used, as one white leader explained, to provide black real estate companies with "material benefits." Further, although business leaders would not launch a drive to establish a revolving fund for rehabilitation loans and related purposes, a few of the large firms did set up a fund that was used to provide "seed money" for some black housing developments. As the agency acquiring land for redevelopment, the Housing Authority appeared especially eager to appease certain opinion leaders. Some of the ministers of black churches in clearance areas felt that their churches were generously compensated in order to make relocation more palatable. Expansion land for the Atlanta University institutions was also part of a deliberate strategy of disaggregating black opposition to renewal.

While attacks by the Localities Committee on the early renewal and relocation plans indicated that opposition could be allayed only partially, cooptation of black leaders continued even after the outbreak of overt conflict. With particular regard to the members of the Localities Committee, federal race-relations specialists urged local officials to steer "the energies of some of the active and interested citizens and citizen groups into exploration of the Section 221 multi-family possibilities."[5] Black leaders responded favorably, but approximately three years lapsed before a firm proposal was developed from the various projects considered. One of the large churches, whose pastor had been a major force in the Localities Committee, emerged as a sponsor for multifamily, moderate-income housing (under the FHA 221(d)3 program) on renewal land. The proposed project was one that engendered considerable pride in the black community as an example of the capacity of southern blacks to plan and develop a major nonprofit housing project.[6] Nevertheless, action was not taken until informal discussions within the white business community produced agreement that the project would serve to increase "interracial goodwill." Business support also came in another way. Two member firms in the CAIA provided the construction loan.

Business influence was not, then, a simple occurrence of good fortune. Shared interests with both City Hall and the news media were exploited and supplemented by politically astute contributions and investments in order to establish a central role for the CAIA in shaping renewal policy. The importance of business leaders as allies, especially to City Hall, provided the CAIA with such complete access to renewal planning that other groups were included in the program only to the extent that they could add support to the program without detracting from CAIA objectives.

There was more than one option in setting policy for the acquisition and clearance of land in the CBD. It was less expensive and less divisive of the white business community to clear land housing low-income blacks than to clear deteriorated commercial areas: clearance of black residences was the policy CAIA favored and that was the policy adopted. The alternative, to clear blighted nonresidential areas, though admittedly more expensive, would have minimized interracial tension through lessening the relocation problem, but that course was never seriously considered. Higher economic costs would have been offset by much lower social costs, but social costs were largely neglected because the principal concern was to maintain business unity behind the program.

Business influence was evident not only in the choice of what was cleared for CBD renewal but also in the neglect of other policy objectives. No public officials came forward with a program of neighborhood conservation and improvement, even though such a program was suggested by various neighborhood spokesmen and the need for it was recognized by professional planners. Finally, although blacks, some white property owners, and many white neighborhood leaders opposed the displacement of low-income blacks from around the CBD and repeatedly spoke against the relocation of blacks into a few areas of the city, they were unable to coalesce and mobilize support for a relocation policy different from the one backed by the CAIA. White neighborhoods could obtain nothing more than ad hoc support in an occasional fight against specific relocation proposals. Because many black leaders and institutions stood to gain from particular aspects of the renewal program, the black community was unable to solidify and sustain its own opposition to clearance around the CBD.

Public officials, including federal officials, not only were unwilling to champion the cause of such groups as the Localities Committee, but they were important actors in carrying out the strategy of disaggregating black opposition to renewal. Throughout the Hartsfield mayoralty, public officials and community leaders displayed a marked unwillingness to work against the expressed interests of the CAIA. Thus, although the CAIA was not overtly powerful enough to prevent conflict or to prevail consistently when conflict did take place, the controversies that occurred left the renewal objectives of the CAIA essentially intact.

The Hartsfield Era of Urban Renewal in Theoretical Perspective

Overall, the Hartsfield era produced an urban renewal policy under which CBD interests received substantial benefits and other interests fared poorly. While some particular decisions represented mutual accommodations among contending groups, the cumulative movement of renewal policy was in the direction favored by the CAIA. This association of businesses possessed substantial influence by means of the wealth and economic power they commanded, by their ability to enlist the support of the news media, by virtue of being major producers of revenue, and by means of the prestige and reputation they enjoyed in the community. Blacks and white neighborhood groups were not without political resources, but they appeared unable to maintain a steady pressure on the city's decision makers.

The political resources of the business community were not converted directly into policy benefits. Instead, resources were used to maneuver into and maintain a favorable political position from which the CAIA had exceptionally good, almost unlimited, access to city decision makers (and through them reasonably good access to federal officials as well). From this favorable political position, business influence extended over the process by which conflict was managed. In this way, some opposition was forestalled and some aborted, but not all opposition could be prevented. However, the overall direction of conflict was that described earlier: the business community remained united, the black community was divided, and tensions between blacks and nonaffluent white neighborhoods were exacerbated.

The business community's maneuvering into and maintaining of a favorable position was in part a matter of supporting and strengthening the institutions and practices of reform politics. The reform institutions and practices, in turn, made it easy for the business community to gain or place spokesmen in key positions inside governmental circles. The close alliance with City Hall also facilitated formal and informal discussions between business and political leaders at all stages of the renewal process. Finally, the maneuvering consisted in part of the cooptation of nonbusiness figures who, through their memberships in such organizations as the CACUR or through their staff positions in social agencies, could lend important support to business-backed proposals. However, these nonbusiness figures were often in a weak position to mount any kind of challenge to these proposals.

Conflict management may be defined as the collection of activities by which attempts are made to control the scope and direction of overt conflict. In this sense, all groups engage in conflict management. Each tries to broaden or narrow issues in accordance with calculations about where the balance of power lies. Each seeks to gain allies and to discredit or divide opponents. Each attempts to time issues for maximum advantage.

What is distinctive about the Atlanta urban renewal experience under Hartsfield is the extent to which public officials shaped issues, timed proposals, and worked to divert and divide opposition (that is, managed conflict) in such a way as to see that business objectives were furthered. To a large extent, political skills are skills in conflict management. While public officials have no monopoly on these skills, they are certainly in a good position to develop and make use of them.

As acknowledged earlier, public officials do not necessarily act in concert, nor do they necessarily act in alliance with only one interest. Nevertheless, in the Hartsfield era, the city's political and administrative leaders did act in concert with one another and with the business community to manage conflict on terms that furthered the renewal objectives of the CAIA. In this enterprise, officials also had the full and active support of the news media.

Despite occasional acts of recalcitrance on the part of individual officials, the overall pattern of conflict management is clear. Policy was framed in terms that maintained business solidarity. Concessions were made (some more apparent than real) and proposals added in order to build a coalition around a program of expanding and upgrading the CBD. Opposition was yielded to in some instances, but the major proposals were revised and altered until the objectives originally sought were accomplished. Resources were used to disaggregate the opposition and to discredit some enemies of the renewal program. In short, city officials acted, not as brokers among competing interests, but as fairly consistent promoters of CAIA objectives. Policy conflict and its relation to community power need to be understood on those terms. Coalition formation, bargaining, and negotiation—far from indicating official responsiveness to the full range of citizen interests—were the very practices whereby business interests secured extraordinary control over the renewal process.

7. BUSINESS POWER AND BLACK PROTESTS, 1962–1966

Ivan Allen became mayor at a moment when protests—that is, the use of unconventional means for making grievances known—became a major factor in the city's politics. These protests represented a highly observable attempt to mobilize previously unused resources ("take up slack") in order to change the course of public policy.[1] If, as the pluralists have argued, "the prizes in politics go to the interested and the active,"[2] then these protests should have had a significant impact on policymaking in Atlanta.

As the case narrative suggests, however, it is not enough to look at immediate impact.[3] Short-term actions in particular decisions should not be confused with long-range policy changes. Protests have to be evaluated as a means of influence by the extent to which they lead to lasting change.

In Atlanta during the mid-1960s, protests were used to try to overcome positional disadvantages. They were aimed at increasing the visibility of renewal policy and its consequences, at modifying the procedures through which renewal planning and decision making occurred, and above all, at changing City Hall priorities. The old policy of promoting CBD revitalization by moving low-income families away from the center of the city to outlying and racially segregated areas was challenged forthrightly; in its stead a new policy of improving neighborhood conditions and increasing housing opportunities was proposed. The Allen era thus lends itself to a consideration of protests as means for correcting imbalances in influence and for promoting policy change. It affords an especially good opportunity to look at and reassess the pluralist notion of "slack in the system."

Throughout this and the next four chapters, we shall be concerned with the attempts by and on behalf of previously unfavored groups to improve their position in the city's renewal process. In the present chapter and the one immediately following, the case narrative centers on the emergence of protest politics, the recounting of demands that accompanied protest activities, and the immediate responses of city officials to these demands, including some proposed new directions in urban renewal policy. The two subsequent chapters discuss the protracted struggle to get those new policies implemented.

Political Leadership in the Allen Era

Even before Ivan Allen emerged as a mayoral candidate, Atlanta was edging into a new political era. Student-led protests in 1960 introduced the tactics of confrontation and direct action. Along with a steady increase in black voting strength, they encouraged the black community's highly diverse leadership to assert itself vocally and publicly.

Blacks occasionally attempted to unify their efforts through various "summit conferences" and some of these efforts were successful for a short duration, but fragmentation was the hallmark of the period. Antagonism and mistrust among black leaders, especially between the old and the new, could not be completely contained. The old pattern whereby a few leaders could negotiate for and bring into line the black community did not survive. Divisions among city-wide black leaders, black disenchantment with some of the older organizations such as the Atlanta Negro Voters League, and a general climate of opinion favorable to protest activities provided a context in which black neighborhoods gave direct and unrestrained expression to their dissatisfactions.

In 1962, the Hartsfield era gave way officially to the Allen mayoralty. A businessman who had long been active in civic affairs, Ivan Allen was president of the Chamber of Commerce when he was elected mayor. And at the time of his election, he was already the principal force behind a Forward Atlanta program. In office, he gained national attention for Atlanta by endorsing the public accommodations section of the 1964 Civil Rights Act and by being a conspicuous southern supporter of various pieces of federal urban legislation. Many of his constituents were somewhat awed by the fact that Allen was both a business leader and the city's chief executive. A man of uncommon personal courage and political audacity, he was more builder, even missionary, than politician. In action, he much preferred the role of promoter to that of mediator. Lacking Hartsfield's finesse at mediation, Allen nevertheless moved headlong into the various crises confronting the city.

Ivan Allen was above all a nonapologetic spokesman for business interests. He genuinely believed that what was good for business was good for Atlanta, and he just as genuinely believed that what was good for Atlanta was good for business. In some ways he was a throwback to New Deal liberalism: he believed in an active government, one that would promote economic growth, improve race relations, and combat poverty.

In the 1960s, renewal policy was thus made under circumstances outwardly quite different from those of the previous decade. The Allen mayoralty was a time of intense activity, widespread protests, and sharp confrontation. During those turbulent years, the coalition of blacks and white businessmen did not dissolve, but it was fraught with tension and did temporarily divide in the 1969 campaign to choose a successor to Allen.

Urban Renewal in the 1960s

New federal programs and innovations in old ones were also a significant element in Atlanta's urban renewal experience of the 1960s. The

Community Action Program (1964), Model Cities (1966), and the Neighborhood Development Program (1968)[4] were significant innovations, intended to increase participation by lower-class citizens and neighborhood groups in local governmental affairs. In response to various sources of criticism, federal officials also attempted to make the renewal program itself more flexible administratively and to give more attention to the needs of the urban poor. Before the decade was over, several efforts were made to assure that the federal government would give priority to projects helpful in the housing of low-income families.[5]

In the early years of the Allen administration, federal officials nationally were most concerned with trying to induce local governments to be attentive to the needs of comprehensive planning. As early as 1954, federal legislation had included as a prerequisite to financial assistance the proviso that communities have a Workable Program for Community Improvement; and the Workable Program in turn required a comprehensive community plan and a set of neighborhood analyses. Concerned that cities—despite general planning requirements—were looking only at the short-run consequences of individual renewal projects, administrative officials requested and Congress in 1959 authorized federal grants for a form of renewal planning known as the Community Renewal Program. A grant under this program enabled a locality to look at blight on a city-wide basis, inventory community needs and resources, and draw up a long-range schedule of renewal activity. In 1956 Congress had authorized the funding of General Neighborhood Renewal Plans for areas that might be too big for a single project but that nevertheless needed to be considered as a single planning unit. A large and complex area could thus be renewed in a planned succession of projects. Administratively, some flexibility was retained in the face of various planning requirements and inducements by a procedure termed Early Land Acquisition. This procedure was a device through which a locality could, with federal approval, acquire and clear portions of land in a proposed project area while the planning of the whole project was still underway. As the following chapters indicate, Atlanta made use of a wide variety of programs and procedures—though not always with full regard to the concerns embodied in federal legislation.

Competing Demands on the Urban Renewal Program

The first few years of the Allen administration started out as a repeat of the Hartsfield administration. Competing demands were sifted, arranged, and packaged so as to maintain business unity around a program of CBD rejuvenation. Further, by making concessions to some nonbusiness groups, city officials were able for a time to delay outbreaks of overt opposition. Eventually, however, the opposition came, and urban renewal became a prime target in the protest politics of the city. The present chapter focuses mainly on a chain of events leading up to and following the decision to build a new civic center in the Buttermilk Bottom area, an area important to white business leaders because it is immediately east of the CBD and important to black leaders because it is the northern hinterland of Auburn Avenue. The construction of the civic center directly precipitated one protest that involved city-wide black leaders, and it triggered a series of actions that led eventually to the formation of a neighborhood protest group concerned with containing the eastward spread of the business district.

Ivan Allen brought to office in January of 1962 a six-point program to promote economic prosperity and racial moderation. It was one he had developed more than a year earlier for his presidency of the Chamber of Commerce. The program included a call for a "vigorous" renewal effort and the construction of a stadium and a new civic center. The mayor's activist stance, even with business endorsement, was not sufficient to achieve immediate results. In his first year in office, Allen suffered a defeat in a bond referendum that would have provided funds for urban renewal and civic center construction. Never as ardent in wooing constituent support as his predecessor had been, Mayor Allen failed to obtain the strong backing of the Atlanta Negro Voters League for the bond election, and he failed to activate fully some sources of white support. Moreover, the urban renewal program itself was subject to much criticism and a wide array of demands.

A Welfare Department report became the basis for a public charge that slum clearance activities were simply creating new slums. Noting that renewal activities often resulted only in the further overcrowding of already-crowded housing on the fringe of clearance areas, the chairman of the County Welfare Board called for new public housing, especially housing that could help the poorest of the poor.

Concerned over the fact that much of the land cleared under urban renewal had not been redeveloped, the Urban Renewal Committee of the Chamber of Commerce urged that projects in execution be evaluated and the purposes of the program be clarified "before embarking on a new set of projects."[6] Members of the Planning Department staff thus found ready allies for their argument that the city should apply for Community Renewal Program (CRP) funds and undertake appropriate studies before a new round of projects was begun. Rodney Cook, the new chairman of the aldermanic urban renewal committee, became a spokesman for the CRP supporters. Cook was appointed chairman of the committee by Allen and remained chairman throughout the entire Allen mayoralty. The two men never had an open disagreement on renewal policy. Cook, like Allen, was part of white, affluent, Northside Atlanta. While Cook's party affiliation was Republican, his important political identification was with the progressive coalition of blacks and white businessmen. He was especially close to some of the younger members of the Chamber of Commerce.

Less concerned with the niceties of overall planning was a diverse collection of individuals—the head of the city's misleadingly named Urban Renewal Department,[7] a school official, a spokesman for the West End Businessmen's Association, and others on an ad hoc basis—who, each with a different goal in mind, urged quick action on several projects in various areas of the city. In addition, the CAIA and the Urban League complained about not being advised of much of the preliminary renewal planning then in process, and both organizations cautioned against a thinly spread renewal effort.

One business leader, a member both of the CAIA and the city's CACUR, voiced a widely held concern that the urban renewal program had ceased to have a clear direction. In an open meeting of the CACUR, he commented, "I feel that what's been happening is that you do a little dab here, then run out there someplace else and do a little dab there for political reasons." He added, "I personally feel that the core of the city ought to get priority."[8]

For quite different reasons, major business interests and the Urban League favored a renewal effort concentrated on the Buttermilk Bottom area to the east of the CBD. A 1958 planning study had identified the area as one that was severely blighted and that had major drainage problems. The proximity to the business district and to an expressway interchange gave Buttermilk Bottom an obvious commercial value. The CAIA regarded the area as the prime site for a "continued battle against the ring of blight encircling downtown Atlanta."[9] The Central Atlanta Plan of the 1950s had pinpointed this area as one into which the CBD should be expanded. Another diligent promoter of renewal action for Buttermilk Bottom was the Uptown Association, an organization whose membership overlapped substantially with the CAIA. The Uptown Association was especially concerned with the area in and around the northeast section of the CBD.[10]

The Urban League and members of the City Planning Department regarded the nearly three thousand families, over half of whom were living in dilapidated structures, as the most urgent problem in Buttermilk Bottom. Both the Urban League and city planners were especially worried about these families and the impact they could have on adjoining neighborhoods. While they were not unaware of the commercial value of redevelopment in Buttermilk Bottom, the staff members of the Urban League and the City Planning Department had a broad view of the purpose of urban renewal. They wanted a large area treated as one well-executed and carefully coordinated project in which full attention would be given to relocation needs and to rehabilitation possibilities.

No matter how it was handled, relocation was bound to be a point of contention. Some members of the business community, including at least one highly active Housing Authority commissioner, were reluctant to see the city's supply of public housing increased. Moreover, the Egleston site controversy had made all concerned keenly aware of the problems of securing sites. Yet clearance in the Buttermilk Bottom area would displace a large number of poor families who would have to be accommodated in some manner.

Federal officials were, of necessity, a major ingredient in any policy settlement. The balance of power between the city and federal authorities had shifted somewhat since the city had first embarked on urban renewal. The program had reached the take-off point so that the demand for funds was outrunning the supply. Federal officials were thus in a position to exert some influence, and they were beginning to become somewhat more sensitive to criticism from civil rights organizations. Although the federal Urban Renewal Administration was quite sympathetic to redevelopment for nonresidential purposes, under Robert Weaver's headship of the Housing and Home Finance Agency (the predecessor to the Department of Housing and Urban Development), renewal officials were encouraged to be more careful about relocation requirements.

In 1963, federal officials thus did not hesitate to let the city know that the approval of further renewal applications would be contingent upon a request for additional public housing. Hints were even passed to the city that Workable Program recertification, that is, the meeting of federal requirements, might be in question. In October of 1963, the Regional Office set forth a list of shortcomings in the city's administrative, planning, and code enforcement performance.

In summary, during the 1960s, it had become increasingly difficult for city officials to ignore demands for renewal purposes other than CBD rejuvenation. The right to acquire land and alter its use was a powerful policy tool, the control of which was widely sought after. The past policy of using urban renewal mainly for upgrading and expanding the CBD had disappointed some groups, who would have preferred a multipurpose program. Some other groups were apprehensive about the prospect of further clearance activity. Keeping the renewal program politically viable was no easy task, but it was faced unflinchingly by Mayor Allen. His initial actions were fully consistent with the past. He set about putting together a renewal package that would maintain business solidarity, but would contain enough concessions to forestall the open opposition of competing interests. His strategy succeeded, but the opposition was only forestalled, not prevented. Eventually, Mayor Allen had to cope with a much more vehement form of protest politics than his predecessor ever faced.

Buttermilk Bottom and the overlapping area known as Bedford-Pine, containing much valued land to the east of the CBD, thus became the site for a transition in the city's renewal program and a testing ground for the effectiveness of black protest actions.

Business Influence and Early Renewal Policy in the Allen Mayoralty

In the opening phase of Ivan Allen's mayoralty, the major concern of the city administration was the decline in Atlanta's economic growth rate. Allen regarded the proposed civic center (auditorium and accompanying exhibition hall and convention facilities) and stadium as essential stimulants to the city's commercial life. Both the Chamber of Commerce and the CAIA shared the mayor's strong interest in new civic facilities as well as his concern over the general economic situation. The business community not only supported the new facilities; it supported the location of the new facilities in the center of the city despite the fact that less costly sites were available in outlying areas. When the Citizens Bond Study Commission recommended funds for the new civic center, they attached the recommendation that convention facilities be located within walking distance of the CBD. The Uptown Association, in particular, lobbied for Buttermilk Bottom to be chosen as the site for the new civic center.

The mayor proceeded to work out a series of policy settlements that would receive the unified support of the business community and would enlist enough allies to win approval of a bond issue when a second election was held. An understanding between the mayor and West End leaders was reached; the mayor appointed a member of the West End Businessmen's Association to head the bond election campaign in 1963. Immediately after the bond proposal was approved at the polls, Mayor Allen earmarked funds for both the Buttermilk Bottom and West End renewal projects. In addition, the leader of the West End Businessmen's Association had been assured that public-works and school-construction funds would be expended in the area, thus providing noncash credits toward the city's share of renewal project costs.

An ingenious combination of proposals allowed the mayor to generate active support from the CAIA, the Uptown Association, and the Chamber of Commerce and at the same time meet federal conditions for continued renewal funding. The Buttermilk Bottom site for the civic center was accepted, a decision that would expand the CBD in a northeastward direction, thus pleasing the Uptown Association. It would place the new convention facilities close to existing hotel and shopping areas in the center of the city, thus pleasing the CAIA and the Chamber of Commerce. The mayor also proposed that vacant renewal land immediately south of the business district be used for the stadium (the eastern ''wing'' of the Rawson-Washington renewal project that was expanded for stadium parking facilities—see map 5.1), thereby giving downtown as well as uptown business interests an immediate and substantial stake in the package of proposals. Administrative changes and an application for CRP funds satisfied some federal expectations, but the provision of relocation resources was the severe test of Allen's ability as a coalition builder and conflict manager. The mayor called for an additional thousand units of public housing and proposed that most of the units be built on renewal land cleared but never developed for industrial purposes (the McDaniel Street area in the western ''wing'' of the Rawson-Washington renewal project—see map 5.1). Although the suggested site was not immediately adjacent to the business district, it was relatively close in; and because renewal land was involved, it constituted a policy matter of importance to the business community.

The Housing Authority Board, it should be recalled, had made a ''gentleman's agreement,'' to reassure realtors and members of the Chamber of Commerce, that public housing would not be built on renewal land and that the Housing Authority itself would initiate no requests for additional units of public housing. The mayor's proposal was thus regarded by business interests as a ''community decision,'' which in the Hartsfield mayoralty had meant a matter to be cleared with the major elements in the city's business leadership.

The Housing Authority prepared a staff paper on relocation and public housing that became the subject for informal discussion in business circles. Then the CAIA circulated a statement to its members, citing both ''a heavy ground swell'' for additional renewal projects and the consequent relocation problem. The CAIA statement said in part:

Despite all the problems of additional Public Housing it now appears that without it the City *cannot* have any more Urban Renewal projects. This is a fact the City, and for that matter the whole community, must face up to. And quite probably the most realistic approach to supplying the Public Housing required to support the City's program is to put it into Urban Renewal project areas. If this should be the final decision, it should be done forthrightly and with full knowledge of the consequences.

As of now we have lived up to our publicly stated policy regarding Public Housing in Urban Renewal projects. The only exception, which was cleared with the Chamber of Commerce and other interested groups, was the single high-rise building for Negro elderly on Hilliard Street. At the time this policy was instituted there were in prospect three Urban Renewal projects. Since then three additional projects have been undertaken. Now, with the proposed addition of West End, Georgia Tech, Buttermilk Bottom and five projects, including school sites, the relocation problem has taken on such proportions that the continuation of this policy seems impossible. If steps are to be taken by the City which will lead inexorably to Public Housing in Urban Renewal project areas then the City should, in advance, recognize this and assume the responsibility of clearing the path for this change in policy. The decision for such a change should be a community decision.[11]

The CAIA statement also noted that there were some financial advantages to the city in locating public-housing units in renewal areas. The sites, for example, would be acquired at a written-down cost. Moreover, the statement made the argument that it would be possible to make use of "some of the least salable areas in our present [renewal] projects if such areas were otherwise suited to Public Housing."[12]

Subsequently when the mayor met with representatives of the general business community, it was not really to seek their approval. Rather it was (with unstated backing from key CAIA members) to announce that "the gentleman's agreement" was no longer applicable to renewal land. The overriding objective he set forth was the rapid completion of the new civic center and stadium.

The mayor's actions indicated that City Hall/Main Street relations had changed from the Hartsfield days. Allen was an incautious leader who cared little about ideological dogmas. As an aggressive promoter of economic growth, he felt no need to tread softly among his former colleagues in business. In response to Allen's conduct as mayor, the business community moved up a rung on the ladder of progressivism. However, too much should not be made of the new policy on public housing. The Board of Aldermen adopted the resolution requesting a one thousand-unit reservation of public housing from federal authorities, but did so with the understanding that the city was not obligated to build the units reserved. At the same time, none of the units reserved in 1959 had been completed. Moreover, federal officials proved lenient with the city once the mayor had set his course of action. Thus, while the mayor and the CAIA were aware of the need to bargain and make some concessions outside the business community, the mayor's renewal policy was essentially a continuation of past policy. It was justified in business terms, based upon business support, and in its unfolding little influenced by federal authorities until black resistance was eventually generated. Even as change came about in such matters as the use of renewal land for public housing, justification came in a form—the need to dispose of cleared but unsold holdings of land—that would appeal to business interests.

Alternative Approaches to Conflict Management in the Renewal of Buttermilk Bottom

During the summer of 1963 business and aldermanic support for renewal in Buttermilk Bottom was strengthened to the point that the only questions remaining were those of when and exactly how the area would be redeveloped. News media coverage of flooding in the area served to dramatize once again the plight of the slum dweller and the profits of the slum owner. The CAIA, through its members on the city's Planning Board and the CACUR, was able to generate endorsements for quick action. The Uptown Association, for its part, supplied city officials with detailed information on Buttermilk Bottom as a possible site for the civic center and in the process tied the case for redevelopment in the area to the long-standing verbal crusade against slumlords.

The mayor's decision to locate the civic center in the Buttermilk Bottom urban renewal area appeared to the general public to be widely supported, but in fact it came at the end of a long internal battle inside City Hall. Competing expectations about resource allocation, land use, and relocation were all involved in the struggle over how Buttermilk Bottom would be redeveloped. And the struggle also involved the issue of how conflict would be managed. Renewal in Buttermilk Bottom might therefore have been carried out in any of several ways and divergent tactics might have been used in an attempt to manage conflict. In the actual course of events, the city tried to confine renewal activity in Buttermilk Bottom to that of providing land for the civic center, thereby, it was hoped, lessening the chances of an open controversy. Another approach had been advocated within City Hall, however.

Members of the city planning staff had, in the first place, argued against both the Buttermilk Bottom site for the civic center and the south-of-the-business-district site for the stadium on the ground that traffic could not be handled satisfactorily. Moreover, a planning staff memorandum offered the view that "if the Buttermilk Bottom area is to be devoted to a non-residential use, the persons to be relocated from the area should be given the option and privilege of relocating in a similar relationship to the central business district."[13] Several sites near the CBD, one of which was the cleared land on which Atlanta Stadium was eventually built, were suggested at various times as suitable for low-rent housing. (The principal proponent of this idea was a planner who subsequently left City Hall in a dispute over housing policy.) Even with Buttermilk Bottom as the site for the civic center, professional planners and the Urban League argued for planning and renewing an area east of the CBD as one large but carefully executed project. Planners and Urban League officials, it should be emphasized, were not opposed to clearance in Buttermilk Bottom. On the contrary, they favored extensive renewal action because that area contained badly dilapidated and substandard housing. But previous experience had shown them that, unless attention was given to the interrelated problems of relocation and the conservation of residences adjacent to clearance areas, housing problems would be intensified through a cycle of overcrowding and deterioration. The Urban League was especially direct in its plea that the city should devote its resources to one good project for the entire inner-city area to the east of the CBD. But the case for comprehensive planning and renewal of the area was not convincing to other participants.

The strategy of undertaking one large renewal project was opposed by the director of the city's misnamed Urban Renewal Department.[14] He argued that a large project would simply increase apprehensions and stir up controversy. Instead of a combined program of clearance, rehousing, and rehabilitation, he sought a project of just enough clearance to solidify business support, but not enough displacement to arouse public concern with the relocation problem.

Beginning shortly after Ivan Allen's inauguration as mayor, the urban renewal "director" urged that the civic center be located in Buttermilk Bottom and argued that the relocation problem was not of great magnitude. Not being secretive about which interest he represented, the director suggested that the Buttermilk Bottom site would not only provide a central location and eliminate a slum, but would also "protect the Uptown Association area."[15] Hence one element in City Hall embraced the argument that Buttermilk Bottom's low income black population constituted a threat to the stability of the Uptown area. They argued that the clearance and nonresidential redevelopment of Buttermilk Bottom "would be the salvation of the Georgia Baptist Hospital" and "should forestall invasion of northeast Atlanta by blighting influences from [Buttermilk Bottom]."[16]

At the same time, the director of the Urban Renewal Department was firmly opposed to massive clearance or even to renewal planning for Buttermilk Bottom in its entirety. He argued that the black community east of the CBD (encompassing both some of the oldest black institutions and some of the poorest black families in Atlanta) would be likely to resist large-scale renewal. Remembering that Auburn Avenue business, political, and church leaders had always vehemently opposed extensive displacement of the population around the traditional "Main Street" of black life in Atlanta, he reasoned that "there is no need at this time to get a large segment of the population in that area exercised and riled up over the possibility of having to move eventually as a result of future developments that could possibly take place in the next five to ten years. This could be disastrous and could conceivably kill the entire project before it really gets started."[17] Controversy over renewal, the director feared, might adversely affect opportunities for "high tax-producing" development in Buttermilk Bottom.[18]

Instead, then, of designating a large area for planning and redevelopment, the Urban Renewal Department suggested that the city concentrate on obtaining land for the civic center. Specifically, the department called for a small project area and the use of the Early Land Acquisition procedure for obtaining the building site.[19] The department's director was confident that, if controversy could be forestalled for a time, the construction of the civic center would "dictate the complexion which redevelopment of the entire area should take."[20] The Urban Renewal Department was also inclined to avoid comprehensive planning for fear that an attempt to detail the number of displacees and the locations in which they would be rehoused might engender white resistance. The relocation problem, the department maintained, could be handled by public housing already in construction, if renewal activity were confined to the proposed civic center and stadium sites.[21]

The Urban Renewal Department's strategy for redevelopment and civic center construction not only had substantial business and aldermanic support, but also offered a way to minimize land costs and shorten acquisition time. The mayor embraced the department's approach, but he had to make additional concessions to federal renewal authorities. In addition to the request for the one thousand units of public housing mentioned earlier, the city agreed to file a General Neighborhood Renewal Program application (which in itself involved only a study and planning exercise) for the larger area to the east of the business district.[22] In return, and under extensive lobbying by city officials and the Atlanta area congressman, federal officials gave quick approval to the Early Land Acquisition procedure. The mayor then made it clear that civic center construction was absolutely top priority and required full cooperation from all agencies. For its part the Atlanta Housing Authority was to expedite land acquisition and to reserve for urban renewal displacees three hundred public housing units in a newly completed Westside project (Bowen Homes)—the outlying project approved more than four years earlier at the time of the Egleston controversy.[23] The housing proposed for an earlier wave of displacement was thus to be used to meet relocation requirements incident to a new wave of clearance and dislocation. While the city had been required to request additional units of public housing, the city was not required to build the additional units before starting another round of displacement activities.

The mayor's actions were strongly supported by the business community, the Board of Aldermen, and the news media. Planning and relocation stipulations set by federal officials, coming as they did in addition to an application for Community Renewal Program funds, seemed to provide some concessions to the viewpoint of socially concerned planners and the Urban League. While these concessions all related to future rather than immediate city activities, they were sufficient to enable the Buttermilk Bottom project to begin without overt opposition.

Protests over the Closing of the C. W. Hill School

Federal approval of Early Land Acquisition was given in the fall of 1964. In line with the Urban Renewal Department's strategy and at the mayor's urging, the Housing Authority cleared the area for auditorium construction within a month after receiving federal approval. The site chosen was adjacent to the C. W. Hill School (see map 7.1), the elementary school serving the Buttermilk Bottom area. Simultaneously with the planning of auditorium construction, the Housing Authority approached city school officials about the possibility of abandoning the elementary school. Concerned over the high replacement costs, school officials resisted the idea initially. However, once auditorium construction was underway, the Board of Education was unable to resist the city's request to close C. W. Hill. The mayor insisted that the civic center was of the highest priority. And, with auditorium construction already begun, there were strong prospects that the clearance of surrounding residential areas would decrease the school's population. At its February meeting in 1965, the board voted to close the school effective at the end of the school year, and they adopted a provision for the following year to use temporary facilities several blocks to the south. A major protest move by Atlanta's black community resulted.

The president of the C. W. Hill PTA went to Jesse Hill, an official in the Atlanta Negro Voters League (still at that time the major organizational link between black voters and city elections) and asked for help. Hill, an Auburn Avenue businessman, agreed to help and drafted a petition that was presented to the Board of Education "on behalf of the C. W. Hill PTA and citizens of the community."[24]

The petition cited the inadequacies of the proposed temporary facilities—"problems of sanitation, cafeteria facilities, restrooms and other important normal school support facilities"—and the drawbacks of a distant location for young children from low-income families.[25] For the times, the statement was worded in strong terms. The board was urged "to spare Atlanta's history of the pending ugly scar" brought on by "the pressure of commercial power and other prestige interests," and by "poor planning or the lack of proper regard for the 800 Negro elementary school children ages 5 to 13."[26] Yet the demand itself was a very

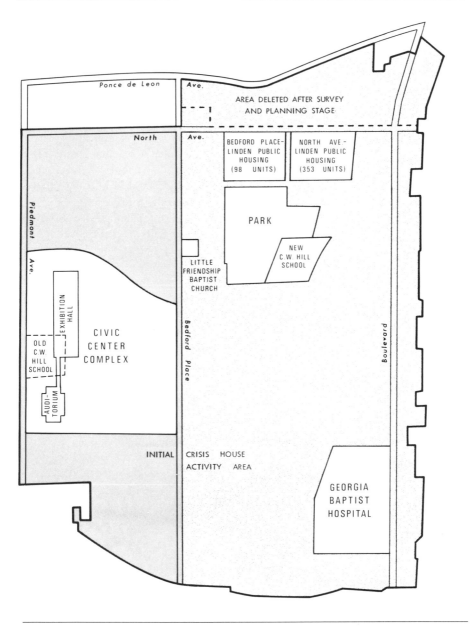

Map 7.1. The Buttermilk Bottom / Bedford-Pine Renewal Area

☐ ORIGINAL BUTTERMILK BOTTOM
URBAN RENEWAL PROJECT

☐ ORIGINAL BEDFORD-PINE
URBAN RENEWAL PROJECT

modest one: "We simply ask that you pass a resolution setting up a committee from your board to include three citizens named by the C. W. Hill PTA to review with City of Atlanta Officials the problem of the C. W. Hill School toward the end of seeking a better solution than the one now underway."[27]

In one respect the demand called for a departure from past practice: blacks were asking for freedom to name their own representatives in a biracial, problem-solving committee. The Board of Education took no action at that time, however. Although some board members did indicate an interest in resisting the closing of the school, the chairman, a CAIA member, offered the opinion that the Board of Education had no choice but to vacate, albeit reluctantly, the site for the civic center.

Jesse Hill proved to be one who was not lulled into passivity by expressions of sympathy. He touched base with the major black leaders in the city as a first step, and within a few days wrote the regional director of Urban Renewal. After specifying inadequacies in the proposed temporary facilities and after charging the city with a failure to consult the affected community, Hill stated, "We do not feel that it is in the interest of the Urban Renewal Program and the Federal government to take part in and subsidize projects that work undue hardships and handicaps on parents and children, especially when there are reasonable alternatives. However, City officials and powerful commercial interests are accelerating the auditorium completion, even though the bulk of the school property will be used for parking area and not the main auditorium building."[28]

Hill did not hesitate to show his determination to pursue the issue to a satisfactory conclusion. He not only requested an immediate investigation of the acquisition of the school site, but he also asked for disapproval or delay of the acquisition until a suitable relocation plan was worked out and "agreed upon." To emphasize the strength of his resolve, Hill also asked about appeal procedures "if your Atlanta office is not the proper office or if you cannot effect an immediate investigation."[29]

Hill closed his letter with the claim that the protest enjoyed wide support among black organizations, and he added credence to the protest by stating, "I have decided to give full-time to this problem during the next few weeks, so feel free to call upon me for conferences, etc."[30]

Federal officials responded with an assurance that the school acquisition would not receive their approval until a relocation solution satisfactory to the black community had been devised. The city proved less malleable.

Maintaining a stance of complete reasonableness in communicating with the mayor and the school board, Hill suggested several alternatives among which were the postponement of school closing for a year, moving the building to another location close by in the project area (an alternative first suggested by the city's chief of construction), and the busing of the students to a nearby school facility located in a white neighborhood but not in use for regular classroom purposes.

Representatives of the school board did meet with planning and redevelopment officials. Consideration was given to the possibility of locating a permanent school site in the General Neighborhood Renewal Program (GNRP) area to the east of the auditorium, but the consensus was that a year would be required to do the necessary planning. The position of school officials was that they lacked funds for a new building in the area because the purchase price for the old school was only $500,000, but its replacement cost would amount to $1,500,000. The most that the school system would offer at the time was to design a new school that would have high priority for development funds out of a new bond issue.

In the face of continued recalcitrance by officials, the PTA group threatened legal action and "protests detrimental to the public relations of our city and [which] could endanger the orderly progress of the new auditorium complex."[31] With that threat having been circulated beforehand, Hill appeared at the Board of Education meeting in April and urged the board to take legal action to prevent the Housing Authority from taking the school. He suggested further that blacks were ready to stage civil rights demonstrations to get their point across. The meeting came to a heated end when the board chairman responded angrily, "I resent and deplore the threats of civil rights demonstrations over the matter of C. W. Hill. I resent it bitterly. I think it's a grand-standing play."[32]

Hill responded with the comment that negotiations were at an end. Some school board members maintained that communications had not broken down, but they had also made it clear earlier in the meeting that the mayor and Board of Aldermen, not the Board of Education, were forcing the relocation move.

The next day the city's major black leaders called a press conference. In turn they assured that civil rights demonstrations were "not a cheap threat but . . . a coming fact," and that Jesse Hill had gone to the Board of Education to express genuine concerns of the black community, for which "all he received was abuse from the School Board president."[33] As a consequence, they stated, "The next step is to communicate through demonstrations. We need to go to the school board and demand complete desegregation."[34]

Immediately afterward, the chairman of the Board of Education removed himself from negotiations in the hope that further talks would occur. The mayor then appointed three members of the school board to serve on a special committee with representatives chosen by the black community to work out a satisfactory solution. The entire school board asked the mayor to delay further construction (an exhibition hall adjoining the auditorium was the project affected), and the mayor agreed to meet with the contractor for the civic center. A few days later the mayor came back with the unconvincing response that it was not practical to delay demolition of the school because the city "would be subject to breach of contract for failure to deliver the land."[35]

The tangled legal relationships among the various city agencies, between the city and the contractor, and between the city and the federal Urban Renewal Administration remained unclarified. Neither demonstrations nor legal action occurred. Instead serious negotiations took place between school officials and representatives of the black community. At no point did the school officials consider an attempt to pressure the mayor or Housing Authority into altering plans for the civic center. The construction schedule as well as the location itself was thus treated as nonnegotiable.

The only concession offered by city redevelopment authorities was to the School Department. The Urban Renewal Policy Committee passed a formal resolution to reassure the School Department that the GNRP area east of the auditorium would remain predominantly residential, and therefore in need of a permanent school facility. Further, the Housing Authority, the School Department, and federal officials agreed to co-operate in order to permit the school site to be obtained under the Early Land Acquisition procedure as part of a renewal project in the area.

By early summer a survey and planning application for a renewal project in the area, identified by two of its major streets as Bedford-Pine, was ready for approval. The terms of an agreement had been worked out. A new, air-conditioned school was to be built in the Bedford-Pine area, east of the civic center (see map 7.1). The school was to be built in six months after a contract was let, to be ready for the 1966 fall term.[36] The temporary structure originally proposed by the city would be used for the 1965–66 academic year, but a committee representing the PTA was to work with the School Department on plans for renovating the facilities. The major concession, however, was to accelerate city-wide school desegregation. In place of the original desegregation plan under which open transfer rights would have been extended to two grades per year, beginning with kindergarten and first grade in 1965–66, the school board agreed to transfers for all grades. A committee of black leaders was to work with parents and school authorities on transfers for children in the C. W. Hill area.

U-Rescue: The Formation of a Neighborhood Protest Organization

In November 1965 the Bedford-Pine Survey and Planning application got federal approval. The consequences were unanticipated. A routine newspaper item on the proposed project, containing a reference to the displacement of 966 families, became the subject for concerned discussions among two white merchants and three black ministers of large churches serving the neighborhood. One of the ministers was also a state legislator representing the area. Each of the ministers pastored a church that had been displaced by an earlier wave of urban renewal. The five men, all quite aware of what had happened to other neighborhoods, determined to challenge the city's renewal plans. They did not attempt to work through city-wide black leaders, but chose to operate as a strictly neighborhood group. While they as individuals had extensive contacts in the area, they wanted a more formal and broadly based organization. They contributed money to organize a protest under the name of U-Rescue: Urban Renewal Emergency, Stop, Consider, Understand, Evaluate.

The strategy that the U-Rescue founders decided on was to hold a mass meeting for the neighborhood in one of the churches and invite city officials to attend. The group, because of its composition, could make use of church announcements to arouse the neighborhood, but they also publicized the meeting by distributing pamphlets that contained the leading statement, "Learn about the danger of losing our Neighborhood because of Urban Renewal." In addition, on the day of the meeting, they rented a sound truck to go through the neighborhood and urge full attendance. An overflow and wrought-up crowd resulted. One of the ministers, an especially passionate orator, proved highly effective in building feeling further as he talked of Atlanta's "urban removal" program, of unkept promises to maintain the residential character of areas, and of the many cases of personal hardships caused by displacement he had witnessed. Several individuals spoke out—homeowners of long standing, proprietors of small businesses, and others who made it clear that they had important stakes in maintaining the neighborhood. An attitude of "you can't trust City Hall" permeated the proceedings.

The news media gave the meeting extensive coverage, and the morning newspaper presented a "task force" report on the proposed project.[37] The "task force" was prepared by reporters and was based largely on interviews with U-Rescue leaders and other neighborhood residents. Under headings such as "It Hurts When They Must Up and Move," reporters offered descriptions of the potential impact of the renewal project on families in the area.

The initial mass meeting was followed by three others, and a series of resolutions to the city was unanimously adopted. The first set of resolutions contained U-Rescue's basic platform, which in brief was:

1. The creation of a citizens' advisory committee to serve as a liaison between the neighborhood and urban renewal office;
2. No change in the area from a residential neighborhood to nonresidential purposes;
3. No replacement of substandard dwelling units with housing beyond the financial means of the people displaced;
4. No widening of a street (Bedford Place) eastward, which would have an adverse effect on one of the small churches in the area (Little Friendship Baptist Church).[38]

The resolutions were carefully worded not to be entirely negative in tone; they expressed general approval of the idea of eliminating blight and specific approval of the new school and adjoining playground.

Drawing on public records in City Hall, U-Rescue strengthened its position first by detailing past instances in which the city had planned to redevelop an area for residential purposes and subsequently either had amended the plan to permit other reuses (the stadium area) or had left land undeveloped (Rockdale). U-Rescue broadened its leadership into a twelve-member executive committee reflecting various political, business, and church groups from the neighborhood. Despite some initial aloofness, city officials came to be convinced that U-Rescue represented genuine grassroots resistance to displacement and that the leadership of the organization had the skill and the incentives to fight effectively against any large-scale clearance.

The city's renewal planning worried the U-Rescue leadership in two respects. While the Survey and Planning application called for the area to remain predominantly residential with rehabilitation in most of the neighborhood, the displacement figure of 966 was regarded as much too high. But, more than that, U-Rescue genuinely feared that the designated area of clearance, a strip along the western edge of the project near the civic center, was only a prelude to total clearance. They saw the civic center as part of a Chamber of Commerce/CAIA/Uptown Association move to extend the business district all the way to Boulevard Street, the easternmost boundary of the proposed project. They also realized that the Uptown Association wanted to create a wide commercial zone extending into the northern portions of the neighborhood. (A little later they were confronted with ambitious expansion plans by Georgia Baptist Hospital in the southern portion of the project area.) Furthermore, with the Egleston-site experience clearly in mind, they feared that a majority of the Board of Aldermen harbored antiblack sentiments and would be quite willing to support efforts to move blacks to Atlanta's Westside.

To gain some assurance that the proposed project would not disrupt the neighborhood, U-Rescue followed a procedure of meeting privately with aldermen and with the city's planning and redevelopment staff. Since various city officials were also invited to attend mass meetings in the neighborhood, assurances given privately thus had to be repeated publicly. U-Rescue regarded the mayor as someone who had to be dealt with gingerly and therefore not to be put on the spot. Consequently, attention centered on Rodney Cook, chairman of the aldermanic urban renewal committee, and on the two aldermen who resided in the ward containing Bedford-Pine. U-Rescue pursued a hard line with the aldermen. In effect, the aldermen were told to be at the mass meetings and state their commitment to maintaining Bedford-Pine as a residential neighborhood for its current population. U-Rescue would construe failure to make this public commitment as opposition to its goals.

Once the general commitment was secured, U-Rescue began to negotiate with Alderman Cook and the Housing Authority over specific points. The city's initial position, as expressed by Alderman Cook, was allegedly one of "don't worry, we'll take care of you." He admitted that some business interests had brought pressure on the city to clear the area for commercial redevelopment, but he maintained that this pressure had been resisted. The city, Cook argued further, would not have committed $2,000,000 or more for a school and park in the middle of the area if it had plans to change the neighborhood from residential to commercial purposes. However, U-Rescue was not at all sure that new housing would be available at a price that would serve current neighborhood residents. To statements that there was nothing to worry about, U-Rescue responded with a demand that the organization wanted to be consulted and involved in the planning of the project. The Housing Authority countered with the suggestion that in place of U-Rescue a large advisory committee for the neighborhood be created. U-Rescue's leadership insisted that the organization would not under any circumstances disband and that, if they served as a neighborhood advisory committee, they ought to be able to make recommendations that would be followed. In short, U-Rescue took the stance that unless they were effectively involved in renewal planning, they would "raise hell." Specifically, U-Rescue's leaders felt that they possessed both voting power in local politics and the capacity to invoke federal regulations.

The city appointed and accepted U-Rescue's leadership as a liaison committee, one that could speak for the neighborhood as redevelopment was planned and executed. In addition there was early agreement to the point that, while the project would consist largely of rehabilitation, the clearance portion would be staged on a block-by-block basis. The Reverend J. D. Grier, spokesman for U-Rescue, and Alderman Cook joined in making a statement that the city would seek to develop procedures whereby one area would be cleared and developed before the next area was cleared. In this way, as people were displaced, there would be housing available in the neighborhood for them to relocate in.

U-Rescue followed up its victories on general points with victories on particular points. A proposed widening of Bedford Street, the street forming the boundary between the Bedford-Pine project and the Buttermilk Bottom project, was postponed indefinitely at U-Rescue's request.[39] When the chairman of the Aldermanic Parks and Recreation Committee stated that the proposed park of twelve acres was not large enough, that it should be twenty-five acres or none, U-Rescue was able to veto the suggestion and maintain the original size.

U-Rescue's most substantial victory, however, was that of gaining the city's agreement to build public housing in the project and to place it in an area covering the northeast sector of the project. Unable to persuade the city to decrease the amount of displacement, U-Rescue turned its attention to the type of residential development that would occur. The organization presented to the Urban Renewal Policy Committee a resolution calling for public housing to "be placed on site within the Bedford-Pine Urban Renewal Project area."[40] The U-Rescue resolution also explicitly demanded that "as soon as the number of families in the area eligible for low-rent housing can be determined . . . not less than this number be scheduled for construction."[41] Finally, the resolution requested that a 650-unit reservation from the Federal Public Housing Administration be obtained to meet the area's needs. The city did agree to 350 units[42] and also suggested that at a later time moderate-income units could be built under the 221(d)3 program.

Opposition from within the business community appeared, not against the request for public-housing units, but against the location of units along North Avenue—the northern boundary of the renewal area. Even before U-Rescue had been formed, the Uptown Association made clear its desire to have the south side of North Avenue, that is, the portion in the Bedford-Pine renewal area, included in a Ponce de Leon/North Avenue commercial corridor (see map 7.1). The Uptown Association engaged in prolonged and determined opposition to low-income housing in that location; on one occasion, the Uptown Association generated a proposal to build a new post office facility in the area planned for housing. Next, the Uptown Association suggested that the renewal project be held in abeyance until public housing could be built elsewhere, either in the project or in an outlying area. City officials rejected both overtures.

U-Rescue's leadership had purposefully selected the North Avenue site for housing in order to prevent further commercial incursion into the neighborhood. Both the proposal for an enlarged park and for the post office facility were viewed as threats to the residential character of the neighborhood. Conversely, public housing in the northern edge of the project was seen as a reasonably good guarantee that the area would remain residential. Although the Uptown Association had staunch support for its position on the Board of Commissioners of the Housing Authority, U-Rescue exerted its influence with the Board of Aldermen, in particular with the chairman of the renewal committee. A divided Urban Renewal Policy Committee supported the North Avenue public-housing site.

In Georgia Baptist Hospital, U-Rescue faced another threat to the residential character of Bedford-Pine. Situated in the southeast sector of the project, Georgia Baptist Hospital first requested a total of thirty-five acres of land for expansion purposes.[43] Although U-Rescue initially opposed selling any renewal land to the hospital, the organization did accede to the sale of fifteen acres, most of which was commercial property and already in nonresidential use. The compromise provided the hospital with land deemed quite adequate for its immediate needs and at the same time generated no real resistance by U-Rescue, because residential displacement was minimal. However, two years later when the Housing Authority proposed expanding the eastern boundary of the renewal project to encompass land sought (purportedly privately) by the hospital for further expansion, U-Rescue strongly and successfully opposed the suggestion.

Overall, U-Rescue prevailed or at least gained significant concessions on most of the points at issue in Bedford-Pine renewal. By contrast, the Uptown Association, while it had attained a much desired objective with the construction of the civic center in Buttermilk Bottom, was rebuffed in its attempts to extend nonresidential reuses into the Bedford-Pine project.

U-Rescue's accomplishments are best appreciated by considering the interests arrayed against the maintenance of Bedford-Pine as a predominantly low-income neighborhood of essentially undiminished population. The Uptown Association, which was especially closely identified with one bank and one department store, included on its board of directors representatives of five banks and two other financial institutions, a major department store and a major national corporation, several "small" but important businesses, attorneys and other professionals, and real estate companies of varying sizes. In brief, the association represented the portion of the CAIA oriented toward the upper sector of the business district. U-Rescue was strictly a neighborhood organization; the twelve-member executive committee was composed of black church and political leaders and black and white businessmen who, without exception, represented small owner-operated businesses dependent upon the immediate vicinity for their customers.

A strictly neighborhood-based organization was thus able to gain important concessions from the city and thwart the demands of an influential element in the business community. Further, while U-Rescue had no active allies, the organization did receive sympathetic and extensive coverage from the news media, editorial endorsements of its general renewal objectives, and timely expressions of support from some business figures on the CACUR and from the Urban Renewal Committee of the Chamber of Commerce. Compared to the Localities Committee of the 1950s, U-Rescue had made a major breakthrough in the local political scene.

The C. W. Hill and U-Rescue Protests: A Tentative Assessment

Opposition to the closing of the C. W. Hill School and to residential displacement in Bedford-Pine, coming within months of one another, signaled an important change in community power relations. During the 1950s, blacks rarely achieved policy concessions in the process of opposing business objectives. Some gains were registered against status quo-oriented whites and some benefits were bestowed on selected black interests in the process of building alliances. But blacks were conspicuously unsuccessful in changing or even modifying the direction of urban renewal policy.

Standing alone, the C. W. Hill protest was not a spectacular success. The school was closed, and the civic center was constructed in a location and on a time schedule quite pleasing to the business community. Important concessions were gained primarily at the expense of the School Department rather than business groups, though the location of the new C. W. Hill elementary school had important ramifications not entirely pleasing to some business interests. Moreover, only federal support made the opposition to closing the school as effective as it was. Had relocation hardships not been so obvious, federal officials might not have proved sympathetic to black protests.

U-Rescue's success, while not complete, was substantial, and it could not be attributed to a single factor such as federal relocation requirements. At the same time, U-Rescue was not pitted against a unified and mobilized business community although it did possess formidable opponents in the Uptown Association and Georgia Baptist Hospital. That the general objectives of U-Rescue received editorial and some business support was not a sign of divided business interests as much as an acknowledgment that blacks had contributed more than their share to civic progress and that they now possessed the capacity to say, "enough is enough."

Before U-Rescue was organized, the news media and others in the community were raising questions about the social impact of renewal and about the balance among various objectives of the program. While the newspapers never waivered in their support for the new civic center and stadium and the use of urban renewal to promote CBD revitalization, in the midst of the C. W. Hill controversy a columnist for the morning newspaper sounded a warning that was subsequently to be repeated and elaborated. Granting that substantial economic benefits had been obtained through Atlanta's renewal program, he asked, "But what of the people who used to live in those old slums?" And he continued by citing urbanist James Q. Wilson's concerns about redevelopment, the "break-up of natural neighborhoods," and the consequent weakening of various neighborhood institutions "that are essential to dealing with fundamental human problems." The columnist concluded, cautioning, "So while we take pride in the new Phoenix Strip of Atlanta [the area along the eastern edge of the business district], we should also think of the problems yet to be solved."[44]

U-Rescue succeeded in pressing the claims of one of those natural neighborhoods against the counterclaims of important business and institutional interests. U-Rescue did more, however, than invoke a moral claim; the organization's leadership displayed skill and exercised considerable power. Yet, in retrospect, it seems reasonably clear that the maintenance of Bedford-Pine as a residential area was part of a tacit bargain between the black community and white civic leaders: if blacks would accept the fact that the civic center had set the character of Buttermilk Bottom redevelopment as nonresidential, then commercial expansion would not be pushed further eastward into Bedford-Pine. In negotiating with U-Rescue, Alderman Cook quite explicitly maintained the posture that the contending interests should be reasonable and that all would receive some consideration. Whereas the Uptown Association was refused its desired land usage south of North Avenue, U-Rescue had to accept the fact that the area above North Avenue was reserved for commercial redevelopment as an already-standing commitment to the Uptown Association. Further, the nonresidential redevelopment of Buttermilk Bottom was considered a settled matter, not subject to negotiations.

U-Rescue's considerable power was thus sufficient to veto significant business demands, but U-Rescue's noteworthy achievement did not amount to a redirection of urban renewal policy. While new and important concessions had been made to a black neighborhood, later events would determine whether or not the urban renewal program would be turned around to become essentially neighborhood-oriented. Further, the obtaining of verbal concessions to the rehousing needs of low-income residents is a long step away from the actual provision of improved facilities. Favorable actions in the early phases of decision making are not necessarily succeeded by equally favorable actions at the implementation stage. In a subsequent chapter, we shall take a later look at the Bedford-Pine renewal project; but first we need to turn to some general efforts to reorient urban renewal in Atlanta.

In the mid-1960s, Atlanta, the town that prided itself on being "too busy to hate," was charged with being "too busy to care." As the new civic center and stadium were under construction, even some public officials began to question the city's priorities. During this time period, Atlanta was hit by a series of civil disorders, mild in comparison to those experienced by some other cities, but nonetheless disturbing to city officials. In Atlanta, as in many places, the disorders were officially attributed to "outside agitators." Still, many of the city's leaders were greatly concerned. They realized that much of the discontent was in fact "home grown." After all, citizen protests as well as a number of official studies had shown—prior to any outbreak of violence—that several Atlanta neighborhoods were genuinely dissatisfied. Thus, before any disorder occurred, leading officials were already aware of unrest in the large number of low-income neighborhoods that made up a substantial part of the city. Events beginning in 1965 provided a good test case of the capacity of neighborhood groups to alter program direction by a campaign of public pressure on city officials.

The events narrated in the present chapter overlapped in time the events described in the previous chapter. There was no formal link between the two sets of events, though, of course, both were occurring in and contributing to the same environment of decision making. Sometimes neighborhoods collaborated in exerting pressure on City Hall, but most often the different groups acted alone. Occasionally, neighborhoods requested assistance from prominent black leaders, and some civil rights organizations took part in the verbal controversies that became so numerous in the mid-sixties. The news media also provided some timely attention to various problems and issues. While neighborhoods were not without allies, there was no organized area-wide effort to bring about a change in city policy. Neighborhood discontent assumed a character that was largely autonomous. In this period, while city-wide black leaders were a significant force, they did not control neighborhood behavior. The present chapter is thus not concerned as much with political organization as with the impact of a loosely connected and more-or-less spontaneous set of events on the climate of official opinion in Atlanta.

Part of the context within which these local events occurred was, of course, a considerable national effort to reorient urban policy in general and renewal policy specifically. The anti-poverty and Model Cities programs provided neighborhood groups with a form of quasi-official representation. Housing subsidy programs were expanded in number and flexibility. And both the Congress and the Department of Housing and Urban Development took steps to redirect urban renewal and have it used as one of the principal tools under the Model Cities program.

Federal officials encouraged cities to undertake projects "which contribute to conserving and increasing the existing housing supply for low- and moderate-income families"; and the Department of Housing and Urban Development came eventually to adopt the position that it would give priority to projects in "areas of physical decay, high tension, and great social need, and in which the locality is prepared to utilize all available resources—Federal, State and local in improving conditions."[1]

Neighborhood Consciousness

As the previous chapter has indicated, in the first few years of the Allen mayoralty the city gave few signs of becoming involved to any large degree in the problems of low-income neighborhoods. Instead the policy that first emerged in the Allen administration was mainly an extension of the policy pursued in the 1950s. While some rhetorical tokens were tossed in the direction of low-income housing and relocation problems, the main concerns were those of building new civic facilities and enlarging the CBD.

The two protest drives already discussed provided some indication that change was in the air, but these protests were not aimed at bringing about a basic redirection of the urban renewal program. Rather they were organized for the limited purpose of halting nonresidential expansion in one section of the city. In other parts of the city, however, some political actors had already begun to entertain ideas about fundamental change. As we shall see, at one point a coalition of neighborhood groups—concerned especially about housing conditions—presented the city with a list of grievances and the threat of a rent strike. Dissatisfaction with the city's urban renewal program had been building for some time. It was articulated in concrete form by neighborhood groups only after a considerable amount of social research and news media discussion had raised the level of general community awareness about the problems of low-income areas.

In order to mobilize support for urban renewal, the news media for more than a decade had publicized slum conditions in Atlanta. The evil of slumlords had been the rallying point for each major drive to undertake renewal action. Opponents to urban renewal had always been depicted by the news media as self-serving and shortsighted interests, but in the summer of 1965 opposition to renewal began to take on a new public image. Under the city's Community Renewal Program, the Community Council of the Atlanta Area (the city's quasi-public agency for social planning) had been commissioned to do a neighborhood analysis and social blight study. The research staff chose as a target area for intensive study two neighborhoods adjacent to the newly constructed

Atlanta stadium. The area bordered an existing renewal project. Interviews with residents yielded more than the usual list of problems for a low-income community. Additional clearance for the stadium parking lot had occurred so recently that the social impact of renewal was readily visible. The low-income housing supply, a preliminary report found, had been reduced with the result that there was a widespread doubling up of families. Houses were being divided and subdivided into apartments; and, according to some of the long-term residents, the changes in the area had "caused a good many of the stable people to move away."[2] Researchers also reported "an extremely high turnover among renters and a loss of homeowners," with a consequent "loss of group pride and neighborhood identification."[3]

Social research usually goes unnoticed by the general public, but the news media have some capacity to determine what is noticeable. Importantly, the newspapers and other media in Atlanta were not a monolithic force, interested only in supporting CAIA projects. On the contrary, some of the reporters were greatly concerned with social problems and were sympathetic to the views reflected in the Community Council research on housing and renewal. An incident in May of 1965 had shown that newspaper coverage had some capacity to prompt City Hall action on social problems: when a newspaper item on health conditions in one of Atlanta's quaintly named slums, Blue Heaven (an area subsequently designated as the Edgewood project area—see map 4.2), proved embarrassing to City Hall, the mayor organized a clean-up campaign, initiated an intensive code enforcement program for the area, and sponsored a guided tour of the neighborhood for various department heads. With quiet cooperation from the Community Council, newspaper reporters followed up that incident with a special ten-part series entitled, "Housing: People, Problems, and Profits."[4]

The series began with an article under the headline, "Thousands Live in Shacks" and contrasted the living conditions of one couple with "Atlanta's gleaming new stadium" nearby. The authors commented: "Atlanta, a City that takes pride in the reputation of being too busy to hate, often is too busy to look at its shelter for low-income people."[5]

The next day an editorial appeared under the headline "Atlanta's Not Too Busy To Care, But Slum Ills Too Big For Old Remedies." The editor asked, "Is Atlanta, the City too busy to hate, also the City too busy to care?" While admitting that there were 40,000 officially labeled substandard units housing 160,000 people, the editorial referred to the mayor's recent interest and concern and turned to the traditional whipping boys: "There are, it is true, slum landlords who profit from suffering and decay. They resist improvement. And there are also political pressures to maintain the status quo in the slums because so many slum dwellers are Negroes, and if they moved, many would move into previously all-white neighborhoods."[6]

The editorial was, however, only one expression of opinion. If there were any need for evidence that newspapers are not monolithic, the subsequent articles in the special series provided it. The later pieces were by no means confined to slumlords and racial bigotry. Rather the urban renewal program itself, which had always been strongly supported by the newspaper officialdom, became the subject of extensive discussion; and critics were given their day in print. The Community Council director was quoted as saying that "all urban renewal does is chase the slums around. It creates as many slums as it clears."[7] Corroborating statements came from the County Welfare director and a member of the City Planning Department directing the Community Renewal Program. Thus the mayor was not entirely convincing when he remarked, "every time we clean up one slum area, we raise our overall standards."[8]

Critics of urban renewal not only cited instances of deterioration in neighborhoods adjoining clearance areas but they also pointed to cases in which dilapidated neighborhoods had been bypassed and given low renewal priority because they lacked high redevelopment value. As a particularly pointed example of the latter, reporters called Vine City

one of Atlanta's worst slum districts packed with 5,000 or more people. . . . The area . . . was considered to be bad enough to be included in the original urban renewal proposed in 1957. It was deleted for economic reasons. . . . Other areas proposed for clearance or rehabilitation had more prospective value for redevelopment—for instance, construction of a motel or a municipal auditorium. . . . There was no reason for renewing the life of Vine City—except to provide people who exist there a better place to live.[9]

The series authors capsuled their urban renewal argument in this manner:

Basically, urban renewal critics fall into two categories: those who feel it is doing too much, and those who think it is not doing enough.

In the latter category, the usual criticisms are two-fold. One is that slum-clearance is motivated almost exclusively by economic considerations—demands for the land on which the slums sit. Thus, land was needed for the stadium so the Rawson-Washington area was cleared, while Vine City sits and grows worse because the land is not yet in demand.

The second is that urban renewal removes more housing than is replaced in the city's housing inventory, thus creating increasing density problems.[10]

The mayor's initial reaction to the attention focused on slum conditions was to order an "all-out attack" on ten of the city's "worst slum areas."[11] However, ten did not exhaust the number of hard-core slum areas, and the "all-out attack" consisted of only stepped-up code enforcement that, its chief administrative officer stated publicly, was better suited for the conservation of housing not yet deteriorated than for the upgrading of housing already dilapidated. Everyone recognized that even concerted clean-up campaigns were not durable and these campaigns were not satisfactory substitutes for needed neighborhood facilities. The Planning Department had given preliminary attention to five neighborhoods as potential renewal project areas, but relocation and funding problems would have had to be surmounted before further renewal activity could be undertaken.[12] Moreover, the Housing Authority's redevelopment director was on record as saying that the urban renewal program was "near maximum capacity" and that "Urban Renewal is no panacea to the low-cost housing problem. The only answer to that is an abundant supply of low-cost housing."[13]

The Federal Regional Office reinforced the view that renewal activity and the low-income housing supply were completely intertwined in Atlanta. Federal officials made final approval of projects already in process contingent upon a request for an additional fifteen hundred units of public housing.

Meanwhile a news article based upon a preliminary analysis of Atlanta's relocation experience, past and proposed, drew public attention to the shortage of standard housing for low-income families. The news media further dramatized the problem by reporting a fatal fire in an overcrowded structure that had provided housing for some displacees from the inner city.

To add urgency to the situation, the Watts outbreak in Los Angeles occurred a week after the end of the "Housing: People, Problems, and Profits" series. A month later the CACUR heard a presentation by its first chairman on conditions in Atlanta that resembled those in Watts. He directed attention to the "appearance of doing things and not getting them done." Among his examples were landlords in the stadium area whose "houses were painted in front and no other place."[14]

Neighborhood Actions

During the summer of 1965 discussions of means for improving housing conditions led to some consideration of rent strikes. Youth volunteers who were working with a neighborhood self-help organization suggested the idea to some low-income citizens, but the idea was first discarded as impractical. However, talk of a rent strike revived in the early fall and was coupled with a proposal for a "tent-in" on the City Hall lawn. On 7 October, at a meeting of the CACUR, representatives of several neighborhood organizations and a black state legislator presented a list of grievances, which began: "We the people of Mechanicsville, Summerhill, South Atlanta, Peoplestown and Vine City appeal to

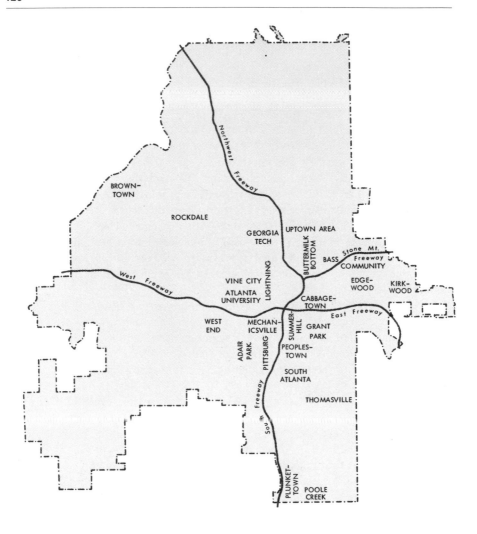

Map 8.1. Selected Nonaffluent Neighborhoods

you, the Mayor, Aldermen, and Citizens Advisory Committee for Urban Renewal of our city, for help in improving our living conditions."[15] [Map 8.1 shows the location of many of Atlanta's nonaffluent neighborhoods.]

The group requested that housing conditions be upgraded and public housing be operated more flexibly, that absentee landlords be forced to comply with the Housing Code, that city services in low-income areas be improved, that regular public meetings such as those of the Board of Aldermen be held in the evening, that special hearings be held in neighborhoods of the city, and that neighborhood advisory committees be appointed. To make the point that city priorities were unbalanced, the petition stated, "Our children have no place to play but the street," and it added, "We would like to use the parking lots of the new stadium and would like to have some help from the city recreation department."[16] The petition also included a specific plea to the city to build the 650 units of public housing promised and planned for McDaniel Street (see map 4.2). Although the petition was written and presented in a moderate tone, it concluded with a warning:

We feel these conditions must be met or we will be forced to withhold our rent in an escrow fund until the landlords have put their houses in living condition. We are ready to be evicted if we have to live in tents and church basements and store our furniture in warehouses, if that is what it takes to get these conditions changed. We do not want to do this and we do not believe that the people of Atlanta will let this happen to their fellow citizens.[17]

Officials responded in a restrained manner. They expressed sympathy with the group's goals and indicated a willingness to keep channels of communication open. City officials did offer assurances that the McDaniel Street public-housing project with supporting facilities would be built and that neighborhood renewal was being considered, but officials also said that additional time and funds would be required before action could be taken. In a shift of his public position, the mayor came to accept the view that the city's urban renewal program had been unbalanced. A year earlier the chairman of the Planning and Development Committee (the recently renamed aldermanic committee on urban renewal), Rodney Cook, had gone on record as being opposed to the use of urban renewal for essentially nonresidential purposes, but neither the mayor's nor the alderman's rhetoric had been accompanied by tangible results. When 1965 came to a close, the forces seeking a new direction in Atlanta's renewal program had brought about a new climate of public opinion in which City Hall decisions would be made. Still, they had neither achieved substantive policy results, nor had they imbued City Hall with a sense of urgency.

In early 1966, no rent strike had materialized, and neighborhood leaders from the stadium area were still meeting with the CACUR and seeking a firm city commitment to begin a program of community improvements. Immediately after President Johnson's message proposing the Model Cities program, residents petitioned City Hall to designate their neighborhoods as the Atlanta Model Cities area. When housing conditions were given renewed public attention, it was not in the stadium vicinity, however, but in a dilapidated area immediately west of the CBD.

A late January cold snap brought near zero weather and a startling eighteen deaths statewide from the cold and exposure. Hector Black, a white Quaker and an organizer of a neighborhood-based self-help group, had been talking about housing conditions with residents in the adjoining poverty neighborhoods of Lightning and Vine City. A landlord with extensive holdings in the area asserted that several of his tenants had complained about civil rights organizers. In the midst of the cold snap, he encountered Black in one of his buildings and had him arrested and jailed for trespassing. Black, as the news media were quick to pick up, had been distributing blankets shortly before he was charged with trespassing. The Vine City Council, the organization Black had helped form, set up pickets immediately, and called for assistance from Martin Luther King and the Southern Christian Leadership Conference, and from Julian Bond and the Student Nonviolent Coordinating Committee (SNCC). (Bond was at that time a newly elected but still unseated member of the Georgia legislature. The near Westside slum on which attention centered was in Bond's district.) Bond was temporarily snow-bound in Washington and at that time could only send a wire to the mayor, but King visited the area immediately. Newspaper and television reporters were in full attendance, not only recording King's comments but also detailing the tenants' grim living conditions.

King, who had been working in Chicago against slum conditions the previous week, described the Atlanta housing as the worst he had seen. He asked the residents if they would be willing to support a rent strike, and remarked to reporters: "I want Mayor Allen to see this. I don't believe he knows such conditions exist in Atlanta."[18]

The mayor's response, according to reporters, was curt: "I'm pleased to have every Atlanta citizen fully inform themselves [sic] on slum conditions that still exist despite all the efforts that have been made to eliminate them."[19] Nevertheless, the day after the arrest of Hector Black and the visit to Lightning by Martin Luther King, city building inspectors and clean-up crews were ordered into the area by the mayor. Community Action aides were also sent in so that a house-to-house survey of resident needs could be conducted. Allen stated that a "great number of services are available for needy slum dwellers,"[20] and he mentioned the fact that there were vacancies in rental units with the Housing Authority. However, a newspaper article subsequently pointed out that the Housing Authority resources were no panacea. While 350 units were vacant, the authority had a waiting list of 950 families, families whose size and locational needs did not match public-housing vacancies.

Continued protest activity in the area was accompanied by news coverage that, through the reporters' penchant for human interest stories, publicized several weaknesses of the Housing Authority as a resource for poor people. Not only were vacant public-housing units small and in distant areas, but some residents, it was pointed out, were too poor to move into public housing or to pay even public-housing rent. Others were reluctant to leave their present neighborhood or to subject themselves to public-housing regulations.

During this time, the city's code enforcement effort served mainly to raise the level of neighborhood apprehension. Part of the enforcement procedure was to present residents with a letter, stating in part that "this unit does not meet the minimum standards required by the housing code . . . it is a violation for this unit to be occupied. Continued occupancy of this dwelling unit will subject you to being summoned to appear before the Municipal Court of the City of Atlanta to answer the charge of violating said ordinance."[21]

A delegation of residents met with city officials and were assured that they would not be forced out of their homes, that landlords in violation of the code would be brought into housing court, and that residents would be given ample time and "every facility the City has" to relocate.[22] When questioned about tenants paying rent on housing in violation of the city code, the chief building inspector responded that "this was a matter between tenant and landlord."[23] Meeting with the mayor two days later, residents presented a list of housing grievances and announced the beginning of a rent strike. They again questioned their obligation to pay rent on housing in violation of the city code, and the mayor replied, "I think if you have rented a house and promised to pay rent on it, then I think you should."[24] He added his assurance that no one would be forced to leave a condemned unit until other housing for him had been located. The mayor then told the group that he commended them for their effort to improve conditions, but said that he did not want them "to think in terms of a rent strike."[25] He urged residents to rely upon "legal methods" and indicated that they were "legally responsible for paying rent."[26]

On the same day residents met with Mayor Allen, Julian Bond held a sidewalk press conference in the area. He asked the mayor to declare publicly that the city would protect the right of individuals to adequate housing with proper heating and plumbing. The mayor, he announced, should declare Vine City a "disaster area." Specifically, he called for an "Operation Fix-It" which consisted of (I) a program to "force slum lords to comply with the City's housing code in the next six months," (2) a multimillion dollar request for public housing to be built before anyone was moved out of current housing, and (3) the erection of a "freedom village" in the community to house people temporarily while new structures were built. His program included a sweeping request that "all the resources of the . . . City be directed toward changing living conditions in this area, as well as other areas of poor housing in the City."[27]

Slum housing conditions were frequent topics in the news and on the editorial pages for well over a month. Two weeks after the announcement of the rent strike, the Vine City Council sponsored two days of picketing in front of the Northside home of Lightning's principal landlord. This event was followed by a press conference and another presentation of demands that the city "do something about the crisis in low-rent housing and these intolerable living conditions."[28]

On 28 February, Hector Black was found innocent of the much-publicized trespassing charge brought against him. But the following day the housing protest received a major legal setback. Eviction procedures were upheld for the two families who had persisted with the rent strike. Although legal appeals delayed the actual eviction for a few days, dispossessory warrants were served on 7 March. The rent strike was over. Pickets and furniture in the street provided one final opportunity for news coverage of housing conditions. A few houses were repaired, but housing code enforcement was soon stilled by legal entanglements.

A New Level of Official Concern with Low-Income Areas

Protestors of slum conditions had not won a battle, but there were indications that they might win a war. They had shown that they could obtain extensive and basically sympathetic news coverage, and the mayor appeared responsive to this coverage. Moreover, poverty problems continued to receive close attention.

No sooner was the Westside rent strike at an end than the Community Council report on the stadium area was officially released. An extensive newspaper piece followed under the headline, "City's Shame in Shadow of Its Pride: Atlanta's Plush Stadium Towers over Slum's Poor."[29] The chairman of the Chamber of Commerce's Urban Renewal Committee also read the report on the stadium area, and he gave it extensive distribution among his business colleagues. Citing a lack of communication between community leaders and the residents of low-income areas, the Community Council report expressed concern over the alienation of neighborhood residents and their distrust of the city.

The report made two recommendations for immediate action:

1. *A Program of Public Information on Future Plans for Urban Clearance* should

be initiated to acquaint the residents of each neighborhood with all existing plans for their neighborhood and the status of these plans. This program should be conducted through a series of meetings held in each of the neighborhoods with well organized advance notice given to the residents. . . .

II. *A Program of Open Dialogue Between the Major Community Resources and the Low Income Neighborhoods* should be initiated to: (1) acquaint the residents with the objectives, methods, regulations, and future plans for service and (2) obtain the reactions and suggestions of the residents. This program . . . should be conducted through both large and small meetings and develop into a continuous program. . . .[30]

The report was first presented to a subcommittee of the CACUR on the Community Renewal Program. Several stadium-area groups were in attendance. Subsequently the report was submitted to the full CACUR. Both the subcommittee and the full CACUR received the report cordially, and the CACUR passed a resolution that urged the city to expedite the still-lagging McDaniel Street public-housing/school and park project. Included in the resolution was a strong admonition to the city:

The committee points out that considerable time has passed in the consideration and planning stages, that a large area of land has lain cleared and unused for many months and residents of the area are understandably insistent that an early start should now be made on the project.

The committee reminds all concerned that long and frequently unexplained delays on projects either in the planning or building stages have done and are doing immense harm to the whole concept of urban renewal. The Rawson-Washington area [near the stadium] would appear to be a prime example of the overdue need to replace promises with fulfillment.[31]

The mayor's office in the meantime was following the legislative progress of the Model Cities program with great interest. Stadium-area residents were continuing to lobby for designation as Atlanta's Model Neighborhood, and City Hall proved quite receptive to their entreaties. The only question among the mayor's staff was that of how large an area could be encompassed. Two of the mayor's aides flew to Washington with a tentative proposal in July, nearly three months before the program was enacted. Four black (Mechanicsville, Pittsburg, Summerhill, and Peoplestown) and two white (Grant Park and Adair Park—see map 8.1) neighborhoods in the stadium vicinity became the tentative project area before the summer ended.

One additional Community Renewal Program matter of importance remained to be clarified. The private planning consultants who were devising the system of urban renewal project priorities released a preliminary report in which redevelopment potential was weighted more heavily than the intensity of physical blight and social problems. The report, which was repudiated by key officials, took no account of changing City Hall attitudes. In May of 1966, for example, the mayor provided a cue for later actions when he issued a memorandum to all department heads suggesting that precedence go to substandard areas in services and other city efforts. A Community Council attack on the scheme of renewal priorities proposed by the private consultants was not only condoned, it was encouraged by the City Planning Department; and it was joined in by the chairman of the aldermanic Committee on Planning and Development. Subsequently the Community Renewal Program report on project priorities was completely revised. The City Planning Department during the summer was preparing Urban Renewal Survey and Planning applications for four of the city's most blighted neighborhoods. In addition, the first steps were made to plan a multi-purpose community center in Vine City.

In mid-July, when the Recreation Department seemed to be unduly slow in implementing the mayor's priorities, one of the stadium-area neighborhood leaders staged a traffic-stopping "football game." By the end of the following day an already-promised play area had been graded, and the city offered its assurance that the project would be completed the following morning.

Concerned about summer violence, the mayor's office had become keenly interested in recreation lots and other signs of city responsiveness to low-income areas. City Hall efforts notwithstanding, in September of 1966, Atlanta experienced two serious outbreaks of civil disorder—the first in the stadium area (Summerhill) and the second in the fringe of the Bedford-Pine project. The first outbreak was particularly traumatic for Allen. Not only did it show that established city-wide black leaders lacked rapport with discontented black crowds, but it demonstrated dramatically that the mayor's own leadership was severely limited. After Allen climbed up onto his car to try to calm a street crowd, several members of his intended audience rocked the mayor off the top of his automobile. Efforts to remind blacks that Atlanta was a progressive city were greeted with a call for another Watts and the charge that "Atlanta is just a cracker town."[32]

Disorder was explained editorially by the *Atlanta Constitution* as the product of SNCC agitation, but many concerned citizens refused to accept that argument. For example, the Council on Human Relations of Greater Atlanta offered an immediate rebuttal to the *Constitution*'s editorial interpretation of the stadium-area incident. The council charged that "the basic responsibility lies with Atlanta's lack of concern over miserable conditions in slum areas."[33] The organization detailed instances of city neglect and delay as well as "the wearying succession of meetings and surveys and petitions of residents of that area and of other citizens during the past months.''[34]

In fact, officials did not dismiss the ''riot'' as a meaningless agitation. The mayor talked with neighborhood leaders to find out what grievances residents had, and housing emerged at the top of the list.[35]

In reporting to the department's central office on the ''riot,'' regional officials of the federal Department of Housing and Urban Development (HUD) made a revealing assessment of precipitating circumstances in the stadium area. They observed that the site of the disturbance, Summerhill, was not in a project area and that no departmental programs were involved in the incident. Regional and local officials alike, however, had long regarded the area as a potential trouble spot. It was a ''port of entry'' for new migrants to the city and had few stabilizing influences. Yet the city had built no neighborhood facilities and provided no social service programs specifically for area residents. City Hall, regional officials reported, realized that the area had major needs, but they had not given it high priority. Sensing and hoping that city priorities were beginning to change, regional officials came forward with an offer to expedite housing or other project applications.

Before the outbreaks of civil disorder, city policy toward low-income areas was in fact already in the process of reversal. Yet it also appears clearly the case that the September events gave the mayor's office a sense of urgency that had been missing earlier. Moreover, staff members and others in the community who were socially concerned found their hands considerably strengthened. The Community Council neighborhood analysis and recommendations made earlier in the year were given wide circulation. A second Community Renewal Program report, a thorough and forthright assessment of Atlanta's relocation experience, also received close attention.[36] The report was completed in September, and it was read by the mayor during the time that he was searching for a concrete and visible way to respond to conditions in the city's poverty areas.

The relocation report included a number of specific recommendations, one of which was to call a ''Mayor's Conference on Housing.'' The conference would ''focus attention on the city's desperate need for low-income housing.''[37] The conference could also serve ''to identify, encourage, and assist private developers'' of low-income housing programs and ''to speed up'' the construction of public-housing units.[38] The mayor put this recommendation together with the finding that ''an estimated 17,000 housing units in the city have major slum conditions or major deterioration.'' After arranging for the aldermanic Planning and Development Committee to declare that no further urban renewal could be undertaken until relocation resources were expanded, the mayor called the recommended housing conference for November 1966. To meet relocation needs and to replace the existing substandard units, the mayor set a five-year goal of 17,000 new units of low- and moderate-income housing. In addition a crash program of 9,800 units was set for completion in two years. To facilitate the accomplishment of the conference goals, Mayor Allen appointed a Housing Resources Committee. This committee, comprising many of Atlanta's most progressive civic leaders, was given a multifaceted charge to

organize . . . business and civic leaders to help stimulate private development of housing units within reach of citizens on the lower rungs of the economic ladder . . . , [and] recommend changes in existing policies and programs and also new programs which will offer promise of helping us reach all our goals. . . . The Housing Resources Committee and its staff will provide direct and continuing technical assistance to any qualified private group which wishes to sponsor "221" housing. It will help locate land and financing. It will assist sponsors in preparing and filing applications with the Federal Agencies.[39]

As 1966 came to an end, the turnaround seemed complete in Atlanta's renewal program. The mayor had embraced housing and relocation goals that presumably would enable the city to eliminate its slums. The stadium area was designated for Model Cities action, and plans for a combined school and neighborhood facilities center in Vine City would allow urban renewal to begin in that long-bypassed area. Other projects, it appeared, would follow in succession as the city embarked on a five-year program of renewal and code enforcement to replace or upgrade substandard housing. The Community Renewal Program studies provided a technical and professional rationale for a redirected urban renewal program.

It was equally significant that concerned whites and leaders in black neighborhoods seemingly had gained a sympathetic hearing from the city's top officials. The Community Council, the firm of planning consultants that had prepared the Community Renewal Program relocation study, members of the City Planning Department, and the newly created Housing Resources Committee enjoyed rapport with one another, and they enjoyed favor with both newspaper and television reporters. Under the leadership of some of its younger members, even the Chamber of Commerce proved responsive to a more socially oriented renewal program.

The change had come abruptly. As late as the 1965 Declaration of Policy in the city's Workable Program document, Atlanta's urban renewal program was explained primarily in terms of the "encouragement of economic expansion," physical planning and development, and "the overall economic ability of the City to support . . . urban development and renewal activities.'' By the close of 1966 the urban renewal program was completely recast; neighborhood improvements, grass roots participation, and expanded supply of standard housing for low- and moderate-income families appeared to be central elements in a new renewal policy. However, at this time, the new directions were only paper declarations, untried against the stresses and strains of concrete application. The next few years would test the durability of concessions won through the politics of protest and public pressure.

For Atlanta, 1966 had apparently been a year of turning points. Planning studies and policy declarations by public officials indicated that the city was on a new redevelopment course—neighborhood improvements and an expanded supply of safe and decent low-income housing apparently would enjoy the same prominent position among the city's priorities that expanding and upgrading the CBD had occupied earlier. Neighborhood renewal and low-income housing proved, however, to be less firmly established than the earlier goals of economic growth and business district revitalization. As it turned out, the events of 1966 were not a prologue to the city's future policy of urban renewal. Instead the 1966 concerns with housing and neighborhood conditions proved vulnerable to subsequent concerns about economic balance and metropolitan reorganization.

As the decade neared a close and the threat of disorder receded, the mayor seemed to lose interest in efforts to better low-income areas. Instead his strategically important actions (and inactions) followed the drift of opinion in the business community. During his final years in office, Mayor Allen made it clear that he regarded economic prosperity as a more fundamental community need than relieving poverty or improving neighborhoods. On the occasion of his farewell address, Allen stated forthrightly that the best way to upgrade social conditions was through economic growth. He elaborated: "The key is balance. Atlanta must continue to produce more jobs, a growing tax base, cultural and athletic activities, a profitable business environment and pride in the community. To neglect these factors in favor of putting all emphasis on social improvement only retards that very improvement."[1]

Allen's farewell address as mayor was more than rhetoric. It was a justification for a reversal of policy in which business priorities had once again gained ascendancy. The latter years of the Allen era were thus a time in which the direct and immediate interests of blacks and other neighborhood groups in improved residential facilities and expanded housing opportunities were sacrificed to the less direct and less immediate interests of businessmen in a "balanced" community.

The present chapter treats these final years of the Allen mayoralty. During these years, neighborhood/City Hall relations were punctuated by a number of controversies—a few of which were intensified by intraneighborhood rivalry. The involvement of residential areas in the planning of renewal activities was a friction-ridden process in which City Hall proved to have no sustained interest. The tension surrounding efforts to plan neighborhood redevelopment was, however, not the principal barrier in the way of rehousing the poor and improving the quality of residential life. The most debilitating force at work on these new program goals was an indirect one, the lack of business support. Business priorities and the priorities articulated by spokesmen for low-income neighborhoods did not coincide. Consequently, the city failed to undertake and sustain the actions needed to put into effect systematic programs of neighborhood improvement and expanded housing opportunities. In the closing years of the Allen administration, overt conflict again proved to be only one face of power. The quiet and subtle influence of the business community was a major determinant of policy.

Neighborhood Improvement and Citizen Participation

As noted earlier, the mayor, eager to demonstrate concern for slum areas in a concrete way, had worked hard and fast to have Atlanta selected as one of the first recipients of Model Cities funds. The planning application was prepared quickly and without the participation of representatives from the Model Neighborhood area. The city did not entirely ignore its new policy of open dialogue with low-income neighborhoods and of not undertaking renewal or rehabilitation programs without evidence of neighborhood support. After the planning application was submitted, a series of meetings was held in the proposed project area. Black neighborhood leaders were generally supportive of the Model Neighborhood designation. Whites were openly distrustful.

Some members of both races displayed fears that the area would be cleared rather than rehabilitated. As one resident commented: "They're going to come in here with bulldozers and clear the whole area out and put in motels, shopping centers and apartment buildings."[2] The mayor offered public reassurance, and at one meeting stated: "It is the full intent of our Model Neighborhood program in Atlanta that not one family will be moved out of this area."[3] Questionnaires were distributed to enable residents to indicate which areas of action were most urgently needed. Housing, to no one's surprise, was rated first and was given top priority in the various stages of planning.

The public meetings revealed some concern over how soon and how effectively the city would act to reverse the neglect and deterioration of the community. The attempt to establish priorities encountered some resistance. One resident, in response to an invitation to speak about priorities, remarked: "We cannot say. . . . No more than we can say meat is more important. Or water. Or bread. We've been without for so long." Another resident, impatient with delay, offered: "We've been the stepchild out here for so long. . . . Why can't they just tell us we're illegitimate and stop asking us for taxes."[4]

In contrast with the unspecific demands for a larger share of the city's resources and services, the demand for a greater voice in the Model Cities program was pointed out and carefully promoted. The city, unaccustomed to the involvement of the poor in decision making, initially made no provision for neighborhood representation on the Model Neighborhood Executive Board.[5] Requests for neighborhood representation were made through the Community Council and the Community Action agency without results.

After some delay and a HUD request for a more precise explanation of how citizen participation would be accomplished, the mayor's office suggested the addition to the executive board of one member selected by area residents. Though there was also to be a Model Neighborhood Area Council with undefined advisory powers, black leaders concentrated their efforts on increased representation in the executive board. First, these leaders persuaded the city to agree to a "Mass Convention," that is, a meeting open to all residents, for purposes of organizing the Model Neighborhood area. Then, working through the Community Action agency to mobilize the black neighborhoods, they were able to obtain a large turnout of residents preadvised to support a resolution calling for six neighborhood representatives to the executive board to be elected in a subsequent mass convention. The resolution passed and the city acquiesced.

With backing from the mayor and the chairman of the aldermanic Planning and Development Committee, the proposal was adopted by a divided Board of Aldermen. Opposition centered on the fact that the proposal would enlarge the Model Cities Executive Board to fourteen members; and, since only six would be public officials, private citizens would outnumber officials. However, the two members of the original eight selected as private sector representatives were appointees of the public officials (in reality appointed by the mayor). The conflict remained low-keyed throughout. Neither City Hall nor area residents saw the issue as one of community control. Some uncertainty surrounded the relationship between the Model Neighborhood Executive Board and the Board of Aldermen, but the uncertainty was tolerated. Area residents made no challenge to the ultimate authority of City Hall over the program.

The city's willingness to involve neighborhoods directly in project planning was put to a more severe test in the Vine City area. Once City Hall had selected the Model Neighborhood area, the mayor directed the Planning Department to prepare renewal applications for Vine City and the East Atlanta neighborhood of Edgewood, two of the communities that had been highly vocal in accusing the city of neglecting them. The applications were not acted on in 1966 because relocation resources were not available. However, preliminary renewal planning was begun for Vine City and was accompanied by the preparation of an application for a community facilities grant. The Planning Department proposed the establishment of a multipurpose community center as part of the construction of a new junior high school in the area. Though one of the purposes of the center was said to be decentralization of services and the encouragement of neighborhood/City Hall dialogue, site selection took place without community involvement.

The Planning Department considered three sites and recommended one that would (1) be centrally located for the area to be served, (2) be inexpensive to acquire ($310,000), (3) involve the least displacement, but (4) also involve clearance of the largest number of standard structures and displacement of the highest percentage of homeowners (55 percent).

As soon as the choice became known, some of the homeowners and churches in the area formed a resistance group. Black members of the CACUR voiced concerns that, as in the case of Bedford-Pine, neighborhood interests were being neglected and that a neighborhood-based protest would be organized. School Board and Planning Department members met with groups in the neighborhood but made no change in the proposed school site and thus failed to allay opposition. The resistance group argued that new construction should be used to eliminate substandard structures, not to displace stable members of the community. The group tried unsuccessfully to persuade officials to adopt an alternative site—one with only 9 percent homeowners (but one that had an acquisition cost of $545,000). However, because city officials were mainly concerned with the relocation problem involved in moving a large number of low-income families, they rejected the suggested alternative.

Although the school site controversy was still unresolved, the mayor decided that renewal planning should move ahead. Planning encompassed an area larger than Vine City, an area officially designated as Nash-Bans. Even though the planning of the renewal project was intertwined with the construction of the new school and the establishment of the community center, the city proceeded as if the school site and renewal planning were unrelated matters.

Under a dual mandate from the mayor and from the aldermanic committee, the Planning Department set out to devise a mechanism for neighborhood participation in renewal planning. But the effort to provide for community participation involved no attempt to settle the dispute over the school site. Indeed, the preliminary plans to establish neighborhood participation completely overlooked the group opposed to the school site selected by the city.

The aldermanic Planning and Development Committee had stated its position as that of making "final approval of the planning application request'' contingent upon ''evidence of neighborhood support'' of urban renewal.[6] ''Evidence of neighborhood support'' went undefined, however. Planning and mayoral staff members consulted with the Community Council, which, in turn, communicated with the Vine City Foundation (formerly the Vine City Council, which had gained visibility in the area's brief but highly publicized rent strike), the neighborhood Community Action center, and a state legislator who had long-standing contacts with college officials and other prominent business and professional men in the Nash-Bans area. Subsequently, a temporary steering committee was established for the purpose of initiating procedures whereby neighborhood groups could become involved in planning the renewal project.[7]

Since the Vine City Foundation had been critical of the Community Action program for failing to involve persons who were genuinely poor, the city had some reason to think that a steering committee that contained members acceptable to both the Community Action center and the Vine City Foundation was reasonably representative. However, while the committee contained officers from a variety of organizations, some organizations were unrepresented. For example, no member of the school-site resistance group was included in the steering committee. Further, the city was unaware that the Vine City Foundation had engendered opposition to itself. Some neighborhood leaders were quite open in their feeling that their leadership was threatened by the Vine City Foundation, which was a newcomer among the neighborhood's organizations. By including representation for the foundation, the steering committee thus intensified the distrust already stirred up by the school site controversy.

City officials, though anticipating some criticism and some opposition, followed through on the formation of the steering committee by sponsoring an open meeting for the neighborhood. At the meeting, the mayor gave an assurance that the neighborhood would be involved in planning its future, and he presented both the steering committee membership and an illustrative urban renewal plan—the latter as an example of what could be accomplished through urban renewal if the neighborhood so chose to move in that direction. The result was a tempestuous meeting. Angry residents impugned City Hall motives, and confronted the mayor with the fact that many past promises to improve conditions in Vine City had been unfulfilled. Opposition to the school site surfaced quickly and was obviously a major force among the audience. Many residents expressed the fear that urban renewal was simply a device through which they would be moved out of the area. The mayor's announcement of the steering committee membership, whose function was supposed to be that of helping to form a representative neighborhood committee, was greeted with the charge that the city was once again acting on the basis of a "plantation mentality."[8] Residents cited the list of committee members as evidence that the neighborhood would not be permitted to choose its own representatives. Try as he did, the mayor could not explain the purpose of the steering committee satisfactorily to a hostile and suspicious audience. The mayor was also unable to explain the purpose behind drawing up an "illustrative" renewal plan. Residents would not accept the plan as a "point of departure" for discussion, and they accused the city of being already committed to a course of action for the neighborhood. Otherwise, residents argued, there would be no need for a plan to have been drawn up. Code enforcement also came under severe attack. Slum landlords, residents maintained, received no attention while homeowners were subject to harassment. It was clear that an overriding concern was that of making sure that residents were able to stay in the area.

During the session, feelings—including the mayor's—ran extremely high. At one point, the mayor took the renewal plan, which he had intended only as an example, crumpled it, and presented it to one of his most vocal critics. And, after two hours of exchange, the mayor turned to another of his antagonists, the president of the Community Civic League, and one of the principal opponents of the school site, and said tartly: "We could talk all night, Mr. Laws; you get that committee [to represent the neighborhood]."[9]

The mayor won no friends and influenced few people during the Vine City meeting. Yet he showed no signs of anxiety over constituent dissatisfaction. He made no effort to have the school site reconsidered or to negotiate a compromise with discontented residents.

Relations between the mayor and the neighborhood opponents of the school site remained tense and largely antagonistic. The mayor did abide by his hastily made delegation of responsibility for the formation of a neighborhood committee; and, when pressed on the point, he gave official recognition to the newly formed neighborhood organization. Designated the Nash-Bans Coordinating Committee, the organization was composed of ministers, businessmen, PTA officers, and officers in various other civic and fraternal clubs in the community. Although city officials realized that the new committee represented basically a homeowner's faction, no effort was made to broaden the committee's representation. Indeed, the mayor's staff concluded that one of the lessons to be drawn from the open meeting was that the city needed "to place more emphasis on homeowners and small business owners and take another look at the strength of our [Community Action] neighborhood centers."[10] Yet neither the mayor nor his principal staff aides played an active role in working out future City Hall/Nash-Bans Coordinating

Committee relations. In fact, the mayor understandably avoided further meetings with the neighborhood group, and the neighborhood group was then forced to deal with the mayor through formal and impersonal channels.

A black member of the city's planning staff was assigned to work with the Coordinating Committee. The effort never went beyond a descriptive study of the area and its problems because the committee was occupied mainly with opposition to the school site. The committee attempted to gain a veto over all planning and development in the area by the city, and it generated a torrent of letters and petitions, including a threat to hold massive "antisocial" mass demonstrations.[11] City Hall responded with repeated statements that neither the mayor nor the Board of Aldermen possessed the authority to halt projects in progress, and that the School Board was an independent body over which the mayor and the other city departments had "no authority."[12] (Mayoral/School Board relations during the C. W. Hill School closing controversy two years earlier provide an interesting contrast.) An appeal to HUD as the source of Neighborhood Facilities Funds and a court challenge also failed to yield any success in the campaign against the school site.

Since the Nash-Bans Coordinating Committee maintained that no other matter could be taken up until the school site conflict was resolved and since the city became increasingly specific on and adamant in the position that the center would have to be a fixed part of any plan, a complete impasse resulted. Committee members sought to meet directly with policymakers and to bypass the planner assigned to work with them. The mayor, in turn, insisted that the committee work through the planner, who, as everyone concerned understood, had no authority to re-open the question concerning the location of the school-and-community-center facility. After nearly a year of unremitting controversy, City Hall was quite willing to let the renewal proposals for Nash-Bans rest in limbo.

The following year, 1968, after Congress enacted a redirected and supposedly neighborhood-oriented version of urban renewal,[13] the Vine City Foundation faction confronted the city with new demands that housing conditions in the area be improved. And two potential nonprofit sponsors of low- and moderate-income housing, which were working with the Vine City Foundation, requested the city to include Vine City in the recently enacted Neighborhood Development Program (NDP). They presented to the mayor's staff a concrete proposal for the development of housing in the midst of the most poverty-stricken section of Vine City.

Meanwhile City Hall continued to be criticized for neglecting the black community. Neighborhood residents in hearings before the city's

Human Relations Committee, the Housing Resources Committee members, and black leaders both informally and in statements to the press indicated that they expected the mayor's office to respond more forcefully to conditions in various black neighborhoods. Feeling that some concrete response was needed, particularly in Vine City and in the eastern part of Atlanta, areas in which vocal and articulate black spokesmen lived, City Hall designated a section of each area for inclusion in the NDP.

Federal regulations for the NDP required the selection of a Project Area Committee (PAC) to provide an established means for citizen participation. In the East Atlanta neighborhood of Edgewood, the selection proceeded without controversy. Vine City, however, once again became the locus of conflict. The Nash-Bans Coordinating Committee argued that it was entitled to become the PAC, but the mayor issued a statement saying that the NDP approach to urban renewal necessitated planning projects smaller than the original Nash-Bans area. The statement also made the point that the new federal regulations required "the establishment of a Project Area Committee (PAC) made up of citizens who live within a project area."[14]

By designating an area smaller than Nash-Bans and by invoking the rule that PAC members be residents of the area (a rule not enforced in other NDP areas in Atlanta), City Hall hoped to circumvent the opposition group to the school site. However, the proposed Vine City NDP project boundaries extended beyond the hard-core poverty area in which the Vine City Foundation was centered and included an area of homeowners in the school site vicinity.[15] The stage was set for another bitter factional struggle that would stretch out over several months. Neither faction trusted City Hall, but the Vine City Foundation group felt the need for action, particularly to improve housing opportunities for low-income families. The Coordinating Committee remnant was interested in continuing the struggle over the school site. However, the competition between the two elements was based on more than different objectives. Neighborhood leadership was at stake. Moreover, the Coordinating Committee element was concerned that the Vine City Foundation, because of its involvement with multiproblem poverty families, conveyed the wrong image of the neighborhood. Indeed they felt that organizations like the Vine City Foundation served only to reinforce unfortunate stereotypes of blacks.

Unwilling to recognize the Coordinating Committee as the PAC for the new renewal area and unable to recognize the Vine City Foundation faction without some form of election, City Hall was forced to play the role of mediator. The two factions reached no agreement, however, in spite of lengthy negotiations. Finally, despite the continuing struggle between the two groups, the city decided to hold a public meeting for the purpose of electing a PAC. One member of the Coordinating Committee slate and two leaders of the Vine City Foundation were removed from consideration on the ground that they did not *reside* inside the boundaries of the proposed renewal project. The remaining nominees of both slates plus a few individuals nominated from the floor were all then elected as the PAC. No set committee size had been decided on before the election took place, and the Coordinating Committee slate constituted a clear majority of the PAC. It was therefore able to elect officers and organize the new committee without difficulty. The Vine City Foundation members, outnumbered and deprived of their two main leaders, did not even attend PAC meetings.

Relations between City Hall and the Coordinating Committee, though still plagued by mutual feelings of mistrust and hostility, lessened in tension enough for renewal planning to begin. A small area was selected for some rehabilitation and the redevelopment of some housing in the first year of action under the NDP. Temporary housing was to be used to ameliorate the relocation problem. Cutbacks in federal funds forced a decrease in the size of the action area and temporary housing was not provided, but no further controversy was engendered.

Some Observations about Neighborhood Improvement and Citizen Participation

The city's approach to federally inspired forms of citizen participation was well-intentioned enough but in some ways politically inept. Because city agencies and even the Community Council had such limited experience with neighborhood groups, officials had little understanding of the complexity of neighborhood politics. Moreover, they had no sense of urgency about allaying fears and building trust. City Hall was responding to external pressures of no little consequence, but the felt need was one that grew out of a public relations problem. It was not born out of some feeling that the community's well-being consisted of improved neighborhoods and expanded housing opportunities. The mayor's office was thus content with a show of concern. If the neighborhood responded in a constructive and cooperative manner, then an effort would be made so long as federal funds did not run short. But if the neighborhood, as in the case of Vine City, proved uncooperative and quarrelsome, then the neighborhood could bear the blame for inaction. City Hall might play the role of mediator between competing factions, but it was at heart a passive role. No elaborate strategies of coalition building were concocted. No commitments of resources, nor concessions on land use, were offered to avert opposition. Increased representation on advisory committees and a willingness to expend federal monies were the extent to which the city was willing to go on behalf of neighborhood renewal.

To understand fully what was involved in the city's faltering effort to renew old neighborhoods, it is important to put the outbreaks of conflict into context. The 1965–66 pressures on City Hall were not maintained at a high level. Although the controversies associated with Vine City renewal were intense, overt conflict was confined to a few particular issues. While demands for improved housing conditions continued to be made by the Vine City Foundation, decreased federal funding and a corresponding decline in the city's renewal activity led to no open conflict.

The city also failed to undertake improvement programs in other neighborhoods, and the failure was not contested overtly. Two black neighborhoods of severe blight and very high incidence of poverty (Lightning and Plunkettown—see map 8.1) and a white working-class neighborhood (the Bass Community) in a state of accelerated decline due in part to proposed freeway construction were unable to obtain more than a verbal acknowledgment of their need for attention. No citizen committees were recognized, and none of the three neighborhoods was given planning assistance. The Planning Department simply responded to requests for assistance and action with the statement that its resources were too limited for further undertakings. Yet the city was at this same time negotiating quietly with federal authorities for a second Georgia State University renewal project in order to expand further the campus of this downtown institution.[16]

To be sure, criticisms of the city for neglecting the eastern section of Atlanta plus the availability of noncash credits, did lead the city to designate another neighborhood, the Edgewood area,[17] for inclusion in NDP planning along with Vine City. Edgewood, of course, faced the same decrease in funds and city activity that had occurred in Vine City. And, as in Vine City, the contraction of renewal activity to the token level went uncontested.

While the city provided for a neighborhood voice in renewal planning, neighborhood participation did not extend to the question of the overall allocation of community resources. Neighborhood groups received some form of official recognition and had some small benefits that they could control the distribution of, but they could not and did not challenge the amount of resources allocated to them. At most, then, neighborhood groups managed to gain token inclusion in the city's renewal process.

Discontent in the 1965–66 period had generated a widespread move to change City Hall priorities. A loosely coordinated effort to document and publicize neighborhood needs and to mobilize support for new city programs had produced a paper change in renewal policy. But the city's officials made no effort to stabilize and unify the neighborhood movement as a political force. Neighborhoods were dealt with on an individual basis; some demands were yielded to, others were not. Persistence was sometimes rewarded. It was not encouraged.

The Failure to Provide Local Funds for Neighborhood Renewal

The failure of the city to follow up planning with substantial efforts to renew neighborhoods is worth a closer look. City officials were not unmindful of the needs of poverty areas. Nor were they totally unconcerned about the conditions of residential life. But they were unwilling to move forward and commit local resources without business support. This unwillingness was demonstrated in the decisions (appropriately in these cases, nondecisions) not to undertake a local bond issue and not to earmark available bond funds for neighborhood renewal.

The small scope of renewal activity in Vine City and Edgewood and the absence of activity in other neighborhoods was explained publicly as a matter of insufficient federal funds. The most telling shortage of resources, however, was in the area of capital improvements. The Neighborhood Analysis and other elements in the Community Renewal Program lent documentary support to what was widely recognized in City Hall and in the larger community, namely, that vast sections of the city were undercapitalized and thus lacking in much-needed public facilities. Atlanta's application for Model Cities planning funds openly acknowledged the neglect of neighborhoods:

The people living in slums and poverty areas, especially those living in Negro slums have never received an equal share of services in the city. . . . Coupled with the absence of service have been unfulfilled promises to improve conditions. Bond issues have been sold on the promise of improved schools or streets or parks, but these services have not materialized. Public officials have stated their desires to improve this or that situation, but conditions remain essentially unchanged. It should be no surprise that almost everyone living in the slums of Atlanta is skeptical of the local government's motivation.[18]

The Planning Department staff along with the CACUR subcommittee on the Community Renewal Program sought through the device of an "Atlanta Goals Conference" to sell the business community on the necessity of implementing recommendations from the Community Renewal studies. A series of seminars was set up with the business community to cover various phases of the Community Renewal Program—from the relocation report to a study of the city's governmental structure. One session was devoted to the general need for a major bond issue, including funds for schools, streets, parks, sewers, and other public improvements as well as for urban renewal itself. The bond funds were then to be used in a systematic fashion to reverse the decline of the city's residential areas.

In calling attention to the need to undertake a far-reaching program of neighborhood improvement, the planning staff called for a new direction in city policy:

One by one, Atlanta's neighborhoods have lost their ability to renew them-selves—not all at once, but over a 40–50 year period—slowly. Our public poli-cies have been directed towards creating jobs, expanding businesses, moving traffic, increasing our tax base—but generally not to making the city habitable.

But if we are to continue to expand jobs and businesses and the tax base, and, at the same time, cut traffic congestion—if the city is, in fact, destined to grow and prosper, then it must also be habitable.[19]

The presentation continued:

. . . if we are ever to solve our problems of deterioration, we will have to end the practice of individual segmented planning. *All* community resources must be brought to bear on the Summerhills and the Kirkwoods. Most of our bond commitments have been spent elsewhere, and scattered, and not related to other projects. We will need to *concentrate our efforts, focus them,* and *coordinate them.* . . . We must begin immediately to create a *detailed plan* for *each* neighborhood and to commit our resources sharply.[20]

The response of the business community was one of neither opposi-tion nor support. Rather the reaction of businessmen was that they did not understand the point of the conference. For a time the Planning Department staff continued with the assumption that a bond proposal was forthcoming, and they discussed with various discontented neigh-borhood groups the improvements that would be made once the new bond issue was approved. Yet the mayor never gave the "go ahead" to prepare a specific proposal. Instead, he first maintained that bond rates were too high, and then he described the "political climate" as not fa-vorable for a bond election. State legislation did authorize the city to do a small amount of capital lending annually, but no funds from this process were earmarked for a systematic program of neighborhood improvement.

Sponsors of the Atlanta Goals Conference had approached the busi-ness community with the statement that "the City requires the help of the leadership of the community to pin down the courses which the city should take in doing something about its physical environment, to *evaluate these choices* and to *select priorities.* That is the purpose of this workshop."[21] When the business leadership of Atlanta failed to give their approval to a program of systematic neighborhood improvement financed through a bond issue, the proposal was allowed to wither. No attempt was made to seek alternative sources of support. The leadership of the black community was especially conspicuous in its absence from the deliberations over the improvement program.

Sites for Low-Income Housing

Just as the first of the mayor's post-protest goals, neighborhood improvements, faltered, so did the second one, an adequate supply of new low- and moderate-income housing. Inevitably this one brought to the surface the policy question of where such housing should be located. A number of considerations came into play. Federal guidelines prohibited the building of public housing in areas already concentrated with minority residences.[22] Yet one of the objectives of the new renewal policy was to build standard housing in or near areas of the existing dilapidation. However, because there was little open land close in and because the renewal process itself was so slow, builders centered their attention on undeveloped areas in outlying sections of the city. Builders were particularly eager to develop housing on the predominantly black Westside where sites could be acquired with relatively little difficulty.

For several years, civil rights groups in Atlanta had with little success opposed the concentration of new public housing on the Westside of Atlanta and had called for the dispersion of low-cost housing into all sections of the city. With a new set of projects in the offing and with white developers seeking the assistance of the Housing Resources Committee in rezoning, several black leaders made a broadside attack on the city's administration of housing and renewal programs. The attack was triggered by the failure of the Housing Authority to accept a redevelopment proposal submitted by some prominent members of the black community.

Northwest Atlanta contained a renewal area (Rockdale), originally intended for 221 single-family homes, which had remained undeveloped. Finally, in 1967, the land was put up for bid to be redeveloped under the 221(d)3 multifamily housing program. Since the Housing Authority was offering the land at a set price, the winning bid was to be selected on the basis of quality and attractiveness in design. The choice narrowed down to two developers, one black and endorsed by the CACUR and the other white. When the Housing Authority selected the proposal submitted by the white developer, blacks leveled the charge that the agency had discriminated against blacks in a variety of ways in a wide range of HUD-sponsored programs. An already existing coalition of city-wide black leaders, organized as the Summit Leadership Conference, appeared before the Urban Renewal Policy Committee, and accused the Housing Authority in particular of being overtly hostile to the well-being of blacks. One spokesman, the sole black alderman at that time, complained that "Negroes have gotten nothing but the brunt of being kicked off the land" from the renewal and relocation process. He criticized the Housing Authority in particular, and stated that "Atlanta must let Negroes participate and become part of urban renewal if it is to survive."[23]

In a meeting with the mayor, Summit Leadership Conference spokesmen raised questions about employment practices and about the need to disperse low-income housing. The mayor proved more malleable and encouraging on employment than on housing. He described sites on the well-to-do Northside as too costly, and on that basis rejected the concept of scattered site housing.

Black leaders, still not focusing their attention on a single issue, next turned to federal authorities and accused the city of acts of discrimination. Specifically, blacks charged the city with violating civil rights laws and with disregarding Workable Program and other administrative requirements devised by the Department of Housing and Urban Development. On behalf of the Summit Leadership Conference, the NAACP branch president filed a formal complaint covering public housing, renewal, and Model Cities. The city was charged (retroactively) with having excluded blacks from the planning stage of the Model Cities program, thus leaving blacks with "little hope of receiving representation on the staff of this project,"[24] with having virtually excluded blacks from employment and business opportunities in urban renewal, with having practiced discriminatory and arbitrary tenant policies in public housing, and with having constructed "ungilded ghettos" under the public-housing program. On the latter point, the complaint specifically stated that Westside was "saturated with Public Housing," and that the city had "failed to develop a Para-Housing, Education, Recreation, Transportation Program" for housing projects.[25]

The bid award and the city's Workable Program certification survived investigation, and plans to develop public housing on the Westside continued. In fact, during the fall of 1967, the HUD regional office loosened the prohibition against building public housing in areas of racial concentration. Atlanta's Westside was not a typical ghetto in any case. Not only was there substantial undeveloped land, but there were also white and transitional residential areas located near some of the vacant land sites. Other factors, however, impinged on the building of low- and moderate-income housing.

Within the business community, informal discussion began to touch on the eventuality that Atlanta would become a predominantly black city. Specific concern was expressed over the possibility that new low-cost housing would serve as a magnet for poor blacks, attracting them into the city from surrounding areas. Although no concerted opposition was mounted (one Northside alderman did express publicly his disagreement with city policy), members of the Housing Resources Committee and Housing Authority staff did feel that it was necessary to attempt to allay fears. As some reassurance, Housing Authority commissioners adopted a one-year residency requirement for public-housing occupancy. (Federal courts subsequently invalidated all such requirements.)

Focused opposition to new housing came only in the form of neighborhood groups who resisted rezoning for specific proposals. One public-housing project of five hundred units was approved over mild neighborhood opposition, but a second proposal for a similar-sized project was met with vociferous and highly organized resistance. A group of black homeowners from a modest income area known as Browntown turned out in large numbers to make their objections known. Many of the residents had moved away from more densely settled inner-city areas and resented the attempt to place low-rent units in their neighborhood, but their most telling point was the argument that school, recreation, and sanitation facilities were already inadequate. The high school, for example, was on double session. The Board of Aldermen deferred action until the city could respond to some of the complaints about inadequate facilities.

The Planning Department assigned a black staff member to work with the neighborhood residents through a special Planning Committee for the Northwest-Browntown area. The special committee systematically identified inadequacies in the area's facilities and made the consequent recommendations, but the magnitude of the facilities needed, especially to accommodate proposed population increases, was such (nearly $25,000,000 to cover both immediate and future needs!) that little could be done without major new bond issues for schools and other public works. The planning report, moreover, noted that the Northwest sector of the city already contained a disproportionate share of low-rent housing, and included the recommendation that "every effort be made to develop a healthier mixture of low- and middle-income housing types throughout the City."[26]

When the Browntown public-housing proposal was reconsidered in December 1967, residents had no difficulty persuading the aldermanic Zoning Committee to delay action for six additional months. As that time neared expiration, a member of the mayor's staff prepared a progress report on improvements in the area, but, with a much-discussed and still unscheduled bond election in the indefinite future, residents maintained their stance of opposition. In fact, when flooding accentuated the continuing drainage problems of the area and some city officials failed to attend a neighborhood meeting, residents threatened a march on City Hall unless remedial steps were taken immediately. School overcrowding also remained a grievance and was the source of a protest lodged with the School Board. Since city officials had assured area residents that the housing project would not be approved until problems had been met to their satisfaction, the proposal was allowed to die.

The initial controversy over public housing in the Browntown vicinity was followed by a series of neighborhood protests against housing projects (see table 9.1). The most highly organized opposition came from residents of a Southwest neighborhood—a middle-class area undergoing some racial transition but containing organizations seeking to stabilize the area as an interracial one. Housing project opponents not only turned out in large numbers for aldermanic sessions, but they lobbied with individual city representatives. The Board of Aldermen accepted the argument that racial stability would be upset, and it rejected both a public-housing and a 221(d)3 proposal for the area.

The Browntown and Southwest rejections were significant defeats for the mayor, but in themselves did not cause him to weaken in his support for new low-income housing. He requested a black member of the Planning Department staff to come up with additional suggestions for

Table 9.1. Rezoning Controversies Affecting Mayor Allen's Low- and Moderate-Income Housing Goal

Proposed Project	Number of Units and Type of Housing	Section of City	Racial Composition of Opposition Group	Intensity of Opposition	Final Disposition and Date
Bankhead Highway	500 public	West-side	black	low	approved October 1967
Browntown	510 public	West-side	black	high	disapproved June 1968
Sewell Road	650 public	South-west	integrated	high	disapproved November 1967
Fairburn Road	558 221(d)3	South-west	integrated	high	disapproved February 1969
Jonesboro Road	160 public	South-side	white	high	approved June 1968
East Lake	800 public	East	white	high	approved June 1968
DeKalb Avenue	205 public	East	white	high	disapproved August 1968

meeting the declared housing goal, a step that resulted in a proposal that several lots, specifically identified and including at least one in each of the city's then eight wards, be rezoned as a package. The proposal was designed to meet Westside objections that public housing was being concentrated in a few areas.

The mayor was cool toward the package rezoning proposal, but did lend forceful support to proposed projects in Southside and East Atlanta. During the spring of 1968, white residents, led by aldermen from the affected areas, delayed temporarily but could not prevent the necessary rezoning. It was not until August of 1968 that a white neighborhood, one in East Atlanta, succeeded in having a rezoning application rejected. By that time, the mayor's support for rezoning had waned.

The Mayor's Declining Interest in Low-Income Housing

In contrast with the open controversy over specific sites for low-income housing, the package rezoning proposal remained a quiet, inside-the-official-family issue. Proposed by a member of the city's Planning Department and strongly supported by the Housing Resources Committee, the proposal to rezone areas in all sections of the city never received significant backing from the mayor. His public position on the proposal seesawed from opposition to endorsement and back to opposition. Neither his support nor his opposition was addressed to the principle of dispersed housing. Rather the mayor always confined his remarks to the question of an increased number of housing units. He explained his coolness toward the proposal, both initially and later, as a fear that the scattered forces opposing low-income housing would be consolidated and might defeat the entire program. The mayor thus argued for the one-site-at-a-time strategy. Since no one pressed him on this point, he never had to explain why the individual proposals he backed never included one in affluent Northside Atlanta. Similarly, Northside aldermen who had supported projects in other sections of the city were unchallenged publicly on their unwillingness to consider low-income housing for Northside Atlanta. As production began to lag behind the mayor's housing goal, the official explanation was that neighborhood opposition, notably from Atlanta's predominantly black Westside, had made it infeasible to build the needed units.

In a sense, of course, the housing site issue did turn upon the power of the black community. If the Browntown and later proposed projects for the Southwest Atlanta area had not been successfully opposed, it is quite likely that more new low-income housing would have been built. But it would have been concentrated on the Westside.

The power apparent in vetoing specific sites should not obscure the fact that the black community failed to gain acceptance for a policy of dispersed housing for low-income families. While the Housing Authority did build on two sites not on the Westside, one was in an area of rapid racial transition and the other in a predominantly white working-class area. Both sites were in areas long regarded by city officials as suitable "Negro expansion areas."

Support for the principle of dispersed housing had had a long history. In the 1950s, blacks had opposed a housing market segregated by race. During the 1960s, specific attention was given to the city's tendency to concentrate lower-income housing on Atlanta's Westside. Fearful that ghetto patterns of racial concentration, overcrowding, and inadequate services and facilities were being extended to outlying areas, blacks called for smaller public-housing sites scattered over all sections of the city. As early as 1964, blacks had proposed that a specific site in Northside Atlanta be used to build public housing for the elderly. Subsequently, blacks within the CACUR argued for the principle of dispersed public housing, and the CACUR endorsed the package rezoning proposal specifically.

The package rezoning proposal itself received active support. The mayor's Housing Resources Committee was the principal proponent of package rezoning and in the spring of 1968 was able to gain some organizational backing for the proposal. The major drive of the committee was to garner business endorsements. Careful lobbying through the Chamber of Commerce Urban Renewal Committee resulted in the chamber's Board of Directors supporting "the principle" of package rezoning to provide multifamily housing in all portions of the city.[27] While the Chamber of Commerce stopped short of supporting particular low-income housing sites, the resolution did specify that the package rezoning proposal was needed in order to alleviate the city's low-income housing shortage. Newspapers and television stations added their editorial support.

The strategy of the Housing Resources Committee was to tie together the need to meet the mayor's housing goal (and implicitly the need for the city to respond constructively to the sources of discontent in inner-city ghetto areas), the fairness of the principle that all sections of the city share to some extent the responsibility for housing people of low income, and the generally acknowledged need to update the city's rezoning regulations. Without the mayor's active backing, however, the Chamber of Commerce endorsement proved to be as much business support as the idea could muster. Even the Housing Authority commissioners failed to endorse the package rezoning proposal; they postponed action on the ground that they did not fully understand the plan. The proposal itself was simple enough; a large number of sites would be rezoned for multifamily residences, and some of these sites, including at least one from each of the city's wards, would, as with other sites in the past, be promoted for public housing. The Board of Aldermen would act only on the rezoning aspect. The Housing Authority commissioners would retain full authority to approve or disapprove specific projects.

The Home Builders Association would not link together updated zoning regulations, which they endorsed, with dispersed sites for public housing, which they did not endorse. The CAIA, however, provided the cue as to how the issue would be resolved. In June 1968, the organization did pass an extensively qualified endorsement for "the principle of increasing density within the City to accommodate additional emergency housing needs, in a heterogeneous distribution throughout the various segments of the City."[28] Aside from the specification that housing should be built in accordance with sound planning principles and with sufficient accompanying facilities, the resolution called for "every possible precaution . . . to minimize disruption of existing sound neighborhoods." Moreover, the resolution called for a regional solution to the housing problem, and it specifically noted "that hopes for decent and safe housing for the poor and disadvantaged of the region cannot adequately and successfully be fulfilled over the long term by Corporate Atlanta alone." Finally, the organization urged that special care be taken to make sure that "new low-cost housing intended for relocation purposes" be used for that purpose, that is, used only for displacees from "essential public action."[29]

In their informal discussions, businessmen displayed some concern over the possibility that low-income housing might accelerate the trend toward a predominantly black city. No opposition was mounted against the package rezoning proposal per se, but proponents of the idea encountered what they regarded as a business consensus that other actions were more urgent. Specifically, city-county consolidation or some other form of metropolitan reorganization was regarded as a matter of higher priority, overriding housing in importance. From the summer of 1968 on, mayoral and business support for new low-income housing was confined to proposals to build in areas beyond the city limits.

Without the mayor's support and in the face of growing business apprehension over low-income housing and its consequences for the city, the chairman of the Housing Resources Committee quietly ceased his activities on behalf of package rezoning. No attempt was made to mobilize support in the black community for the proposal. The momentum behind the proposal earlier in the spring was sufficient, however, for the Housing Resources Committee to bring package rezoning before the aldermanic Planning and Development Committee in mid-summer of 1968, but the committee responded only with a motion to refer the matter to the Planning Department for further study.

One final attempt was made to revive the proposal. In December 1968, after no further rezoning measures had been brought forward to meet the mayor's low-income housing goal, a subcommittee of the Housing Resources Committee drafted a resolution calling for the resubmission as part of the package rezoning plan of some of the sites rejected in the past. The resolution called for ''subsidized housing'' to ''be fairly distributed throughout the city,'' and for the package plan to be presented to the aldermanic board by the mayor and the Housing Authority. The resolution also contained the following exhortation:

If the same energy, zeal and leadership of our ''power structure'' and city officials that was mobilized to build our dazzling stadium, luxury apartments, and magnificent hotels and office buildings in our urban redevelopment areas had been applied with equal energy, zeal and leadership to providing subsidized housing for those who were bulldozed out of slums to make room for these majestic structures, the goal of public housing our Mayor publicly proclaimed so long ago would now be nearly reached.[30]

Although the resolution was unanimously passed by the full committee, the mayor did not act on it. When some members of the committee began raising questions about the mayor's commitment to his own housing goals and about the mandate, if any, of the Housing Resources Committee, the mayor did respond in the spring of 1969 both by letter and by meeting with the committee. When quizzed on the specific point, the mayor stated that his goal was still that of developing 16,800 units of low- and moderate-income housing. The mayor was not completely convincing, however, especially since he maintained that ''the procurement and development of sites for housing can best be expected to come along by themselves because of the momentum generated in the initial two years.''[31] If that cue were not clear enough, the mayor's letter also cautioned that ''the new housing units which have been developed were intended as replacement housing for slum properties.'' He urged the committee to concentrate its energies on ''ways and means through which one slum structure would be demolished for each new low-cost housing unit created.''[32]

Interpreting the mayor's stance as one of quietly halting the low-income housing effort, some members of the Housing Resources Committee resigned. They did so in private communications without any further attempt to revive the package rezoning proposal or to challenge the mayor. The Housing Resources Committee was, after all, appointed as a mayor's committee, and it had no standing independent of his support. Several members felt that the mayor, through his informal discussions with business leaders, had come to share the fear that improved housing would attract more poor people into the city.

Although the failure to act on package rezoning was the most conspicuous example of cooling interest in low-income housing, other proposals were also bypassed. In the fall of 1967, the Planning Department completed a comprehensive report as a follow-up to the mayor's Housing Conference. The report embraced the policy of placing low-income housing in all sections of the city, and, in addition to a call for the necessary rezoning, contained the suggestion that "in order to secure a more equitable distribution of low-cost housing throughout Atlanta, the City should consider the purchase of high-cost sites where necessary."[33] Though the package rezoning proposal and related activities had served to identify a number of potential sites in Northside Atlanta, no official attempted to promote subsidized housing in the area.

The Housing Resources Committee saw another of its proposals substantially modified in the face of business concern over the city's increasing black population. The committee successfully promoted the idea of establishing a Housing Development Corporation. However, the committee had in mind a multipurpose organization that could provide not only technical assistance and seed money to nonprofit sponsors but could also operate a revolving fund for low-income homeowners who were faced with the necessity of making repairs beyond their immediate means. In fruition, the Housing Development Corporation was funded completely by business donations and became a little-publicized organization housed with and under the direct influence of the CAIA. The corporation defined its major purpose as that of providing seed money for nonprofit sponsors who wanted to build in the metropolitan area *outside* the city limits.

The city's housing effort thus diminished in force and narrowed to the promotion of subsidized housing in the suburbs.[34] No overt business pressure was evident in this process, and black leaders acquiesced. Since business leaders had long-established ties with the mayor and key aldermen, the absence of pressure is easily accounted for—it was not necessary.

The failure of black leaders to push for package rezoning or for a greater housing effort is less readily explained. The 1960s were a decade in which blacks were an increasing proportion of the city population and apparently were experiencing growing political power. Yet black leaders proved to be keenly aware that power based on protests or even votes was greatly constrained. From their past experience with white political figures, they concluded that a proposal such as package rezoning turned on more than potential voting numbers. They realized that the CACUR, the Housing Resources Committee, and the Community Relations Commission had no authority and no resources to move by themselves.[35] The mayor and aldermen, moreover, were seen as being very much a part of a society separate and distinct from the society of which blacks were a part. Blacks feared that political pressure, even if mobilized, would be countered. Not only white political pressure, but informal, highly personal, and difficult-to-resist social pressures from the friends and acquaintances of white officeholders, blacks believed, would counter-balance any effort they made. Finally, blacks felt that the mayor, the Board of Aldermen, the Housing Authority, and other city agencies could and did on occasion move together, but that the influence needed to bring about the necessary coordination of the various elements of city government was of a magnitude far beyond that possessed by the black community. Blacks, then, had raised questions about both the quantity and the location of lower-income housing, but, when asked in inter-views to comment on the absence of a concerted effort to achieve expressed goals, black leaders proved to be acutely aware of the weak-ness of the organizations through which they had been working. More-over, they were fearful that even a major mobilization of strength would be insufficient to change housing policy. Understandably, they did not want to expend time and resources on a futile effort.

Conclusion

When Ivan Allen's second term as mayor came to a close, his program of slum eradication was lagging far behind early expectations. Housing was being built in neither the numbers nor the locations sought by neighborhood and civil rights leaders. Improvements in older and less affluent neighborhoods were not being undertaken on a systematic and adequately funded basis. Federal and local funds alike were in great shortage. Some requests for governmentally aided planning and renewal projects were rejected outright on the ground that the city lacked the necessary resources.

The mayor himself had become increasingly concerned with the need for metropolitan reorganization. Publicly and openly he questioned the capacity of Atlanta to meet the problems of poverty and discrimination alone. Social problems, the mayor also concluded, were secondary in importance to the need for economic vitality. In his farewell address, Allen argued that social problems could be ameliorated only if the city's economic base were carefully attended to.

Two critical developments signaled the decline of slum eradication as an issue of high priority at City Hall: the mayor failed to seek a new bond issue and he chose not to back some version of the package rezoning proposal. These nonactions of the mayor are best understood not as matters of personal behavior but as consequences of the ways in which interests were organized and represented. Mayor Allen, like his predecessor, identified business well-being with the general interest of the community. Business opinion was considered vital to the reaching of sound judgments. Moreover, liberal staff members and civic activists in the white community regarded business support as essential to any substantial step in housing and redevelopment policy. Consequently, business leaders enjoyed a tacit veto over policy change. The absence of active business support—and it should be remembered that business support was actively sought—thus weakened the efforts to eliminate slums, improve low-income neighborhoods, and rehouse the poor in safe and decent dwellings. Proponents of new housing and redevelopment measures certainly were not without a voice in policy deliberations, but the most consistent advocates of neighborhood and low-income interests were found on bodies like the Housing Resources Committee and the CACUR that were merely advisory. Business interests, by contrast, enjoyed direct and easy access to the mayor and the Housing Authority. Business leaders thus did not have to engage in direct and open opposition to neighborhood groups in order to influence policy.

Not every outcome in the struggle over neighborhood improvement and adequate housing can be traced to the business community's active pursuit of CBD priorities. Sometimes indifference on the part of the business community was enough to stymie the implementation of other groups' goals—indifference, plus the built-in difficulties, in Atlanta, of creating a high-leverage coalition without business support. The story of Bedford-Pine that follows is a case in point.

Until a program moves beyond the stages of being a plan, a proposal, or a declaration, the program has not really been tested. Program execution is the battleground on which a policy must ultimately prove itself. Costs and competing priorities once hidden begin to surface. Victories gained at an earlier time can again be contested. And new conflicts among affected groups emerge. Program execution is thus strategically important ground in the group contest to influence public policy.

The previous chapter has shown that general plans to renew nonaffluent neighborhoods and rehouse slum dwellers were not followed by successful efforts to execute these plans. City officials were unwilling to devote the time, allocate the resources, and incur the resentments needed to push the program forward. Neighborhood groups and the proponents of improved housing opportunities lacked the capacity to maintain the initial momentum toward a new policy direction. In contrast, at an earlier time, when efforts to expand and upgrade the CBD were stymied by the noncooperation of city departments and by the opposition of various neighborhood groups, forceful counteraction from the business community bestirred city officials and unblocked CBD renewal. Later, Mayor Allen made stadium and civic center construction items of top priority in his administration and surmounted many obstacles to move the necessary redevelopment projects ahead rapidly. Yet the mayor made no comparable exertion of leadership on behalf of neighborhood renewal and rehousing goals.

The present chapter continues the consideration of program execution. It contains a detailed examination of redevelopment and rehousing activities in one neighborhood, the Bedford-Pine area. This area was singled out for an in-depth study of implementation for two reasons: (1) Bedford-Pine was a project in which both neighborhood and nonneighborhood interests had substantial stakes; and (2) the Bedford-Pine project was the first neighborhood project on which protests had an impact, and it was therefore further along in the execution phase than other neighborhood projects.

The reader may recall from chapter 7 that a neighborhood organization, U-Rescue, had worked out with the city an urban renewal plan that supposedly would protect the interests of low- and moderate-income residents. The present chapter shows, however, that agreed-upon objectives suffered as planning gave way to execution. Open neighborhood dissatisfaction reoccurred, but it was dissatisfaction that had relatively little impact on city officials. As with the larger relocation and redevelopment program for the city, housing for the Bedford-Pine area was built neither in the numbers nor on a time schedule that matched the early hopes of neighborhood residents.

Major Developments

In August of 1967, the city submitted an Early Land Acquisition application to build public housing, install temporary housing units for relocation purposes, and along Boulevard, the eastern edge of the project (see map 7.1), rehabilitate apartments and do some spot clearance. In April 1968, after a lengthy review, federal officials in Washington at first denied approval to the temporary housing. (The city could, of course, have undertaken the temporary housing on its own, but without federal approval the city would have to bear the entire cost.) With strong urging from the city, including the mayor, federal renewal officials reversed their position and did approve the inclusion of the temporary housing in the project activities. However, before the city completed all of the steps required to implement the Early Land Acquisition, new federal legislation was enacted. The NDP established by the 1968 Housing Act, as a new version of urban renewal, was regarded by federal officials as especially suited for areas such as Bedford-Pine. The city was persuaded to convert the Bedford-Pine project to NDP, with the result that new planning applications had to be prepared and additional hearings held. Meanwhile the visibility of U-Rescue within the neighborhood waned.

When conflict finally surfaced, opposition to city actions was voiced not by U-Rescue but by dissident social action agencies. Two of these agencies, somewhat ironically, were based at Emory University, a predominantly white institution located in the Atlanta suburbs.

An Upward Bound course at Emory in the "Urban Crisis" led to "lab work" in one of the unredeveloped remnants of the area originally known as Buttermilk Bottom. The urban-crisis laboratory was a small neighborhood overlapping the old boundary between the Buttermilk Bottom and Bedford-Pine projects (the two were combined into one project in August 1967). Ed Ducree, director of Emory's Upward Bound program, had good command of the rhetoric of black militancy and also had a flair for dramatizing issues. Under Ducree's leadership, a center for several service activities in the neighborhood, called Crisis House, was established in the southern portion of the renewal project (see map. 7.1). Crisis House was also in contact with the Emory Community Legal Services Center (sponsored by Emory University and funded by the Office of Economic Opportunity), which had an office nearby; and, for a time, Crisis House was assisted by some Vista workers. A Catholic charitable organization, the St. Vincent de Paul Society, was also working in the Bedford-Pine area, but its activities were concentrated in the northern portion of the renewal project.

During 1968, the head of the St. Vincent de Paul neighborhood office and the director of the Community Action neighborhood center in the area made efforts to encourage wider citizen participation in the renewal process. In collaboration with the renewal project office, which was located in the neighborhood, a number of meetings were held during the year, but none was based upon a mutual understanding of what the term "citizen participation" meant. The project office gave the residents minimal information, and let them know that the major decisions about the area had already been made and could not be changed. One group specifically sought to have a small church (Little Friendship Baptist Church) in a clearance portion of the project preserved as part of the neighborhood, but they were told that it was too late to change plans. When some residents pressed the project office for specific examples of what they could participate in, the project office cited as examples the design and decorating features of the new public housing for the area. Some residents complained about the condition of rental property in the area, but they were informed that the Housing Authority could do nothing about code enforcement and that the only service available through the project office was information on where displacees could relocate. One of the larger meetings with residents was not attended by the project director, who left the handling of questions from residents to a Housing Authority trainee serving temporarily in the project office. Block chairmen in the Community Action program, who were important links with poorer residents, did attend meetings for a time, but eventually stopped going to them. The block chairmen came to believe that the meetings had no clear purpose. Insofar as they could see, the meetings consisted of explanations as to why resident questions and requests could not be attended to and were therefore pointless.

None of the meetings with residents involved U-Rescue, and the Community Action representatives were for the most part unaware that U-Rescue existed. In a statement before the Georgia Advisory Committee to the United States Civil Rights Commission, the head of the local St. Vincent de Paul office charged that U-Rescue failed to represent the poorer elements in the neighborhood. He said that the organization was composed mostly of homeowners who "don't associate with the people down in this area." He added, "They . . . do not communicate."[1]

The absence of more extensive neighborhood participation was challenged finally, but not through the Community Action program. In November 1968, Ed Ducree and a number of residents from the Crisis House vicinity made the challenge during the public hearing on the inclusion of Bedford-Pine in NDP. Ducree voiced concern about proposals to move residents out of the southern portion of the Bedford-Pine project and to convert the area to nonresidential uses. He stated further that a board of black people represented the area and that they wanted to keep their neighborhood and rebuild it.

Since the area under discussion was not proposed for action in 1969, the chairman of the Planning and Development Committee (the aldermanic committee on urban renewal), Rodney Cook, attempted to cut off the Crisis House testimony with the statement that Ducree's presentation was "not relevant." Ducree retorted, "I'm not finished. You wait until I finish what I have to say. This is the old game you boys have been playing for a long time. You say I'm out of order because you don't like what I say."[2] Cook returned, "I'm the chairman and I'll make a statement when I want to make a statement." Ducree then charged, "It's a dictatorship."[3] He added that he wanted the aldermen to be aware of the problems and again stated that some citizens were not involved in the planning process. U-Rescue representatives were present, but they kept a distance from Ducree both during the meeting and later. They acknowledged no shortcomings in the representation of neighborhood interests.

Despite the heated nature of the exchange, Cook called Ducree the following day and invited him to discuss the neighborhood further. During the subsequent discussion, Cook, along with the director of redevelopment, assured Ducree that plans were not fixed for the southern portion of the project and that the city was willing to consider a proposal from Crisis House.

Ducree did not follow through. Without a tangible program around which the residents could be rallied, personal animosities came to the forefront, and Crisis House could no longer mobilize overwhelming support from the surrounding area. Since the Emory Community Legal Services Office was an available ally, Crisis House gave some thought to bringing a suit to prevent the execution of the urban renewal project. Ducree, however, expressed qualms about working with whites—the Legal Services staff was white. Moreover, at that point Ducree's stated preference was for using confrontation rather than legal tactics. The issue lapsed, however, for Ducree became occupied mainly with Upward Bound and other matters outside the area.

During the summer of 1969, dissatisfaction among Bedford-Pine residents once again welled up, this time in the northern section of the project in which the St. Vincent de Paul Society was most active and in which some clearance was taking place. The long-promised temporary housing for displacees was opened at the end of May, but only a few units were ready for occupancy. Only sixty units had been purchased, and, of these, ten were three-bedroom units and the rest two-bedroom units. It soon became apparent that not only were the number of units far short of what was needed to keep residents in the neighborhood, but that families were carefully screened before they were placed in the temporary units. Obviously, large families could not be housed in such small units, and "problem" families were excluded.

The publicly stated position of the Housing Authority was that everyone was to be accommodated in temporary housing or at least other housing in the neighborhood. Even large families could be accommodated, it was said in response to public queries, by combining two of the two-bedroom units. However, the in-house policy was that screening was necessary to make temporary housing a success, and that proper maintenance depended upon housing only the smaller and most desirable families as tenants. Both the St. Vincent de Paul and the Community Action workers in the area discovered that the real policy was one of relocating in outlying public-housing projects all larger families and families with any history of social problems. These families, of course, retained the option of refusing that alternative and relocating themselves in private dwellings.

Neither the St. Vincent de Paul Society nor the Community Action office was willing to make an issue of the de facto relocation policy. Both agencies felt that they needed the cooperation of the renewal office, and, in fact, both organizations had service activities housed in facilities provided by the renewal agency. The position of the St. Vincent de Paul Society was that raising an issue might help one or two families in the short run, but that project office cooperation would be lost for long-term service efforts. The St. Vincent de Paul Society, moreover, had only recently weathered one conflict with the Community Action program and was not eager to become embroiled in another controversy.

The Community Action staff was also operating under constraints. The agency's director made it known that he regarded Community Action as essentially a referral agency, dependent upon cooperation from other agencies. In 1969, operating under a budget cut, Community Action felt especially dependent on other agencies. Without exception, the staff working in the Bedford-Pine area recognized that residents needed to be organized to make demands, but also without exception the staff saw community organization as an activity not proper for the Community Action program. From above, they were told that their principal objective was, as one staff member said, "to work *with* and cooperate *with* other agencies." From below, they sensed no pressure. Rather, they saw the low-income residents as apathetic, as unwilling to attend meetings, and, in general, as a dependent population with much to lose if they antagonized the various social service agencies.

Thus, while both the St. Vincent de Paul Society and the Community Action staff were fully aware that residents were apprehensive about the renewal program and while both were dissatisfied with the Housing Authority's relocation policy, they believed that no substantial gains could be made by raising an issue. At this time, the summer of 1969, the two agencies were working closely with one another, but neither saw the other as an ally "with weight." Both saw the Housing Authority as the only agency in the area with sufficient resources and staff to provide social services directly and indirectly on a significant scale, and each saw itself as without the power needed to compel a change in Housing Authority practices. Social agency "constituents" were not regarded as a force that could be mobilized, but simply as people who were, in the words of one staff member, "submissive and shy." One antipoverty worker described the mass of Bedford-Pine residents as having "no power—they don't vote; they are poor, uninformed, non-mobile, alco-holic, et cetera."

In August of 1969, the relocation program came to the direct attention of the Emory Community Legal Services Office. With some assistance from the St. Vincent de Paul Society and after a lapse of several months, a Legal Services lawyer was able to obtain from twelve families in the area depositions with which to challenge the city's relocation practices. In March of 1970, a class-action suit was brought, charging the city with failing to meet relocation obligations under the Workable Program. The legal brief stated: "The city has undertaken a program to reduce the supply of (low to moderate income) housing, stem in-migration of low income citizens, disperse the resident constituency of low income citi-zens and erect protective barriers for downtown commercial interests."[4] The suit further challenged the city's stated policy of only partially enforcing the Housing Code. In particular for urban renewal areas, the city's policy was one of selective enforcement on the grounds that "it is necessary to use all of the city's housing for its residents, even if presently dilapidated."[5] Finally the court action sought to prevent the city from expending funds on nonresidential purposes, in particular for the expansion of Georgia Baptist Hospital and its affiliates.

Working with the Emory Community Legal Service Office, Ed Ducree again became active and initiated two open meetings in the neighbor-hood. However, both meetings—in comparison to the U-Rescue protest meetings in earlier years—were lightly attended. Moreover, at the first meeting, one of the U-Rescue leaders expressed his opposition to the suit against the city. For the second meeting, Ducree persuaded a number of activists in various militant organizations to attend. The new chairman of the aldermanic Planning and Development Committee (Rodney Cook had run unsuccessfully for mayor in the fall of 1969 and was no longer on the Board of Aldermen after January 1970), an attorney from the Housing Authority, and a representative from the Georgia Baptist Hospital were invited to and did attend the meeting to hear residents' grievances. However, in the face of harassment from some of the audience, the two city officials and the Georgia Baptist Hos-pital representative walked out of the meeting.

In a rump session, Ducree then planned to break into a meeting of the Housing Authority commissioners the next day and to present a list of demands. Accompanied by a few people from the neighborhood (including some of the St. Vincent de Paul staff) and by a newspaper reporter and some black militants, Ducree brought off the dramatic confrontation that he had been considering for some time. The group broke into the meeting of the Housing Authority Commission. Some physically imposing militants stood at the door while Ducree presented a list of demands and made a shrill speech in which he announced that they were going to "hold trial for criminals [that is, the Housing Authority]."[6] A black member of the authority was singled out as an "Uncle Tom" and was subject to an especially bitter verbal attack. The commissioners themselves were flustered by the incident, but the Housing Authority director began to talk in a calm and reasoned manner about the individual demands presented.

The demands of the Ducree group were far-reaching. Some were very general, such as the demands that no more renewal money be spent for nonresidential renewal and no additional houses be torn down until the poor had adequate places to live. Some demands were quite specific. For example, the group asked that commercial land, including a supermarket serving the area, not be sold to Georgia Baptist Hospital for redevelopment. Taking advantage of the fact that Bedford-Pine had been converted to NDP renewal, the Ducree group also called for the replacement of U-Rescue with an elected committee to represent the neighborhood. Several of the demands related to housing directly—the group called for the enforcement of the housing code inside renewal areas (the city's policy was not to enforce the code in areas marked eventually for clearance) and the making of retroactive relocation payments "to all people moved by urban renewal who were eligible but did not receive them."[7] The group also sought to reduce housing costs in the area by calling for the Housing Authority not to charge rent on "the 30 slum houses" it owned in Bedford-Pine until the houses were brought up to code "and then [to] charge public housing rent rates."[8] They also asked the Housing Authority to recommend to the Board of Aldermen the passage of a rent control ordinance covering the rehabilitation portions of renewal projects. Finally, to drive home the point that the city had neglected neighborhoods for other priorities, the Ducree group called for the city to provide emergency housing "for all people living in unhealthy or hazardous dwellings in urban renewal or model cities areas by using the Atlanta Civic Center until relocatable housing is sufficient to the need";[9] and the group asked for the civic center to be made available, free, for community meetings.

The Housing Authority offered no concessions on the major questions relating to land use, but several demands relating essentially to procedural matters were acceded to. Rent was stopped in the thirty Bedford-Pine houses, even though some of the units were not substandard. U-Rescue, it was agreed, would cease to be recognized as the Project Area Committee, and an election would be held. Nine months elapsed, however, before the election was held. Retroactive relocation payments were also agreed to, but rent control received no consideration beyond a promise to look into ways of preventing slum owners from raising rents on deteriorating properties in renewal areas. The civic center, it was pointed out, was not under Housing Authority control and therefore could not be offered by them for community meetings, but later an effort was promised to secure the civic center for the election of the Project Area Committee. Code enforcement was also a City Hall function not under Housing Authority jurisdiction, but the Housing Authority promised to and did successfully urge the city department to step up its activity in the area. Without a program of supplemental housing assistance, however, the code enforcement effort led to increased housing costs for and worked hardships on some area residents.

The major negotiating point concerned the provision of emergency relocation facilities. The use of the civic center was, of course, never really considered by either side and was brought into the discussion only as a symbol of the imbalance in the city's renewal program. What the Housing Authority did work out with federal consent was a plan through which two of the new outlying public-housing projects were made available to Ducree for relocation purposes. Ducree formed an organization called the People's Housing Authority, which was given a contract for handling the relocation responsibility for Bedford-Pine, including the direct conduct of moving operations for residents. The Housing Authority agreed to pay moving expenses both to the outlying projects and back into the Bedford-Pine area when new housing was built. Displaced residents were promised priority for new Bedford-Pine units as they became available. Serving still as the director of the Emory Upward Bound project, Ducree had limited time to devote to the actual relocation operations, and the business affairs of the People's Housing Authority were soon ensnarled by some serious mismanagement. The organization became defunct long before facilities were available to move people back into the area. Whether intended that way or not (and they probably were), the relocation arrangements served mainly to divert Ducree from further use of confrontation tactics.

New efforts were made through the Emory Community Legal Services Office to stop the expenditures of renewal funds for nonresidential purposes and to commit City Hall to a housing policy that would increase the supply of low-income housing in all parts of the city. But neither legal action nor direct contact with the mayor's office yielded any significant results. Specific requests for increased participation in the federally-subsidized Section 23 Leased Housing program, for the representation of poor blacks on the CACUR, for the establishment of an emergency housing fund, and for the obtaining of an additional supply of temporary housing of the relocatable type yielded no better results than requests for broad policy changes. The mayor (Sam Massell had succeeded Ivan Allen by this time) showed some interest in a proposal from his own staff to require that Georgia Baptist Hospital provide free clinic services for people in the neighborhood. Beyond that, the only matter that the mayor showed concern about was the representation of poor blacks, but he indicated that he was interested only in the names of individuals who were proven leaders with supporting constituencies.

The Emory Community Legal Services lawyer did obtain full access to city records on relocation and related matters, and sought to handle hardship cases by working with Housing Authority officials. Court procedures proved so cumbersome that the lawyer found it more productive to seek administrative remedies. At the same time he realized that work on individual hardship cases did not lead to replanning of the project area in order to meet the broad needs of the neighborhood's low-income residents. One person working part time could not perform all the legal and historical research required to challenge the city's plans. As allies, he could count only on Ed Ducree and the head of the St. Vincent de Paul Society. The former could devote only a portion of his time to Bedford-Pine, while the latter had to balance opposition to Housing Authority plans against the need for cooperation from the authority's project office. Without funds for publicity and canvassing, it was not possible to rally neighborhood support. Limited resources and political weakness thus dictated the strategy of seeking to relieve individual hardships even though the basic character of neighborhood renewal went unchallenged.

In the meantime, during the summer of 1970, the Community Relations Commission held open hearings in the Bedford-Pine area. Complaints about high rents, substandard housing, and inadequate services and facilities were aired once more. The summer did see the groundbreaking for Bedford-Pine's first permanent public housing. Of the 353 units planned, 283 would serve the elderly. In December of 1970, when an election was finally held for the Project Area Committee, leaders of the old U-Rescue organization dominated the new committee. Some of the Community Action block chairmen were also elected to the PAC, but they offered no challenge to city policies. Social agencies had reverted to the practice of aiding people on an individual basis, and with the coming of winter protest activity ceased.

More than five years had elapsed since residents had first become alarmed over the possibility that the neighborhood would be disrupted and depopulated. Attempts were made to secure the residential character of the area; but, despite the earlier efforts of U-Rescue and the later efforts of various social action agencies, rebuilding and rehousing never kept pace with displacement activities. Although the original objective of keeping the neighborhood intact as a home for a generally nonaffluent population was never publicly repudiated, many of the very poor were quietly moved away.[10]

Conclusion

A number of reasons could be offered for the failure of Bedford-Pine renewal to meet its stated objective of rehousing residents within the neighborhood. The complexity of intergovernmental relations, the shortage of federal funds, and the transitory nature of leadership in a slum community could, for example, be cited as contributing factors. But such particular reasons assume importance only in the light of underlying and continuing conditions that have characterized low-income neighborhoods in Atlanta throughout the time period encompassed by the present research.

A program goal may be displaced either because a powerful group with overriding interests is able to reshape policy or because the group originally intended as the beneficiary of the program is too weak to sustain a policy effort on its own behalf. Bedford-Pine faltered at least as much for the latter reason as for the former. There were, to be sure, competing interests. But these competing interests, as exemplified by Georgia Baptist Hospital, registered gains, not because they were able to defeat neighborhood groups in head-on conflicts, but rather because they were capable of maintaining a persistent and multifaceted effort on behalf of their land expansion and other needs. Low-income residents, by contrast, proved to be an unsteady source of pressure on city officials. Although mobilized from time to time in varying numbers to attend public meetings or hearings, residents were seen even by the social agencies working in the neighborhood as apathetic and dependent. The agencies themselves were short on resources and on numbers of residents who could be induced to act in furtherance of organizational goals. In their capacities as the clients of public agencies—clients who had neither the information nor the material wherewithal to pursue alternative courses of action—low-income residents had much to lose individually. Potential collective gains could not always be readily perceived. As the consumers of publicly provided social services, slum dwellers represent an especially difficult group to organize. Under any set of circumstances, organizing consumers is a substantial task; but consumer organization becomes nearly impossible when the group is poor, dependent, and not highly educated.[11]

Because many of the neighborhood residents had multiple and pressing needs, social agencies working in the area were themselves inclined to pursue actions to meet the immediate needs of residents rather than to seek fundamental and long-term solutions to neighborhood problems. The social agencies were also disinclined to engage in controversy. Their own needs were great, and they forewent active dissent rather than lose opportunities to enhance their own service-providing capabilities.

While several groups in the project area realized that the Housing Authority was guided more by a general public relations concern than by a concern with neighborhood housing needs, project area residents were too weak politically to challenge the Housing Authority. Besides, since many area residents believed that the most they could do was to delay the inevitable, they felt that they might eventually need relocation assistance from the Housing Authority. Some therefore concluded that they would be better off individually if they did not antagonize the agency.

The two aldermen from the ward that included Bedford-Pine had been drawn into initial controversy over renewing the area as allies—at least publicly—of U-Rescue. Both aldermen were white, lived in neighborhoods well to the north of Bedford-Pine, and failed to keep in close touch with the renewal situation. The two aldermen were contrasting political types: one had essentially a "good government" orientation and the other had a more traditional orientation. Neither knew very much about what was occurring in the neighborhood. Neither was on the Planning and Development Committee. The alderman with the "good government" orientation assumed that the renewal of the neighborhood was essentially a matter of promoting rehabilitation, and, in the absence of any cues to the contrary from the chairman of the Planning and Development Committee, he believed that relocation was being handled to the satisfaction of all concerned. He had no ties with groups in the neighborhood, and moved primarily in white-collar and Republican political circles. The other alderman was more the old style, ward-oriented politician, but he did nothing more than talk occasionally with some of the U-Rescue leaders. He was knowledgeable about the civic center, but knew little of the relocation situation.

The mayor's office and the Housing Authority staff were the city officials most immediately concerned with Bedford-Pine renewal, and at no time did they indicate anything less than full sympathy for the goal of rehousing residents within the neighborhood. However, Mayor Allen did not make Bedford-Pine redevelopment an item of top priority as the stadium and the civic center had been, so that neighborhood redevelopment was not pursued with a sense of urgency by his staff. No deadlines were set, and no systematic set of follow-through actions was undertaken. The Housing Authority staff, as employees of an agency esteemed neither by the larger community nor by the residents of low-income neighborhoods, was especially eager to avoid bad publicity around the use of temporary housing for relocation purposes.

What part business influence had in the course of events is difficult to determine. There was no overt business opposition to the originally agreed-on rehousing plans for Bedford-Pine. City officials knew that some individual businessmen favored minimal low-income housing for the area, but no business demand was articulated (that is, during the time period considered here).[12] If there was business pressure, it was indirect. Administrative officials were sure that they were expected to handle rehousing efforts in a manner compatible with the nearby presence of the civic center. And, of course, Georgia Baptist was expressly interested in expanding its facilities and in decreasing the low-income population of the area generally. In the absence of some indication from the mayor or other top level officials that rehousing Bedford-Pine residents was a matter of high priority for the city, program administrators understandably proved to be less than vigilant guardians of rehousing opportunities for large or problem-ridden families. The rehousing of Bedford-Pine residents within the neighborhood faltered, then, partly because the renewal of the neighborhood was not a high priority program for city officials and partly because Bedford-Pine residents lacked the organization and resources to maintain a steady and unrelenting pressure in support of their housing goals.

The present chapter is an overview of the Allen mayoralty, with particular attention to protests and to neighborhoods as political groups. It also sounds the theoretical themes that will be elaborated in the final part of this study.

Despite the fact that Ivan Allen was twice elected mayor with a huge majority of the black vote, the Allen mayoralty was characterized by extensive conflict between blacks and City Hall. Neighborhood groups protested against city actions and inactions alike. Grievances were articulated, alternative program directions were formulated, and new paths of city policy were debated. During the Allen era blacks became a more numerous as well as a more vocal part of the Atlanta citizenry. Yet business influence, particularly that of the CAIA, continued to have a telling, but unobtrusive, effect on city renewal policy.

When basic policy choices had to be made in the face of competing community interests, City Hall most often chose courses of action and inaction that coincided with business preferences. Neighborhood groups, despite an ability to prevail in particular disputes, were unable to pursue their aims successfully through all the stages of policymaking. Hence, some preliminary victories were eventually lost by the absence of follow-through efforts. Further, even though the Allen era was generally a time of protests, some important policy decisions went uncontested. Neighborhood groups and city-wide black leaders dramatized a number of issues, but city officials were still able to resolve some basic policy questions in ways that were not readily observable by the general public and were therefore somewhat insulated from the heat of community controversy.

Protest Politics and Policy Influence

Insofar as urban renewal is concerned, the Allen era began with a "bang" and ended with a "whimper." The "bang" was the further upgrading of the CBD by stadium and civic center construction. The "whimper" was neighborhood renewal and rehousing the poor. Above all else, the Allen era suggests that neighborhood-based protests had little long-range impact but that the influence of business, though indirect, was nonetheless highly durable.

An overview of issue cleavage during the Allen mayoralty indicates that overt conflict between competing community groups became less pronounced than it had been during the Hartsfield years. While the earliest years of the Allen administration were marked by black protests against business-backed redevelopment plans, and thus these years resembled the Hartsfield mayoralty, the Allen administration came later to be marked by a different kind of conflict. This later conflict was directed at City Hall, specifically at the city's inattention to housing and neighborhood problems. Protests during the Allen mayoralty were therefore no longer just veto-minded attempts to stop some unwanted actions. They were attempts to mobilize public officials behind a new program of housing and neighborhood improvements. Thus the city's inactions as well as its actions became subjects of controversy.

The dramatization and documentation of slum conditions served to bring about official consideration and adoption of new programs, but these new program efforts were not sustained. Proponents of the new policy directions were unable to put together a stable coalition of active support. As table 11.1 suggests, neighborhood groups had little success, but rarely did they encounter overt or direct business opposition. Rehousing the poor and renewing nonaffluent neighborhoods faltered because the mayor became preoccupied with other problems and because the business community was unwilling to lend its support to major efforts to reallocate resources. The business veto was no less effective for being a quiet one.

Protests and various forms of disruptive action, according to some observers, are the only way that poor people can gain concessions to their policy interests. In their influential study of welfare policy, Frances Fox Piven and Richard A. Cloward concluded that "a placid poor get nothing, but a turbulent poor sometimes get something."[1] "It's the squeaky wheel that gets the grease" is an adage frequently thought to be applicable to urban communities. Protests, however, have come to be recognized as no panacea for the political weaknesses of poor people.[2] Clearly, unconventional actions such as mass demonstrations can serve to dramatize issues; and, in Atlanta, protests, civil disorders, and other events did bring about official consideration of new policy proposals oriented toward neighborhood groups and low-income blacks. However, such pressures were often unstable. In an important sense, they were external pressures on official decision makers; and, while these pressures were fully capable of determining the outcome of specific issues, they were ill suited to controlling or maintaining a policy direction.

The protests in Atlanta during the 1960s arose from a popular base that was too vulnerable and too incohesive to instill in official decision makers any ongoing sense of obligation to respond to the needs of the nonaffluent. The spokesmen for dissident groups often had an uncertain base of support, and their constituents were subject to the centrifugal forces of personal rivalry, immediate concerns, and unaggregated policy interests. Without a secure form of political organization, without supplementary resources, and without some substantial efforts to bring

Table 11.1. Major Policy Questions during the Allen Mayoralty

Policy Issue	Stance of Various Groups	Status of Group Conflict	Issue Outcome
Further upgrading of the CBD through stadium and civic center construction	Business—active and united support; city-wide black leaders and black neighborhoods—some active opposition; white neighborhoods—no stance	Partially overt	Business success
Providing expansion land for medical and educational institutions in CBD vicinity	Business—generally active and united support; black neighborhoods—some active opposition; white neighborhoods—some active opposition	Partially overt	Limited business success
Dispersion of low-income housing into all sections of city	Business—indirectly opposed; city-wide black leaders—active and united support; white neighborhoods—active and tactical support for the general principle	Overt conflict with City Hall over the concentration of housing in some areas	On balance, failure by blacks and white neighborhoods
Increased supply of standard low-income housing	Business—indirectly opposed; blacks—active and united support by black neighborhoods; white neighborhood groups—no stance on the general principle	Latent (but overt conflict with City Hall)	Mixed
Undertaking systematic program to improve neighborhood conditions and facilities	Business—probably indirectly opposed; black neighborhoods—active and united support; white neighborhoods—some active support	Latent (but overt conflict with City Hall)	Substantial failure by blacks and white neighborhoods
Phase redevelopment to allow renewal area residents to remain in neighborhoods	Business—no opposition to the general principle; black neighborhoods—active and united support; white neighborhoods—no stance	Latent (but some overt conflict with City Hall)	Substantial failure by black neighborhoods

together a coalition as a continuing enterprise, previously uninvolved groups could not be welded into a durable political force. Instead of raising group consciousness, the protests that did take place seemed to increase a collective sense of futility.[3] The neighborhoods and their spokesmen had too few resources. The city and its agencies too often offered only a hearing before an advisory body or provided an opportunity to participate in a complicated and lengthy planning process. Frequently, the officials with whom discontented groups were brought into contact lacked the authority, the direction, or the resources to do something tangible to change living conditions. The mayor's concerns with neighborhood groups were sporadic at best. Aldermen had only tenuous contacts with some neighborhood groups and virtually no contacts with others. Many genuinely poor people were unorganized and unenfranchised. Protests did nothing to change that situation.

Neighborhoods as Political Groupings

Neighborhoods have no natural cohesion as political groups. Particular interests and differences in economic status can as easily divide a neighborhood as they can a business community.[4] Especially if neighborhood residents are nonaffluent and diverse, they will have few inducements to organize themselves into a stable political force. They may come together in opposition to some common threat, as was the case in the early stages of Bedford-Pine renewal; but when the threat ceases to be immediate, neighborhood cohesion declines. And, as was the case with U-Rescue, the neighborhood organization—while it may survive—can easily lose its representative character.

In a situation like the one that prevailed in Vine City, even an immediate "threat" may not produce neighborhood solidarity. Unless policy benefits are aggregated in a way so as to reassure all elements and to convince them that there are substantial collective gains to be made, then unity will not result.

In Atlanta, two factors were involved in the failure of nonaffluent neighborhoods to become politically influential. First, city officials had no incentives to mold neighborhoods into effective political forces. The mayor's office was very much a product of a city-wide constituency. The mayor had especially strong ties with the business community and, although he had some ties with black leaders, without exception they too were leaders with a city-wide rather than neighborhood-based constituency.

While there are absolutely no indications that City Hall sought to incite disunity among neighborhood groups, the city did little, even in the selection of neighborhood advisory committees, to foster unity. In the early stages of Vine City renewal planning, the city simply chose sides in the school-site dispute. Later, when faced with a factional fight over representation on the PAC, city officials adopted a "let them fight it out" stance. In neither instance was there an effort to try to transcend differences and develop potential benefits that could be held out as an inducement for collective action. Compared to the efforts made in the 1950s to bring together a business-centered alliance in support of CBD renewal, efforts in the 1960s to generate support for neighborhood renewal were weak and half-hearted.

The second aspect of neighborhood political ineffectiveness has to do with the position of people who live at the level of hard-core poverty. They are in an almost totally dependent relationship to the institutions of the larger community. In Atlanta, the agencies that were most immediately concerned with the welfare of the poor faced overwhelming needs with few resources. As a consequence, Atlanta's social agencies were themselves far too dependent on the good will and cooperation of others to develop leverage against City Hall. One reason, then, that neighborhoods were politically ineffective is that many of the organizations and agencies active in them had no endogenous strength.

Neighborhoods thus had neither the resources for political organization nor the wherewithal to compel action on the part of recalcitrant officials. In the 1950s when CBD renewal had become ensnarled in official inaction, businessmen had been able to pressure the mayor into reactivating the coalition behind redevelopment. In the 1960s, social agencies were unable to reverse the city's declining interest in low-income housing and community improvements.

Race conceivably could have been a tie between black neighborhoods and black city-wide leaders and organizations. Yet there was little in the experience of the 1960s to suggest that the interest of city-wide black leaders in the needs of nonaffluent neighborhoods was any more durable than was the mayor's interest. Through their support for a new C. W. Hill School, city-wide black leaders perhaps helped to limit CBD expansion in the Buttermilk Bottom/Bedford-Pine area. But their only other visible impact on renewal and relocation policy was in the effort to divert some public-housing construction from the Westside of the city. If blacks had not been so thoroughly junior in their partnership in the city's governing coalition, a different pattern of conduct might have been evident.[5] As it was, city-wide black leaders seemed to feel that their tenuous base of influence had to be used selectively and sparingly. In the Allen era of urban renewal, black solidarity was thus a very limited force behind the efforts to improve housing and neighborhood conditions.

The Allen Era of Urban Renewal in Theoretical Perspective

According to pluralist theory, policy benefits are differentially distributed because interest and issue salience are differentially distributed. As Dahl explained, "nearly every citizen in the community has access to unused [that is, 'slack'] political resources."[6] Political leaders are thereby motivated to diffuse widely the benefits and costs flowing from policy decisions. If a policy affects two groups more or less equally, then public officials supposedly have a strong incentive to work out a position that is mutually satisfactory to the two groups—otherwise, the unsatisfied group would be disposed to use its "slack" resources until a more favorable outcome is achieved.[7] As Wildavsky has argued: "Given the reservoir of resources which most citizens possess, their willingness to use them at a higher rate in the few areas of their concern, and the interest rival leaders have in taking their case if they are dissatisfied, the rule of minority satisfaction should apply."[8]

Under Ivan Allen's leadership, Atlanta's urban renewal program did not conform to the "rule of minority satisfaction." Activity and vocal discontent—the taking up of slack resources—did not lead to lasting policy gains for blacks, neighborhood groups, and other nonbusiness interests who favored improvements in the quality of residential life. The redirection of Atlanta's renewal program thus proved unsuccessful despite a widespread show of interest by affected groups. And, significantly, efforts on behalf of the new program impetus were not confined to protests by neighborhood groups. Many individuals, organizations, and agencies were sympathetic to redirection. Technical studies were conducted, follow-up measures proposed, and favorable publicity secured. The difficulty was that the major public officials were not predisposed to further a new policy direction that seemed to conflict with the interests of the business community. And, neighborhood leaders not only failed to change the predispositions of incumbent officials, but they also lacked the ability to promote the candidacies of persons with different predispositions.

Politically usable resources were not so widely dispersed as to make protests an effective technique for shaping and maintaining a direction in renewal policy. The imbalances in resources available to various groups were too great for officials to feel compelled to do more than make temporary concessions to dissatisfied groups. Thus it was not enough that spokesmen for improved housing and neighborhood conditions possessed some resources or that they "took up slack" and made use of their resources. The resistance that they encountered was simply too deeply embedded in the community's system of governance. "Slack" resources are thus not easily converted into a durable form of influence. As external pressure on public officials loses intensity, officials revert to an unresponsive attitude toward dissatisfied groups. The "taking up of slack" is too costly an exercise to be done repeatedly by groups whose resource base is somewhat meager.

No one could really deny that "slack," in the sense of unused resources, exists, but the important question is whether or not it exists in sufficient amounts for disadvantaged groups to be able to have more than a passing effect on policy. In Atlanta, it apparently did not. Spokesmen for neighborhood interests felt compelled to work within the established system of community leadership and to accede to the noncooperation of city officials. Neighborhood and low-income groups did not have sufficient resources to alter the channels of access and change City Hall's "bias."

By not being able to maneuver into a favorable position, these dissident groups failed to have conflict managed on their terms. City Hall did not obtain allies for these groups and did not try to outmaneuver, circumvent, or lessen the opposition to their objectives. Instead, City Hall chose not to embark on a path that might bring it into conflict with major business interests. The business community was thus in a position to veto indirectly measures that would have reallocated city resources and provided the means for improving the quality of residential life in nonaffluent neighborhoods. Yet overt conflict between businessmen and neighborhood groups was completely absent in the later years of the Allen administration.

Policy, it is generally agreed, is made incrementally. Far-reaching change comes about only after many minor changes take place over a long time period. Further, it is sometimes argued that incremental change occurs without much pattern. Decision making is alleged to be fragmented and decentralized.[9] As Dahl described New Haven under Mayor Lee: "The centrifugal forces in the system were, in short, persistent and powerful; the fullest and most skillful use of all the resources available to the Mayor added barely enough centripetal thrust to keep the various parts from flying off in all directions."[10] Incessant bargaining and unstable coalitions are believed to characterize much of community policymaking and therefore cause change to be not only incremental but disjointed. The power situation is regarded as too fluid to give policy a consistent bias.

In Atlanta, however, political relationships showed themselves to be quite stable. The link between City Hall and the business community was durable. While urban renewal was subject to a variety of influences, official decision making was not so disjointed and undirected as to disregard business preferences. Efforts to reset the course of renewal policy proved short-lived. Whereas the earlier impetus toward upgrading and expanding the CBD met with some temporary reverses but was gradually moved forward over time, the attempt to improve residential life for the nonaffluent simply stalled and came to a halt after a brief spate of official activity. In short, incremental decision making is not incompatible with the fact that some groups are favored consistently while others are neglected. At least within the bounds of Atlanta's urban renewal program, a pronounced bias in favor of business interests was evident in the Allen era as it had been in the Hartsfield era. Although policy was shaped in an incremental fashion, policy gains did not follow the ''rule of minority satisfaction.''

System Bias and Business Influence

The ''rule of minority satisfaction'' may be a satisfactory explanation of how some policies are made, but it does not provide a very useful guide to understanding Atlanta's urban renewal experience. The point is not that the ''rule of minority satisfaction'' oversimplifies a complex reality; system bias is also a simplified description of a complex process. Rather, the point is that the ''rule of minority satisfaction'' offers an inappropriate interpretation of official behavior. It is based on the view that public officials are motivated to accommodate public policy to the interests of groups with the most direct and immediate interests in a given issue area.

The ''rule of minority satisfaction'' thus assumes that official decision makers are concerned mainly with maximizing constituency support and that officials are therefore motivated to respond to group interests in accordance with the intensity of those interests. In the face of group conflict officials are presumably neutral arbiters, eager to seek out compromises that will satisfy everyone as much as possible.[11] However, the Atlanta experience suggests that public officials are not neutral arbiters but are more interested in satisfying some groups than others. And the Atlanta experience suggests further that, while the use of ''slack'' resources was visible—particularly in the form of protest politics, officials felt compelled to do no more than make temporary concessions to dissatisfied groups. As a result, housing and neighborhood improvements failed to come about for two reasons: (1) the groups most directly and immediately affected were unable to remain in a state of politically active readiness—therefore external pressure on officials was not maintained; (2) top-level public officials shared the views and concerns of the business community—therefore as soon as the external pressure on them eased, they reverted to a policy oriented toward business interests. Even though the interests of the business community in neighborhood and housing improvements were relatively remote and indirect, as compared to the interests of neighborhood and low-income groups, business influence proved to be more telling in the long run.

System bias thus seems to offer a better guide than does the ''rule of minority satisfaction'' to how urban renewal policy in Atlanta was made. System bias directs attention to the role that public officials play in advancing some interests at the expense of other no less active and directly affected interests.

In the preceding analysis, business success in renewal policy has been credited to the business community's capacity to secure, maintain, and exploit a positional advantage in Atlanta's politics. By contrast, the failure of neighborhood and low-income groups to achieve improvements in the quality of residential life has been attributed to their politically disadvantaged position. It might be argued, however, that the business community exercised no extraordinary amount of influence. Upgrading the CBD could conceivably have been preferred policy for reasons that had nothing to do with a system bias in favor of business interests. Thus, before a probusiness bias in the political system can be accepted as an explanation for the direction taken by Atlanta's urban renewal program, we need to consider some alternative ways of accounting for the city's tendency to further business interests at the expense of the interests of neighborhood and low-income groups.

A policy such as urban renewal might assume its character as a consequence of any of a number of factors. For example, a policy might take shape from an inherent community tendency toward maintaining the status quo. Alternatively, a policy could result from a majoritarian bias; that is, some groups might be frustrated in pursuing their interests because they encounter the opposition of a popular majority while other groups are successful because their interests enjoy majority support. Still another possibility is that policies such as urban renewal are controlled by economic necessity: as entities with strong revenue needs, cities may be brought inevitably to promote policies of economic growth. Finally, it might be argued that Atlanta's urban renewal program has been an arena of mutual adjustment and that it offers a variation on, rather than a contradiction of, the "rule of minority satisfaction." In one variation, the business community might be considered as a small and cohesive group that is satisfied with tangible benefits while neighborhood and low-income interests comprise a large and diffuse group that is satisfied with symbolic rewards.[1] In another variation, it might be argued that constituency pressures sometimes have a delayed reaction and that the accommodation of nonbusiness groups had to await the election of Ivan Allen's successor.

Status Quo Bias

New York City's political system has been described as having "tendencies toward stasis," as "more favorable to defenders of the *status quo* than to innovators," as "inherently conservative."[2] The characterization is considered by some to be applicable to other communities. "Community agendas," Nelson Polsby has argued, "are hard to change.''[3] Certainly the proponents of improved housing and neighborhood conditions in Atlanta would concur with Polsby's view. Atlanta's protesters in the 1960s were clearly aiming for more than piecemeal change in the city's urban renewal program, and they were disappointed. However, Atlanta's overall urban renewal experience hardly conveys a picture of a policy in which the status quo is simply perpetuated with minor modifications. As Dahl observed, ''Rapid, comprehensive change in the physical pattern of a city is a minor revolution.''[4] In Atlanta, CBD redevelopment and the accompanying relocation program were unquestionably major departures from the status quo. Not only did the city's policy make widespread changes in land use and contribute to neighborhood instability, but the use of eminent domain and public funds to promote private redevelopment were also a substantial departure from past practice. As indicated in chapter 5, there was considerable ideological opposition to the city's early redevelopment program. Business influence was therefore evident as much in innovative policy actions as in efforts to veto changes proposed by other groups. In short, it would appear that business influence rested on more than a system tendency toward stasis.

Majoritarian Bias

A fundamental tenet of pluralism is that public officials formulate policies acceptable to broad cross sections of their constituents. The promotion of economic growth, as a *general* policy aim, no doubt enjoyed widespread support in Atlanta. But, rehousing slum dwellers and the renewal of older neighborhoods, as *general* policy aims, also enjoyed a broad base of community support. Every available community survey in the 1960s indicated that housing conditions were recognized as a problem of first-order seriousness, and a broad array of groups and organizations voiced support for a city effort to eliminate substandard housing and improve the quality of residential life. Unless a nonobservable phenomenon like latent support is appealed to (and even that interpretation would be strained because the rating of problems by seriousness indicates that housing ranked higher than employment or business expansion as a matter of public concern), the available evidence suggests that economic growth, as a *concrete* policy, enjoyed no special amount of popular favor.

A commonly held view is that programs to improve opportunities for the poor do not succeed because they encounter too much opposition, real and potential. Unquestionably, some rehousing measures had a high potential for conflict. Yet there are few indications that city policy was designed to move in the directions least likely to arouse opposition. As we shall see later in more systematic terms, it was CBD revitalization, not neighborhood improvement, that produced the greatest amount of open controversy.

City officials, in fact, realized that the massive displacement of low-income families around the CBD was a disruptive and conflict-producing policy. A program of neighborhood improvement and conservation probably would have excited much less controversy than the policy followed, but neighborhood renewal was consistently neglected. Moreover, displacement around the CBD was maximized, not because that was a popular policy with the general public—indeed, both the clearance and relocation activities of the city generated intense opposition—but because it was the policy that the business community could best agree on.

All things considered, it is difficult to see how Atlanta's urban renewal policy was in any concrete way dictated by public opinion. The general objective of economic growth and the specific means to achieve it seemed to grow out of a special City Hall attentiveness, not to generally prevailing sentiments, but to opinion within the business community.

The Public Interest and Economic Necessity

Conceivably, businessmen, as the city's major revenue producers, exerted a dominant influence because officials recognized that services could not be provided unless revenue is raised. Economic growth, some might argue, is promoted by governmental officials not because the political system favors business interests but because economic growth is objectively in the public interest. Or, as Edward Banfield suggested at one point in his Chicago study, businessmen exert influence "by main force of being right."[5] The poor, it might also be argued, do not carry their own productive weight. Still, it is by no means clear that the economic vitality of Atlanta has been promoted in the one best way.

The argument might be made that some short-run social costs were a worthwhile price to pay for economic growth, but it appears that the social costs as perceived by a variety of community actors were substantial and they were not all short-run. Although community leaders have prided themselves on being defenders of racial harmony, the relocation policy backed by business interests has generated much racial friction. Indeed, it is likely that the white exodus to the suburbs was quickened by the city's relocation policy and by the city's inattention to neighborhood facilities and services. In other words, economic growth as a policy was pursued not just at the cost of social programs for the very poor; it was pursued in a manner that disregarded neighborhood stability for all but the most affluent sections of the city.

Atlanta, moreover, could easily have afforded a more balanced renewal program. In view of the city's relatively low tax rate, it clearly
was not squeezed financially into one alternative to the exclusion of the
other (and did not always choose the least expensive alternative, anyway). Further, while all cities must strike a balance between raising
revenue and providing services, that balance can be achieved in a variety
of ways. Atlanta, a number of participants felt, need not have neglected
its nonaffluent neighborhoods so extensively.[6]

Another factor at work was the fear that additional low-income
housing would serve as a magnet for the poor and endanger the city's
economy. The fear was real enough, but the threat to the city's economy
could be questioned. Indeed some administrative officials argued that
job opportunities affect migration trends more than housing conditions
do. Thus it may be that the movement of poor people into Atlanta was
more a sign of the city's prosperity than a threat to it. At any rate, there
was dispute even within official decision-making circles over the consequences of building new low-rent housing; and some administrators
argued that the composition of the city's population would not be
significantly affected by a continued rehousing program.

Further, while any community is understandably concerned over its
economic strength and tax base, the policy of CBD enhancement has
perhaps been a mixed blessing. University and hospital expansion and
the building of civic facilities on central-city land probably raised the
value of surrounding property, but it is not clear that the net effect has
been financially beneficial to the city. Land was removed from the tax
roll, residential disruption and deterioration were substantial, technical
considerations introduced by planners were sometimes ignored, and, in
the case of civic facilities, less expensive sites could have been purchased. Obviously, there were economic advantages to a program of
CBD revitalization, but there were also economic as well as other
advantages to programs of neighborhood conservation and upgrading.
To the argument that CBD rejuvenation was necessary for the economic
health of the area (and that argument could be disputed),[7] the point
should be made that the CBD could have been upgraded with less
residential dislocation and without moving large numbers of low-income
blacks into selected outlying sections of the city.

The fact of the matter is that CBD renewal in Atlanta has taken a
somewhat unusual form. One of the main objectives of the city's
renewal effort has been the creation of buffers between the city's
commercial core and nearby low-income residential areas. Thus the
major thrust of the city's urban renewal program was not to provide land
for commercial redevelopment. (Some land was provided for this purpose, but two major proposals for commercial redevelopment were

rejected as too costly.) Rather it was, especially in the 1960s, a policy of building "support" facilities—the stadium and the civic center—which could have been located elsewhere with less residential dislocation but which in that event would not have served as buffers between low-income citizens and CBD commercial activity. Possibly the hotel- and office-building boom would not have occurred unless developers had been reassured by the creation of buffer zones, but it is at least possible that the profit opportunities were there, buffers or not, and that the buffers were built mainly because they were an ingrained part of the white business leaders' pattern of thought. At any rate, it is hard to see how, for example, a downtown stadium contributed more than remotely to the "Manhattanization" of the Atlanta CBD. It is not at all certain, then, that extensive new building in the heart of the CBD—most of which occurred on privately acquired land—required the construction of wide buffer zones on the periphery of the business district. Thus, while urban renewal activity *may* have been a necessary catalyst, it is also quite possible that—given the city's favorable location—Atlanta's political and business leaders might have successfully promoted economic growth in ways other than the path they actually followed. Unfortunately, a side effect of the political weakness of neighborhood groups is that we shall never know for sure whether or not economic growth could have been achieved with fewer social costs.

The point of these comments is not to find fault with specific decisions, but to suggest that the public interest is composed of many elements and could have been served in ways other than the particular form Atlanta officials decided upon. Even if community well-being requires economic growth and an expanding tax base, that well-being could have been served by a different combination of decisions than those made in Atlanta. Business success in Atlanta's renewal policy rested on more than a fortuitous coincidence between business interests and those of the general public. And business success was not a matter of the city's inevitably following the path of greatest necessity. CBD redevelopment in Atlanta was promoted without regard to frugality in site selection for civic facilities, was pursued in spite of inconvenient federal regulations, and was furthered in the face of substantial community resistance. Necessity, like beauty, seems to be in the eyes of the beholders.

As suggested above, a case can be made for the view that the overall health of the city (not to mention its social health) would have been better had the urban renewal program been a more balanced one. At the same time, it is possible that the city followed a sound policy in unabashedly promoting CBD revitalization. Yet there was not a clear consensus even among official decision makers that the policy followed was best. "Reasonable men" could and did differ over the city's renewal policy.

Disregard for various neighborhood and low-income interests in the making of redevelopment and relocation policy appears to have been less a matter of necessity or of undoubted economic wisdom than of deliberate choice between competing interests. There has been a great deal of uncertainty about the best way to serve the public interest through the urban renewal program, and, in Atlanta, uncertainty—not necessity—was the floodgate through which business influence entered the policy process. Decisional choices flowed directly from the politically advantaged position enjoyed by the business community.

Mutual Accommodation and Symbolic Satisfaction

Since many of the proposals to improve housing and neighborhood conditions were neglected at one stage or another without causing conflict, it might be argued that these proposals were not in fact strongly supported by their intended beneficiaries. Conceivably these proposals could have been examples of middle-class do-goodism, and therefore of symbolic rather than tangible importance to their supporters. If one accepts the view about slum dwellers that "those people live that way because they like it," then one can argue that lower-class apathy was the root cause. For example, Edward Banfield describes "the imperatives of class" thus: "The lower class individual lives in the slum and sees little or no reason to complain. He does not care how dirty and dilapidated his housing is either inside or out, nor does he mind the inadequacy of such public facilities as schools, parks, and libraries: indeed, where such things exist, he destroys them by acts of vandalism if he can."[8]

Perhaps Atlanta had very few people who were lower class, as that term is defined by Banfield. Certainly the vocal supporters of housing and neighborhood improvements were restricted to no single social or economic stratum. Homeowners, renters, large families, senior citizens, blacks, whites, blue-collar workers, small-business owners and middle-class professionals, persons below the poverty level, spokesmen for neighborhood civic associations, and staff members of social action agencies were all identifiable in significant numbers as proponents of a better quality of residential life for Atlanta's nonaffluent population. Above all, however, the residents in substandard areas were visibly dissatisfied with housing and neighborhood conditions. It might also be noted, as was evident from Housing Authority surveys and public hearings, that these residents were openly opposed to relocation in places distant from the center of the city. During the period when the

Community Action agency was organizing poverty neighborhoods, systematic evidence was accumulated from block-by-block meetings that housing conditions were a major grievance of Atlanta's poor people. After outbreaks of civil disorder, less systematic but equally convincing evidence on this same point was provided to the mayor as a result of his inquiries into the nature of neighborhood discontent. Community Relations Commission hearings offered further documentation of neighborhood dissatisfaction. In brief, support for improvements was widely and consistently expressed over a long period of time. Apathy, in the sense of indifference at least, was not observably a characteristic of the nonaffluent portion of Atlanta's citizenry.

Even if the discontent is admitted to have been genuine, it might still be argued that the expressions of concern by City Hall were sufficient to reassure the loose aggregation of supporters who were behind the call for a new policy direction. But the most nearly applicable theory, Murray Edelman's analysis of political quiescence—the theory that large and diffuse groups can be satisfied by symbolic rewards—does not appear to be appropriate for the Atlanta urban renewal experience. Edelman's analysis is focused on "audience" groups who respond to political actions that are "remote from the individual's immediate experience."[9] As Michael Lipsky has suggested in his adaptation of the Edelman theory, while symbolic responses may be reassuring to the middle-class supporters of social programs (an "audience" group), members of the lower class (those who are directly and tangibly affected) may acquire nothing more than a sense of futility and hopelessness.[10]

In Atlanta, nonaffluent residential and neighborhood interests, although loosely organized and geographically scattered, were not an "audience" group without immediate stakes in housing conditions and community facilities. The evidence from interviews and from public hearings indicates that these groups were both dissatisfied and disappointed. Even middle-class activists, such as the members of the mayor's Housing Resources Committee, were frustrated rather than reassured by the city's actions. There is thus no evidence to suggest that the proponents and supporters of improved housing and neighborhood conditions felt that their interests had been accommodated. While the Edelman theory undoubtedly has applicability to a wide variety of circumstances, the renewal experience of Atlanta's lower-income citizens does not appear to have been one of them. Some casual observers among the general public may have been persuaded that the city was attentive to the needs of its nonaffluent neighborhoods, but neither the residents of those neighborhoods nor the middle-class advocates of neighborhood interests were so persuaded. Renewed disappointment rather than fresh-found contentment marked the end of Atlanta's era of protests. It appears that the proponents of housing and neighborhood improvements were satisfied neither tangibly nor symbolically.

Delayed Constituency Reaction

In 1970, the year that the Census Bureau recorded a black majority in Atlanta's population, Sam Massell became mayor. Massell's accession to that office came after a campaign in which his opponent was endorsed by Ivan Allen, the newspapers, and the business community. Massell— liberal, white, and labor-backed—received strong support in the black community.[11] After one term, Massell was replaced in office by Maynard Jackson, Atlanta's first black mayor.[12] Some fairly strong winds of political change are obviously stirring in Atlanta, and at this stage it is not easy to determine how the city's politics will be transformed. As would be expected from a shift in the community's racial balance, new leaders with new predispositions have assumed office. Although these events lie outside the time and circumstances analyzed here, it may still be worthwhile to see if there were indications of a basic change in policy during the early 1970s. In this way, we can see if the main narrative was cut off just before constituency dissatisfaction brought about a major victory for low-income and neighborhood groups. Conceivably, the Massell mayoralty witnessed the institution of changes in politics and policy that had been sought earlier. We should look briefly at what these changes were and how they fared under Massell.

The neighborhood-based revolt against Atlanta's reformed and centralized politics in the mid-1960s was a three-pronged attack:

Procedural innovation
Neighborhood groups attempted to gain direct representation in the planning and administration of programs. These forces of discontent repudiated the politics-administration dichotomy, and they claimed the right to have a voice in every decision that involved them. Because policy is the final product of a long series of actions, they argued, no decision is too detailed for neighborhood consideration.

Fresh forms of political activism
Throughout the 1950s and in the early 1960s, City Hall was inclined to recognize as black leaders only those individuals who were dependent on the white business community for some economic benefits. But in the mid-1960s new political activists emerged. Many were neighborhood-based leaders, some of whom were skilled in community organization and in the art of dramatizing issues. They defended conflict, open

debate, and confrontation as legitimate tactics for voicing the interests of neglected and unrepresented groups. (New activists in urban renewal were, of course, preceded by the student-led sit-ins.)

New ideas

Prior to the mid-1960s political leaders and top-level administrators alike were unequivocally committed to the substantive idea that economic growth was in the best interest of the whole community. The notion that economic growth was good for everyone was a concrete expression of the more abstract idea that there was a one best way to advance the welfare of the entire community. With regard to matters of proper procedure, Atlanta's leadership simply did not believe that all segments of the community needed to be represented in policy deliberations. Rather, they considered the deliberate representation of all groups to be undesirable practice. Excessive attention to representativeness, they feared, would elevate private interests over the public interest and undercut community-mindedness.

Spokesmen for neighborhood and lower-income groups developed contrasting ideas. They argued that social justice required the correction of past inequities and the provision of greater opportunities for those who historically had been disadvantaged. They depicted the public interest as a matter of equitable treatment for all groups and they asserted the worth of representativeness as a political and an administrative value.

While change is undoubtedly still in the making, the early 1970s indicate that the attempt to subdue Atlanta's centralized institutions and reformed style of politics met no better fate than the effort to redirect renewal policy. As the Allen era came to a close, dissident forces and the principles they propounded were not much in evidence. Even before the national administration had begun to disestablish participatory and antipoverty programs, neighborhood groups ceased to maintain a high level of activity. Some post-1970 protests in the Model Cities area served only to provoke Mayor Massell into an attack against the notion of neighborhood participation. Neither the new political actors nor the new procedures they introduced proved to be lasting parts of the Atlanta political system. Protests and anomic acts of civil disorder served to raise issues for lower-class groups, but protests proved to be costly in terms of civic good will. As the Atlanta experience demonstrates, raising issues and resolving them are quite different kinds of accomplishments. New procedures in the forms of neighborhood advisory committees and neighborhood legal action, like protests, have been ineffective as channels of lower-class representation. They never penetrated the city's system of setting priorities. These procedural innovations were perhaps foredoomed by the political conditions in which they were tried. Neighborhood advisory committees, for example, were nothing more than ad hoc concessions to the ideas of decentralized planning. Control over resource allocation remained centralized within the city government—more precisely within the mayor's office.

The new ideas of representativeness and social equity also failed to have much impact. Indeed, they were modified and brought into line with the reform ethos. Despite the presence of a black majority in the city, representativeness came to mean not citizen involvement in neighborhood decisions, but the appointment of blacks to a fair share of high-level administrative posts in the government of the city. Even the impact of that change was effectively blunted. Mayor Massell admonished black leaders to "think" white and to represent the general views of all portions of the city, not just a distinctly black viewpoint. Some black leaders voiced agreement with the Massell statement.[13] Thus neither the city's principal administrators nor the major figures in the black community were inclined to talk much about the impact of programs on specific sections of the community. Particular needs of blacks or of the poor were neglected in favor of a rhetoric that assumed that programs like mass transit and CBD revitalization were uniformly beneficial.

Social equity as a policy aim that should guide renewal policy apparently gave way to alternative considerations about economic balance. For example, the aldermanic Planning and Development Committee (as well as the Housing Authority) seemingly accepted former mayor Ivan Allen's rationale for not concentrating on the provision of low-income housing. The CAIA was able during the summer of 1973 to gain aldermanic support for a proposal to include a substantial component of middle- and upper-income housing in the further redevelopment of the area east of the CBD—the long struggled-over Bedford-Pine area. In embracing the idea of "economic balance," the committee declared: "It is the policy of the city to maximize the housing possibilities for all income levels."[14] In December 1973, the Housing Authority awarded a bid to redevelop seventy-eight acres of Bedford-Pine land to Park Central Communities, a consortium put together by CAIA for the special purpose of directing "economically balanced" renewal in the Bedford-Pine area.[15] Thus, as the Massell administration came to a close, there was still no policy of systematic neighborhood improvement and no policy of rehousing the poor. Instead, renewal policy had come to center on the notion that "economic balance" was in the best interest of the whole community and that the city therefore should make special efforts to see that middle- and upper-income housing would be built.

In actuality, then, the Massell administration was far from a delayed victory for lower-income and neighborhood groups. Mainly it was a continuation of the policies of the past. It did not bring about a change in renewal policy, and it did not provide the nonaffluent with ready access to the processes of planning and program administration. What the Jackson administration will bring is still a matter of speculation, but the Massell mayoralty apparently failed to integrate lower-class groups into the city's political system. The business community appeared still to be the dominant influence in renewal policy. Atlanta's renewal policy may someday become accommodating to low-income and neighborhood interests. But, if and when that accommodation occurs, it will likely be a result of long-term alterations in the city's politics, alterations brought about by ongoing changes in the community's racial and other characteristics. By itself, constituent dissatisfaction over earlier policies seems to have had little impact on urban renewal during the Massell administration.

System Bias

Renewal policy in Atlanta coincided most closely with business interests, it has been argued here, because the business community enjoyed and exploited a politically advantaged position. The evidence on this point is embedded in the narration of events surrounding the formation of urban renewal policy.

City officials had a variety of policy alternatives before them throughout the twenty-year period. The proposals they enacted and implemented were choices they made on the basis of their own political calculations, but they were choices made more on the basis of inside influence than on external pressure. Yet the city's policy was not the one prescribed by planners and technocrats. The city's renewal planning technicians prescribed a much more balanced program than the one that was actually followed. They recommended giving more attention to neighborhood improvements; they urged that displacement and relocation be more closely synchronized; and they did not favor construction of the stadium and the civic center in areas adjacent to the CBD.

The policy followed clearly was not one that emanated from constituency pressures. City officials spent much of their time trying to maneuver around constituency opposition. On those occasions when officials were openly attempting to rally public opinion behind urban renewal, they never confined their pronouncements to the desirability of revitalizing the CBD. Instead they always spoke of the need to improve housing and neighborhood conditions. However, the more unobtrusive actions of city officials clearly subordinated housing and neighborhood improvements to the policy concerns prevalent in the business community.

To summarize, in Atlanta there were many policy alternatives open to and considered by public officials. The alternatives that were actually followed were, for the most part, not the ones recommended by planners and other technocrats. Nor were they the alternatives behind which there were publicly vocal supporters. Instead the policy followed was the one favored by the business community, which, through its spokesmen and its close alliance with the mayor's office, gained a great amount of "inside" influence in the formulation and implementation of the city's urban renewal program.

PART 3

SYSTEM BIAS: A REVISIONIST PERSPECTIVE

By looking at policy formation over a long time span, we have been able to see that a positional advantage, as the source of a system bias, does not necessarily show up in individual decisions or at the height of controversy. Rather, bias is more likely to become apparent as the eventual outcome of a large number of interrelated decisions—many of which have low visibility. While controversy increases the salience of decision making and subjects officials to public pressures, controversy is a sporadic occurrence. By taking a long-term view of conflict, the researcher is able to observe the process by which a specific controversy can be waited out or maneuvered around.

A long time perspective offers another benefit in that collective interests as collective interests become easier to see as they have more opportunity to keep resurfacing. The resurfacing, in turn, makes it possible for underlying cleavages of interest to become evident. Over a time period greater than the history of a single issue, stable interest cleavages thus have an opportunity to manifest themselves.

Further, a lengthy period of time permits patterns of official behavior to become clearly observable. Official behavior is complex, varying somewhat from circumstance to circumstance and personality to personality. Moreover, officialdom is a collection of many individuals whose predispositions do not fall uniformly into one category. It is only over time that a prevalent predisposition within officialdom has an opportunity to emerge and prove itself as something more than a temporary leaning of one group of officeholders. The present chapter is concerned with the prevalent predispositions among Atlanta's urban renewal decision makers.

In contrast with the earlier discussion, the analysis here will treat the process of demand conversion in a quantitative and somewhat abstract form. In this way, we can examine the conduct of officials at the various stages of policy formation, and we can give special attention to the impact that overt conflict has on policy formation. Then, we can make some general inferences about official decision making under conditions of positional advantage and disadvantage.

Patterns of Demand Conversion

Demand conversion, it should be recalled, is only a portion of the total process of policy formation. An analysis of demand conversion thus does not answer questions about why some demands were articulated and others were not. (Nor does it lead to an examination of the long-term impact of policy.) Instead, it is a scope of analysis that focuses only on how some demands came to be furthered while others were not.

Demand generation is important, but, in the contemporary city, the process by which competing demands are converted into policy measures is of equal or greater importance. Certainly the Atlanta experience suggests no shortage of articulated demands. Therefore, a critically important question was that of how, in a context of limited resources, various proposals and counterproposals would be blended into a policy of urban renewal.

Demand conversion, it was suggested earlier, could be divided for purposes of analysis into three stages: (1) mobilization—the stage at which proposals may or may not generate enough support to be brought up for formal consideration by local authorities; (2) official disposition— the stage at which officials formally decide to approve, either fully or in substantially modified form, or disapprove proposals; and (3) implementation—the stage at which it could be determined whether or not after gaining official approval proposals had been put into effect, and, if so, to what extent. In addition, overt conflict has been identified wherever it occurred, and it has been pinpointed within the context of the three stages of demand conversion.

Over the twenty-year period studied, proposals for particular renewal actions and for commitments of city resources came from a variety of sources for a variety of purposes. Renewal policy could conceivably have moved in any of several directions. Demands, however, fell mainly into two broad policy alternatives.[1] The two alternatives differed substantively, and they differed in the makeup of their group support. As we have seen, the business community generally and the CAIA particularly were consistent backers of efforts to upgrade and expand the CBD and of complementary efforts to relocate low-income blacks into areas away from the CBD but not in Atlanta's affluent Northside. A different and somewhat less fixed constellation of interests—which may be identified in brief as black and white neighborhood groups, city-wide black leaders, and various spokesmen for low-income housing needs— favored actions to conserve and upgrade neighborhoods and to increase the supply of standard low- and moderate-income housing. And with regard to relocation, these nonbusiness groups variously urged that residential opportunities for low-income blacks close to the CBD be preserved and that low-income housing located in outlying areas be dispersed throughout the city, including areas adjacent to affluent white residents.

While both renewal policy alternatives have been embodied in a number of concrete proposals for which careers could be charted, neither policy alternative should be thought of as simply an aggregation of isolated demands. Rather each alternative represented an ongoing attempt to shape the renewal program in accordance with the expressed interests of major community groups. The demand conversion process has thus been examined in order to determine at what points business and nonbusiness groups encountered resistance and with what consequences. Table 13.1 confirms what was strongly suggested by the narrative account of Atlanta's urban renewal program. Proposals to rejuvenate the CBD were much more successful than proposals for neighborhood and residential renewal. Fewer than one-half of the business-backed proposals failed to be at least partially implemented, and most of those that were implemented were put into effect without being seriously modified. By contrast, nearly three-quarters of the neighborhood and residential renewal proposals failed to be implemented, and, of those put into effect, most were watered-down versions of the original proposal.

The real value of table 13.1, however, is that it indicates where the two sets of demands encountered official resistance. Entirely different patterns of demand conversion are evident for the competing policy alternatives. Proposals to upgrade the CBD were rarely turned down at the mobilization stage; more than one-half of the neighborhood and residential renewal demands failed to receive formal consideration by local authorities. Among the proposals that were officially approved and therefore reached the implementation stage, demands with business backing also enjoyed a substantial edge over other demands although not nearly as great an advantage as at the mobilization stage. More than two-thirds of the CBD renewal proposals that moved to the point of implementation were, in fact, put into effect without substantial modification. Most of the remaining one-third were at least partially imple-

Table 13.1. The Conversion of Urban Renewal Demands: Outcome by Policy Alternative and by Conversion Step

Policy Alternative	Number of Specific Demands	Mobili- zation		Official Disposition		Imple- mentation		Overall Outcome	
CBD renewal and selectively decen- tralized relocation (business-supported)	31	P 26	(84%)	P 15	(54%)	P 13	(68%)	P 13	(42%)
		M 2	(6%)	M 4	(14%)	M 4	(21%)	M 4	(13%)
		F 3	(10%)	F 9	(32%)	F 2	(11%)	F 14	(45%)
Residential and neighborhood renewal and diversified relo- cation (nonbusiness- supported)	64	P 26	(41%)	P 17	(57%)	P 7	(29%)	P 7	(11%)
		M 4	(6%)	M 7	(23%)	M 12	(50%)	M 12	(19%)
		F 34	(53%)	F 6	(20%)	F 5	(21%)	F 45	(70%)

Note: P=demands passed through a given stage essentially intact; M=demands advanced through a given stage in modified form, with the modification representing more than a token effort on behalf of the origi- nal demand; F=demands failed to advance through a given stage even in modified form.

mented. On the other hand, fewer than one-third of the neighborhood and residential renewal demands that reached the final stage were fully implemented, although one-half were put into effect to a modified degree. Only at the highly visible stage of official disposition does city action appear to be equally favorable to the two policy alternatives. At this stage, demands in line with business objectives fared no better than the demands supported by nonbusiness groups, and extraordinary business success was undetectable.

Because the Hartsfield and Allen mayoralties represented different styles of community politics, the pattern of demand conversion and the degree of renewal success could conceivably vary significantly over time. In particular, it might be expected that neighborhood and civil rights groups would have a substantial impact on policy in a period of highly active and visible discontent. Demands that were neglected under one set of political circumstances might receive favorable attention in other circumstances. Protest and confrontation seem, however, to have had only marginal or short-term effects on concrete policy actions.

The Hartsfield and Allen mayoralties are compared in table 13.2. While demands originating during the Allen administration did have a

Table 13.2. A Comparison between the Hartsfield and Allen Mayoralties in the Conversion of Urban Renewal Demands

Policy Alternative and Time Period	Number of Specific Demands	Mobili-zation		Official Disposition		Imple-mentation		Overall Outcome	
Business-supported demands originating during the Hartsfield mayoralty	17	P 13 M 1 F 3	(76%) (6%) (18%)	P 9 M 1 F 4	(64%) (7%) (28%)	P 7 M 1 F 2	(70%) (10%) (20%)	P 7 M 1 F 9	(41%) (6%) (53%)
Business-supported demands originating during the Allen mayoralty	14	P 13 M 1 F 0	(93%) (7%) (—)	P 6 M 3 F 5	(43%) (21%) (36%)	P 6 M 3 F 0	(67%) (33%) (—)	P 6 M 3 F 5	(43%) (21%) (36%)
Nonbusiness-supported demands originating during the Hartsfield mayoralty	29	P 11 M 1 F 17	(38%) (3%) (59%)	P 7 M 2 F 3	(58%) (17%) (25%)	P 4 M 2 F 3	(44%) (22%) (33%)	P 4 M 2 F 23	(14%) (7%) (79%)
Nonbusiness-supported demands originating during the Allen mayoralty	35	P 15 M 3 F 17	(43%) (9%) (49%)	P 10 M 5 F 3	(56%) (28%) (17%)	P 3 M 10 F 2	(20%) (67%) (13%)	P 3 M 10 F 22	(9%) (29%) (63%)

Note: P=demands passed through a given stage essentially intact; M=demands advanced through a given stage in modified form, with the modification representing more than a token effort on behalf of the original demand; F=demands failed to advance through a given stage even in modified form.

slightly higher rate of success than demands originating earlier, business as well as nonbusiness-supported demands achieved this higher level of success. The number of specific residential and neighborhood renewal demands rose a little in relation to CBD renewal demands, but this trend is hardly surprising in view of the extensive amount of nonresidential redevelopment that had already occurred. Overall, the two time periods resembled one another closely. In both mayoralties, business-backed demands reached the official disposition stage with little difficulty (even less under Allen than under Hartsfield), but encountered significant resistance at that point (but more during Allen's administration than Hartsfield's). Once acted on, however, they were implemented with a high rate of success. Again in both mayoralties, over half of the nonbusiness-supported demands failed to be acted on at the official disposition stage, but, when acted on, they were approved in the large majority of cases. During implementation, the rate of success dropped off appreciably. Dividing renewal actions into two time periods thus had no effect on the previously described pattern of demand conversion. Under both mayors, proposals to upgrade the CBD received especially favorable attention in the stages of policymaking least accessible to the public view. Contrasting styles of politics and leadership thus did not affect the pattern of demand conversion.

Demands can be arranged and analyzed by categories other than chronological periods. In light of the prominence of conflict as a topic in the literature on community power and policy formation, the relationship between open controversy and demand careers warrants particular attention.

The success of CBD redevelopment and the foundering of neighborhood and residential renewal might be attributable to the effects of community conflict. The one policy might simply have encountered less resistance than the other. For instance, if demands to upgrade the CBD had rarely encountered opposition, then business success might be credited to this absence of opposition. The argument might be made that the policy objectives of the business community were achieved because they embodied a general consensus. This was not the case, however, because CBD renewal was carried out in the face of substantial opposition.

Another possible way of explaining the successful attempt to upgrade the CBD is to show that the power of the business community enabled it to prevail when conflict occurred. In other words, direct exercises of influence could have accounted for business success. Political resources could have been mobilized to such an extent that opposition groups were overwhelmed. Again, however, the data do not support this line of speculation. If attention is focused on those decisional steps in which demands gave rise to overt conflict, then CBD renewal does not appear to have been an especially favored policy. In fact, table 13.3 shows that under conditions of conflict demands for neighborhood and residential renewal were slightly less likely to be rejected than demands for CBD renewal. Moreover, it is worth noting that the two policy alternatives generated different levels of conflict at each stage of demand processing. Most of the controversy around CBD renewal occurred when proposals were up for formal disposition. Conflict over neighborhood and residential renewal was more in evidence before and after official decisions were being made than during the official-disposition stage. Outcomes under conditions of conflict also varied from stage to stage. As was the case in the overall pattern of demand processing, neighborhood and residential demands were least successful in receiving official consideration in the first place (the mobilization stage) whereas CBD renewal demands were most likely to be rejected at the stage of official disposition.

Table 13.3. The Treatment of Urban Renewal Demands for Which Overt Conflict Was Present: Outcome by Policy Alternative

Policy Alternative	Mobili- zation		Official Disposition		Imple- mentation		Sum of Out- comes for All Conflict- accompanied Stages	
CBD renewal (business-supported)	P	2 (100%)	P	8 (44%)	P	2 (40%)	P	12 (48%)
	M	0 (—)	M	3 (17%)	M	3 (60%)	M	6 (24%)
	F	0 (—)	F	7 (39%)	F	0 (—)	F	7 (28%)
Residential and neighborhood renewal (nonbusiness- supported)	P	8 (57%)	P	4 (50%)	P	3 (27%)	P	15 (45%)
	M	1 (7%)	M	3 (38%)	M	8 (73%)	M	12 (36%)
	F	5 (36%)	F	1 (12%)	F	0 (—)	F	6 (18%)

Note: P=demands advanced through a given stage essentially intact; M=demands advanced through a given stage in modified form, with the modification representing more than a token effort on behalf of the original demand; F=demands failed to advance through a given stage even in modified form.

The relationship between demand conversion and overt conflict is best understood if the types of conflict are differentiated. In table 13.4, conflict involving an attempt to defeat a measure that is receiving official consideration is distinguished from conflict involving an attempt by supporters to move forward a demand that is stalled by official inaction. In short, the former is caused by community opposition to a proposal and the latter is caused by an attempt to overcome official resistance by making a demand more forcefully. Table 13.4 thus indi-

Table 13.4. Policy Alternative and Type of Overt Conflict

Policy Alternative	Total Number of Demands	Demands Accompanied by Overt Conflict	
		Conflict Involving Attempt to Defeat a Proposal Receiving Official Consideration	Conflict Involving Attempt to Move Forward a Demand Stalled by Official Inaction
CBD renewal (business-supported)	31	19 (61%)	2 (6%)
Residential and neighborhood renewal (nonbusiness-supported)	64	12 (19%)	17 (27%)

cates that renewal policymaking in Atlanta has a remarkable characteristic: the most successful set of policy proposals, those for CBD renewal, has encountered the greatest community opposition.[2] Neighborhood and residential renewal proposals have met some community opposition, but, in confirmation of earlier findings, the strongest resistance has come from public officials in the form of inaction.

Business success in public policy is sometimes explained as a matter of business objectives being widely ascribed to.[3] Urban renewal policy in Atlanta does not accord with that explanation, however. City decision makers were receptive to business-backed demands that later proved controversial, and these same decision makers resisted nonbusiness-supported demands that generated relatively little controversy once they were officially under consideration. Policy success in Atlanta does not seem to have followed the path of community consensus, nor do officials appear to have been guided by a strategy of conflict avoidance. Thus there is little in the pattern of demand conversion and overt conflict to suggest that officials pursued a policy of least resistance. Moreover, there is not much evidence that officials consistently anticipated strongly felt community needs and wants in developing and considering policy proposals.

Conflict and community opposition were certainly not without an impact on renewal policy. Business-supported proposals were defeated often enough to put to rest claims of business omnipotence. It may be recalled that the business edge over other groups was least under conditions of conflict. However, the major conclusion to be drawn from the pattern of demand conversion is that official decision makers were strongly predisposed to act favorably on business-supported proposals. Only when the full impact of public opposition was felt, generally at the highly visible stage of official disposition, did decision makers show any appreciable tendency to reject business demands.

The study of demand conversion needs to be treated with caution. As units of analysis, demands have some important limitations. They must, for example, be treated as discrete phenomena, but this treatment ignores the interrelated character of demands. Further, as units for quantitative analysis, demands do not display the nuances of policy direction that are more easily shown by a narration of events. Finally, one should not overlook the fact that, in the absence of some method of weighting, all demands are treated equally.[4] Their primary use is to indicate patterns of behavior. It should therefore be borne in mind that the central purpose of the analysis of demand conversion is not to achieve a precise measurement of power. It is rather that more modest aim of understanding at what points and under what circumstances influence is exercised. From this understanding, it should, in turn, be possible to draw a more complete sketch of how the revisionist theory of community power and policy formation applies to Atlanta's urban renewal experience. Specifically, it should be possible to state more exactly what role, under conditions of positional advantage, public officials played in the policy process and what part overt conflict had in giving direction to a policy thrust.

Toward a Revisionist View of Political Brokerage and Interest Advocacy

In responding to the claims of competing interest groups, it was argued earlier, public officials can follow sharply divergent strategies. Officials can be strong partisans of one group or another, that is, interest advocates; or they can be relatively impartial arbiters of group conflict, that is, neutral brokers. Interest advocates and neutral brokers fulfill their official responsibilities and react to conflict in different ways.

In the pluralist version of how power is exercised and policy formed, the major community leaders are professional politicians. A professional politician is one who does not have strong or fixed personal preferences about groups and issues, but is motivated to attract and maintain a broad base of support.[5] According to pluralist theory, political leaders consistently neither favor nor neglect any sizable group of constituents. Instead, to the extent possible, officials propose measures that are mutually accommodated to the interests of the most directly affected groups; and, if mutual accommodation proves impossible, then officials presumably follow the preferences of the most numerous group of active and mobilized citizens. What emerges clearly from the writings of pluralists is a view of public officialdom as a heterogeneous grouping of individuals who do not have sharply defined group preferences and who are not inflexibly inclined to further any policy that lacks widespread public support. Top-level officials, especially those holding elective office, are conceived of as political brokers—that is, as individuals who are bargainers, negotiators, and compromisers, as realists who can and do count constituents and who are eager to increase their popularity and improve their standing with the public.

Unquestionably, the brokerage role is played widely. But it is not a universally performed role, or at least it is not the role played on all occasions. The Atlanta experience certainly suggests that impartial mediation did not typify official conduct in the making of urban renewal policy. At the same time, the brokerage role was not absent from decision making in urban renewal. Indeed, the pattern of demand conversion suggests that the stronger the light of public scrutiny, the closer officials came to being neutral arbiters. The other side of that coin is, of course, that the further removed official behavior was from the surveillance of the general public, the stronger the advocate role became. Indisputably, top-level officials some of the time served as staunch advocates of the business interest in an expanded and upgraded CBD, and they did so in the face of anticipated opposition.

The pattern of demand conversion in Atlanta thus offers a somewhat different view of brokerage and advocacy than that described in earlier analyses of urban politics. That is, instead of officials consistently playing one or the other role, their behavior shifted from one tendency to another in accordance with the visibility of their conduct. High visibility heightened the tendency to serve as broker. Low visibility provided a protective cover under which advocacy could take place relatively free from the sanctions of unfavored groups.

Of course, there may be some circumstances—a racially polarized community politically dominated by one group—in which highly visible advocacy is expected and rewarded.[6] The Atlanta experience is based on an entirely different circumstance, however. Urban renewal policy in Atlanta was formed in a political climate in which no segment of the community expected its interests to be disregarded. All segments sought to have their objectives furthered by incumbent officials. Advocacy did not come about because constituency pressures favored one group over another. There was no majoritarian bias in support of business interests. Rather, the bias was a covert one that manifested itself most strongly in the phases of policy formation most removed from the workings of electoral accountability.

Pluralist forces were at work some of the time, it is important to remember. But the presence of some signs of pluralism is not an indication that officials made policy on the basis of a consistent impulse to reach mutual accommodations among all the groups with a substantial stake in a given policy.

198

The ebb and flow of pluralism in Atlanta's urban renewal program was somewhat as follows:

1. Low- and middle-echelon officials and members of advisory committees represented a broad cross section of backgrounds, points of view, and clientele groups. Demands were thus not only articulated on behalf of several major interests, but these demands were embodied in some very specific and technically elaborate proposals for governmental action. In brief, no single interest group dominated the demand articulation phase of the policy process.

2. Top-level officials represented a more restricted set of interests. Their closest ties were to the business community and other city-wide organizations. They turned to relatively few groups for policy cues. They were responsive to the news media, but they perceived the managers of the news media to be close allies of the business community. In the active promotion of proposals for formal consideration, top-level officials screened out most proposals that lacked business backing. The building of support and the creation of coalitions were complex actions not easily overseen by various elements of the general public. A bias in favor of business interests was thus largely unchecked.

3. Once proposals reached the stage at which they were formally acted upon, then the light of constituency attention served to limit the favoring of one group over others. Officials felt constrained to compromise and even to reject some strongly opposed measures. The pressure of numbers was most telling at the stage of official disposition, and the brokerage role was the politically safest stance to assume.

4. Public oversight of program execution was not nearly as keen as the surveillance of official acceptance of proposals. As a consequence, the biases of top-level officials were reasserted; and programs without strong business backing were not promoted with the energy often required to surmount administrative obstacles.

Top-level officials, according to pluralist thought, are the most broadly representative participants in the decision-making process. Pluralists describe them as participants who feel a "duty to do what 'a broad cross section of the community' wants."[7] The contrasting argument presented here is that lower- and middle-echelon officials collectively were more representative of a wide range of interests. The biases of these officials tended to be multiple and crosscutting. Top-level officials, on the other hand, tended to filter out some biases and reduce the number at work; but what occurred as a result of this filtering was not political brokerage. Rather, the top officials served to accentuate a few biases because they identified strongly with some groups and served as their advocates during the least visible phases of policymaking. Top-level officials were thus more receptive to some demands than to others, and their predilections were evident in the priorities they set and in the proposals on which their political energies were focused. Overall, they were not neutral arbiters. Support was developed and activities coordinated around some policy objectives to the detriment of others. In the process, officials seemed to be less concerned with the avoidance of opposition than with the need to manage conflict in such a way as to advance favored group interests.

Toward a Revisionist View of the Interrelations among Overt Conflict, Group Influence, and Policy Direction

The narrative account of Atlanta's urban renewal program should remove any suspicion that business objectives were favored over neighborhood objectives because businessmen felt more intensely about their interests. Selecting policy alternatives was not a matter of "indifference versus preference."[8] On the contrary, groups contended actively and vigorously over the costs and benefits of urban renewal. The program thus provides a rich opportunity to gain some insight into the relationships among policy direction, group influence, and conflict.

Pluralism accords conflict a central place in the exercise of power and in the formation of policy. Political leaders are generally believed to have an aversion to public controversy and therefore follow a strategy of conflict avoidance. As Raymond Wolfinger observed, "like everyone else, they do not willingly or lightly venture where they anticipate hostility, defeat, and perhaps retribution as well."[9]

More to the point of pluralist theory, conflict is the mechanism by which leaders are controlled by nonleaders.[10] In the world of pluralism, veto groups are rampant. A proposal can supposedly be blocked readily by vigorous opposition. Because consent is easily revoked, even groups who are generally inactive are not "led very far against their will."[11] Policy decisions, Polsby has argued, tend to move in directions "that do not strain the compliance of others in the system."[12] Controversies, according to Banfield, "serve the function of forming and preparing opinion."[13] And Wildavsky has asserted boldly, "conflicts among leaders supply the dynamics of the system [of influence and decision making]."[14] In the eyes of pluralists, power is demonstrated (to other community actors as well as to researchers) by prevailing on a contested point in a community controversy.[15]

In Atlanta's urban renewal program, however, overt conflict did not appear to be a reliable guide to group influence on policy. No group consistently won when issues were contested (see table 13.4). Neighborhood groups demonstrated a capacity to prevail in particular decisional controversies. Yet policy moved, haltingly at times, but nevertheless cumulatively in the direction favored by the business community.

The Atlanta experience thus suggests something quite different from the pluralist view of how conflict and policy are related. Policy direction seemed to shape conflict to a greater extent than conflict appeared to affect policy direction. In the first place, much of the overt conflict was precipitated by specific actions taken to expand the CBD and to relocate low-income families away from the center of the city. Public officials anticipated that this policy would come under heavy attack. And, from its inception in the early 1950s on through the building of the civic center and the efforts to acquire expansion land for Georgia Baptist Hospital, CBD renewal, in fact, was widely opposed, both openly and covertly. The city's political leaders were thus promoting a policy recognized as controversial.

While Mayor Hartsfield's behavior certainly indicated that he had no appetite for community controversy, he was unable to confine his actions to those of a neutral arbiter. Business pressure brought City Hall into action on behalf of CBD renewal, and Hartsfield played a prominent role in managing the ensuing conflict. Mayor Allen's conduct as a promoter of CBD renewal was much less cautious. He preferred to move ahead forcefully, taking an occasional step backward only in order to recoup political strength for another forward move. Under both mayors, CBD renewal was treated as a first priority policy objective, and therefore one that had to be pursued even in the face of intense opposition.

The second major source of controversy was the failure of city officials to heed the warnings about discontent over neighborhood and housing conditions. Some overt conflict thus occurred because the direction of renewal policy was not altered to accommodate demands for neighborhood improvements and expansion of the housing supply. Even when protests and other forms of overt conflict brought about responses from political leaders, the new policy direction was not sustained.

Overall, it is difficult to see how overt conflict served as an indicator of group influence. In Atlanta's urban renewal program, open controversy offered only the signs of pluralism: that is, no group consistently prevailed under these conditions. However, when the pattern of demand conversion is examined, a preponderant business influence is visible. Overt conflict appears in this light to be neither a test of influence nor a guide to policy direction, but a phenomenon that occurs along the outer edge of a policy thrust. Overt conflict may therefore provide a number of friction points and even affect the speed with which a policy objective is reached, but the direction of the policy thrust comes from other sources. The pattern of demand conversion indicates a need to look further at the policy process and the distribution of political resources to determine how it is possible for bias to arise in a system that has free and competitive elections.

"Slack in the System" Reconsidered

In Atlanta, protests and implied threats of electoral sanctions were means by which pressures from a variety of groups were brought to bear on official decision makers. However, pressures exerted by means of protests or elections tend to be direct and simple. While such external pressures are fully capable of determining the outcome of any specific issue, they appear to be ill suited to controlling a policy direction. Influence over policy seems most effectively exercised by groups who have close and intimate access to official decision makers and who are capable of maintaining a steady and undiverted pressure on behalf of their interests. The Atlanta urban renewal experience suggests further that political advantages and disadvantages were not distributed in that community in such a manner as to promote mutual accommodations among equally affected groups.

Because policy is a complex phenomenon more easily shaped by internal than external influence, a dispersion of political resources does not necessarily lead to the exercise of power in a pluralistic fashion. In the first place, the electoral process may fall far short of providing full accountability to various constituency groups. In Atlanta, electoral politics was more or less monopolized by the conflict between "progressive" forces and the defenders of traditional modes of political, social, and economic life.[16] The city's nonpartisan, at-large elections have not been contests in which the interests of neighborhood and low-income groups *as proponents of an improved quality of residential life* enjoyed much prominence. To the extent that urban renewal was ever an open campaign issue, it was in bond elections as part of the "progressive" versus "stand-pat" conflict. Tension between the champions of economic growth and the proponents of improved housing and neighborhood conditions was real enough, but the overt issues were aired mainly by protests. Indeed, protest came about in part because elected officials were essentially unreceptive to demands from neighborhood and civil rights groups.

As structured contests for public office, elections are akin to the policymaking process. That is, they are more easily penetrated on single issues than on overall direction. The impact of constituent discontent may, therefore, be temporary. As soon as a controversial decision loses salience, electoral competition may revert to an earlier pattern of cleavage. For example, during the 1961 campaign in Atlanta, the Egleston rezoning controversy did become an issue on which the incumbent vice-mayor was defeated for reelection, but the 1961 election left previous coalitions and lines of cleavage intact. The influence of blacks on housing and redevelopment policy was not measurably increased by their show of electoral strength.

The use of political resources in the conduct of protest activities may also fail to have any permanent impact. A stable organization does not come about simply because a group is dissatisfied. The U-Rescue example in Atlanta shows that neighborhood groups can form associations that are highly effective in the short run. However, U-Rescue also shows that popular dissatisfaction, especially in a neighborhood both diverse and nonaffluent, is a weak foundation on which to build an enduring organization. Neighborhood organizations, *as organizations*, have few resources for assuring their survival. Unlike institutions such as Georgia Baptist Hospital, they have no paid staff, no way of financing a planning and development operation, and no means for maintaining public relations activities. Neighborhood organizations have to depend on the avocational interests of individuals whose availability is subject to many unforeseen and uncontrollable circumstances. U-Rescue, for example, was deprived of its two most dynamic leaders by the promotion of one and the accidental death of the second. Unlike bureaucratic organizations, neighborhood groups have no systematic method of recruitment and no career ladders. Leadership succession is therefore a highly uncertain matter. In view of the complex and difficult-to-influence character of policy, fluctuations in the availability of effective leadership seem only to add to a sense of futility among economically and socially disadvantaged groups. They are easily discouraged. Except for a few individuals of extraordinary experience, poor and working-class people are understandably bewildered by the complicated nature of an intergovernmental program like urban renewal.[17] A period of intense activity might, then, be followed by inactivity—not because the group is satisfied and not because the group is reassured but simply because the group has spent its resources and feels that it has failed.

If the argument presented here has validity, then the basic premises of the pluralist theory of community power and policy formation must be revised. Electoral competition is not a guarantee of official responsiveness to constituency groups on policy matters. Political resources are not widely dispersed in combinations that enable groups to influence the policymaking process. While "slack" resources (such as time, energy, and initiative) can easily be brought to bear on particular decisions, most outbursts of political activity can be met with temporary concessions, diverted, or waited out. Protests by previously inactive groups are likely to be quieted, not by substantial accommodations to their interests, but by a growing sense of futility. As one of the U-Rescue leaders observed, in reflecting on his group's experience, "You can't fight City Hall and money."[18]

Because the predispositions and orientations of officials on policy matters are not readily changed by means of the electoral process, the notion of dispersed political resources and the concept of "slack in the system" need to be reconsidered. Electoral competition supposedly guarantees indirect influence by constituent groups, but the Atlanta experience suggests that this indirect influence is confined to particular policy decisions with high public visibility. Much of the policy process is not highly visible, however, and different patterns of influence seem to hold for different phases of policy formation. To the extent that Atlanta provides a suitable illustration, discontented groups may have difficulty penetrating some crucial phases of the policy process. They may express objections readily; their interest, energy, and activity may affect particular decisions; but only groups who enjoy close and immediate access to official decision makers are able to alter the direction of policy.

14. CONCLUSION
A REVISIONIST VIEW OF COMMUNITY POLITICS

More than twenty years ago Floyd Hunter found that Atlanta business-men were extraordinarily influential. The present study reaffirms that finding. We should therefore be clear about what is and is not meant by "extraordinarily influential." What it means is that power is less widely dispersed than one would expect on the basis of the tenets of pluralism. What it does *not* mean is that the business community exercises mono-lithic control. Neither the present study nor Hunter's study has argued that Atlanta was governed by a ruling class. Atlanta politics, at least as it has impinged on the urban renewal program, has not been an arena in which superiors ruled subordinates. Instead, it has been an arena in which bargaining, compromise, and coalition building were much in evidence; but they were in evidence against a background of system bias and of significant imbalances in the distribution of political resources.

The concern in the present study has been with group influence and public policy formation. It is therefore not a replication of Hunter's study in either method or scope of analysis even though there are some parallels between the findings here and the findings of Hunter. Specific attention has been given in the present study to the shortcomings of pluralist ideas about mutual adjustment and the "rule of minority satisfaction" as explanations for how public policy is formed. It seems that, contrary to pluralist expectations, equally affected groups are not equally accommodated by the policy decisions of public officials. Con-sequently, some new factor needs to be introduced into the pluralists' community power equation. That factor, Atlanta's urban renewal ex-perience suggests, is positional advantage and disadvantage.

The revisionist theory offered here is both an alternative to and an elaboration of pluralism. The relationship between the two theories can perhaps be clarified best by a brief comparison of the points on which the two theories differ. That comparison, in turn, provides a foundation for a new perspective on incrementalism and for some parting thoughts on political change. The research reported here is, of course, only one step in understanding the "hows, whats, and whys" of system bias. Thus this concluding chapter ends with some guidelines for future research.

Pluralism and Revisionism

All theories are abstractions from and therefore simplifications of re-ality. The revisionist theory offered here has not been presented as a total explanation of how urban renewal policy in Atlanta was formed, and it certainly has not been presented as a complete explanation for how policies are formed in American cities generally. Rather the argument has been that revisionist theory offers an explanation of group influence in the urban renewal program of Atlanta that is more complete than the explanation provided by pluralism. It has not been argued here that pluralism was missing from Atlanta's urban renewal program, but that pluralism was largely a phenomenon of the more visible aspects of policy formation. Influence via positional advantages, it appears, can be effective mainly to the extent that technical complexity and low public visibility reduce the scope of external constituency pressures on public officials. Another way of looking at the present findings would be to acknowledge that to the extent a policy is controlled by one or more key decisions of high salience—as, for example, in a referendum on metropolitan reorganization—then pluralism would be likely to prevail.

Perhaps another clarifying point should be made about the argument developed in the present study. Revisionist theory is intended to direct attention to the phenomenon of system bias as an end product of group influence, but it should not be assumed that the only biases are pro-business or that only business interests are capable of securing positional advantages. Nothing in revisionist theory itself precludes the possibility of a variety of biases in different policy areas in various communities. For that matter, revisionist theory does not preclude the possibility of changing patterns of bias in Atlanta—even in the urban renewal program.

Revisionism, as developed here, differs from pluralism in two important respects regarding positional advantage and system bias. First of all, in the revisionist view, a positional advantage substantial enough to enable a group to gain cumulative policy benefits at the expense of competing groups does not come about easily. Only those groups with substantial, multiple, and expendable political resources are likely to be able to devote their resources to gaining and maintaining a positional advantage. Even then, political success depends on favorable circumstances. Resources and opportunities of this kind are not widely dispersed; though, again, they are not monopolized by business interests.

Second, a positional advantage, according to revisionism, is a relatively stable political phenomenon. While political change can and does occur, activity and discontent do not necessarily bring about political change; indeed, they rarely bring about change unless accompanied by fundamental alterations in community structure and composition. Pluralist theory simply does not provide for relatively stable imbalances in political resources and influence. Biases are supposed to be crosscutting and noncumulative. Electoral accountability, according to pluralist thought, is the balance wheel by means of which dissatisfaction is attended to and flexibility is maintained.

The revisionist theory offered here thus differs substantially from pluralism, but it is not a revival of the stratificationist theories of writers such as the Lynds. Wealth is an important political resource, and the economic notables are often able to mobilize a variety of community institutions in order to further their interests. But the analysis of Atlanta's urban renewal experience did not show economic sanctions to be a substantial factor in business influence. That influence was political. It was based upon the making of alliances and the use of resources in order to gain the willing cooperation of public officials in formulating a program and managing conflict so that a desired public policy objective—the upgrading of the CBD—would be achieved. It is entirely within the range of possibility that resources other than wealth can be put together in combinations that allow groups to secure positional advantages. For instance, under favorable circumstances, an association of public employees might not only be able to exert a collective external pressure on official decision makers, but it might also facilitate the kind of political action that would yield a positional advantage to the employee group. Whether or not this has been the case in some communities is a matter for further research. The point here is that revisionist theory does not exclude such a possibility because it is not a theory that puts a single resource at the center of community influence. Rather, revisionist theory provides only that multiple resources and favorable circumstances can lead to the kind of concerted and durable action necessary to obtain and hold a positional advantage. Thus power may be unequally distributed *even among those groups who are equally interested and active* in a given policy area.

Revisionist theory resembles pluralism in that public office holding is treated as a key factor in the exercise of power, but differs from pluralism in that, according to revisionism, officeholders are considered likely to be advocates of some group interests at the expense of others. In the revisionist framework, the lack of neutrality on the part of public offiicials is possible because some phases of decision making have low visibility. "Slack" resources can be mobilized to pressure public officials, but officials are able to alter the substance and timing of proposals in such a way as to let opposition subside and build new bases of support.

According to revisionist theory, favored groups gain their objectives through the successful management of conflict and an outmaneuvering of opposing interests. Bargaining and compromise may occur, as pluralists contend, but these activities are subordinate to larger efforts to manipulate the lines of conflict and the saliency of issues in such a way as to advance the causes of favored interests. Finally, revisionist theory yields the conclusion that policy decisions are often not mutual accommodations to equally affected groups.

In the allocation of costs and benefits among various community groups, public officials can bring about significant change, but they are likely to do so step by step, in an incremental and cumulative manner (consonant with the dictates of successful conflict management) and not in a sudden or dramatic fashion. The absence of dramatic change is not to be confused with the perpetuation of the status quo, and incremental change is not necessarily without a systematic bias. Change can be gradual without being disconnected or disjointed.

Bias, Opportunity Costs, and Incrementalism

Incentives and opportunities to exert influence are complex phenomena, interrelated with one another and with the social and political structures of the community. Too often it has been assumed that discontent will lead to activity and activity to influence. However, discontent can be diverted. Further, because policymaking is itself such a complicated process, active discontent can be consumed by transitory victories. Protest activity is seldom a durable form of pressure on public officials. Policy success is not likely unless a group is able to exert a steady influence through time and over a range of decisions. To be effective, influence must extend through a variety of activities—from amorphous attempts to set priorities and build appropriate alliances to the seemingly routine and technically detailed matters involved in project execution. This is influence that is exercised more readily *through* public officials than *on* them. It is a kind of influence that is not widely distributed, and it is therefore a kind of influence that yields what has been termed here "system bias."

In an analysis of power and opportunity costs, John C. Harsanyi argued that the influence of two actors should be compared in terms of what they "can achieve at comparable costs," or alternatively "in terms of the costs they have to bear in order to achieve comparable degrees of influence."[1] The Harsanyi argument is directly applicable to an understanding of system bias. Group influence over policy is less costly to the group that holds a positional advantage than to the group that lacks such an advantage. A positional advantage provides a continuing and relatively costless influence over a range of decision-making activities. That influence may be challenged on occasion, and an expenditure of resources may be necessary to meet or circumvent the challenge. But the challenge itself is a costly exercise for some other group. Therefore, unless the other group has enormous resources, the challenge is likely to be short-lived. Even if the challenge recurs, the opposing group is unlikely to equal the advantaged group in total influence on the policy process. Immediacy of interest and intensity of preference, as ingredients in group influence over policy, are thus significantly modified by the factors of positional advantage and disadvantage. Because equally affected groups cannot exert their influence at equal costs, imbalance in the strength of political position moves policy away from the point of mutual accommodation.

Pluralists, it is argued here, misunderstand the problem of system bias because they make faulty assumptions about the visibility of public decision making and because they exaggerate the ease with which an electoral challenge can be mounted. If all phases of decision making were clearly observable and fully understandable to all groups, then public officials would be discouraged from favoring one interest over another. But complex and technically complicated policies can veil acts of favoritism. Complex and technically complicated policies also raise the costs of opposition. Information is likely to be scarce or at least difficult to obtain. Moreover, the actual effecting of a policy may be extended over such a long time period that only sustained controversy could bring a policy to public light. Effective opposition—that is, a successful effort to change a policy by means of external pressure on public officials—may therefore require a heavier expenditure of resources than most groups can afford. Important decisions may be uncontested, and a policy direction may be challenged on only a sporadic basis.

Pluralists have argued that small, cohesive groups are more likely to influence the outcomes of specific decisions than the direction of a policy. Policy direction supposedly follows lines of consent set by the preferences of large, diffuse publics, who can become active and make use of their "slack" resources if their wishes are disregarded. In direct contrast with that position, the Atlanta example suggests that, in most political circumstances, large and loosely organized groups (such as those interested in housing or neighborhood improvements) that lack a positional advantage may have little influence over policy direction because they find long-term influence to be beyond their resource capability. By contrast, the small but well-organized group that has been able to gain a positional advantage is well situated to devote its resources to the long-term influencing of a policy direction.

This is not to say that numbers or popular consent are irrelevant or that they had no impact on urban renewal decision making in Atlanta. Rather, it is to argue that "slack" resources, at least in the form of resources previously unused for political purposes, may be mobilized to influence particular decisions without necessarily having any lasting impact on policy direction. General policy direction appears to come from the workings of system bias, from the less visible and often uncontested phases of decision making. Despite occasional setbacks, an advantaged group may be able to bring about a gradual, step-by-step movement of policy in line with its interest.

If positional advantages and disadvantages are thought of as bearing importantly on the cost of exercising influence, then it might be well to reconsider the character of incremental decision making. Some writers consider incrementalism to be a type of decision making that lends itself especially well to the achievement of maximum overall agreement. They depict incremental policymaking as a process of mutual adjustment through which no group enjoys disproportionate gains or suffers disproportionate losses. According to their view, short-term and counterbalancing concessions to competing group interests produce gradual modifications in policy that supposedly favor the goals of no one segment of the community at the expense of others.[2]

Incremental policymaking does not necessarily occur in a disjointed and undirected fashion, however. Incrementalism clearly could be a part of a general pattern of policymaking in which some groups consistently gained concessions while others just as consistently failed to do so. If anything, incrementalism lends itself to the subtle workings of system bias. Incrementalism certainly should not be equated with policymaking by consensus. Renewal policy in Atlanta, for instance, unfolded step by step, but did not move in the direction of least public resistance. Incrementalism was part of a strategy for the containment and management of conflict, not part of a strategy of conflict avoidance. Or, viewed in another way, incrementalism extended policymaking over a time period long enough to exhaust the "slack," but thin, resources of dissatisfied groups. Especially when policy is made incrementally, it seems that the prizes in politics go, not to the active and interested, but to those groups with durable resources and positional advantages.

Disjointed incrementalism assumes that public officials are motivated to search for compromises and make mutually satisfying adjustments in policy. But, if public officials are not consistently inclined to play a broker or "reactive" role, if competing interests are not equally represented among the major makers of official decisions, or if neglected interests lack the capacity to exert a sustained pressure, then incrementalism is not likely to be disjointed. Instead, it may serve to make system bias less visible at any given time, and it may also serve as a way in which groups lacking a durable political base can be outmaneuvered. Incremental decision making thus need not move in a direction of popular consent. It need not be disjointed, and a policy may evolve incrementally but not come about through a series of disconnected decisions.

Pluralist writers have assumed that, if some significant interest is neglected, complaints on behalf of the neglected interest will build in intensity until the neglect is remedied. But remedying neglect is a lengthy process, and, for those who hold no positional advantage, it is a costly exercise. Acquiescence to a pattern of biased incrementalism may indicate, not that a group is satisfied or indifferent, but that the costs of changing a policy direction are more than the group can afford. "Slack" resources are of limited importance if they do not exist in amounts sufficient for the altering of a cumulative, long-term policy bias.

Some Closing Thoughts on Political Change

Pluralists regard power relationships as too pliant to be described as structured. The argument developed here has been that power relationships are stably (but not inalterably) structured into positional advantages and disadvantages, and that "slack" resources are relatively ineffective as a means for changing a system bias. Both the pluralist argument and revisionist argument presented here are based upon inference from selected portions of the urban political experience, and therefore neither argument can be offered as the final and authoritative word on power and change. But a case can be made for the view that pluralist conclusions are drawn from what were quite exceptional circumstances, circumstances in which fundamental changes in the social order were occurring.

Dahl's New Haven analysis draws heavily on two political developments: (1) the democratization in traditional politics that took place when the ex-plebes replaced the economic notables in public office and (2) the emergence of a version of reform politics under the aegis of Mayor Lee's leadership.[3] Banfield's study of Chicago and Wildavsky's examination of Oberlin also focus on tensions between traditional political leaders and the proponents of modernization and professionalization. The pluralism reported is genuine enough. In communities like New Haven, numbers did come to counterbalance wealth and social esteem as bases of political office holding. And in a large number of communities as diverse as Chicago, Oberlin, and New Haven, the forces of tradition and governmental modernization have been locked in a somewhat inconclusive struggle. Indeed, if there has been an edge in the struggle, it has been on the side of modernization—which is to say, on the side of change. Yet the struggle has not been one-sided. In New Haven, the shift to collective benefits, expertise, and executive leadership has been constrained and halting. Lee's charter reform was defeated, and his successor in office proved to be a more traditional-minded politician than Lee was. As Dahl very accurately concluded, New Haven's executive-centered coalition represented no permanent victory over the centrifugal forces of party, district, and ethnicity.

To say, however, that reform was only a partial success in New Haven, that Mayor Daley is a broker in the contest between reform politics and machine politics, or that Councilman Bill Long of Oberlin gained a meteoric victory over his tradition-minded opponents is not to say that political change occurs easily. It is not even sufficient grounds for reviving ''slack in the system'' as a working concept. The democratization of traditional politics and later the encroachment of reform ideas and practices on traditional politics came about, it seems, not as examples of the capacity of dissatisfied constituents to work their will through the electoral process, but as instances in which a wide accumulation of changes in the social order finally was accompanied by a realignment of political forces.

The revisionist argument here is, then, that power relationships change epochally rather than episodically. Not every outburst of discontent has its impact. Power relationships alter significantly only when dissatisfaction builds up as part of an accumulating change in the basic socioeconomic structure of the community.

Most efforts to mobilize ''slack'' resources and bring about change encounter deep resistance. Incumbent political leaders and positionally advantaged groups are not apt to respond lightly to a threat to established power relationships, and they are likely to have very substantial resources that can be used to preserve these existing relationships. Incumbent leaders have acquired skills, and they have abundant opportunities to use these skills in the timing, shaping, and presenting of proposals in such a way as to build support and disaggregate opposition. It is not an easy task to coalesce dissatisfied groups into a substantial and stable opposition force when the competing group has command of the public domain. In other words, conflict is easier to manage from inside the governmental system than from the outside. It may be argued, of course, that incumbent political leaders can be defeated. However, mounting an electoral challenge is no easy matter, and it stands little chance of success unless there is a relatively cohesive and stable base of support from which to operate and unless multiple resources are at the disposal of the challenging group. These are conditions not easily met.

Electoral challenge might be unnecessary if public officeholders engaged in the unmitigated pursuit of constituent support.[4] But, in fact, officials appear to have strong predilections on matters of policy and group preference. Initially successful with one set of supporters, schooled in one body of issues, and accustomed to an established pattern of relationships, public officials do not adjust open-mindedly to new sources of discontent. Certainly they are not inclined to form quick relationships of mutual trust and confidence with any group that has provoked open controversy and engaged in public attacks on their leadership. Dissident groups are caught in a dilemma. They may find it difficult to gain attention except by disrupting or threatening to disrupt what appear to be the normal and orderly processes through which community affairs are governed. But, if dissidents engage in disruptive behavior, then they are held in low regard by established leaders.

As elected officials consider the problem of maintaining support, they are likely to avoid risks with uncertain payoffs. Thus officials are not unrestrained seekers of constituent favor. They may in reality tend to insulate themselves against the winds of change. As Walter Dean Burnham observed in another setting, elected officials "are not well-equipped, either in ideology or in incentives, to incorporate discordant demands arising from newly mobilized groups."[5] The weight of habit and prudence often comes down heavily on the side of political continuity.

System Bias and Future Research

The type of system bias described here is not simply a bias in policy direction; it is a bias in policy direction that derives from the conduct of political leaders faced with competing demands from active and interested groups at the community level. The bias found in Atlanta's urban renewal program did not come about because all actors adhered to a single ethos or because environmental pressures generated only one set of irresistible pressures. It came about because public officials played an active part in forming policy and in managing the conflicts that policy gave rise to.

If we are genuinely interested in the "black box" of politics, that is, the manner in which competing demands are converted into public policies, then we have to give proper attention to the role that public officials play in managing conflict. The Atlanta experience suggests that conflict is not something that controls and directs public officials, but something they attempt to mold and manage. Conflict does not chart the path that policy will follow. For the most part, conflict appears to be the byplay of policy formation. As indicators of influence, the outcomes of particular controversies are thus less important than the efforts made to contain and direct controversy. System bias comes about through the concrete actions that officials take to build coalitions, orchestrate proposals, and isolate opposition forces in order to move a policy forward in the face of resistance.

The analysis of Atlanta's urban renewal experience has been concerned mainly with how public officials and competing interest groups behave under conditions of system bias. The presentation has been made with the belief that political structures, group influence, and conflict management are important aspects of the total process of policy formation. It is worthwhile, as pluralists have long recognized, to study the observable behavior of public officials as they participate in the making of public policy. If Atlanta's urban renewal experience is a useful guide, the preferences and predispositions of these officials are also a vital piece in the community power puzzle. Indeed, the preferences and predispositions of officials are the connection through which community characteristics and group influence are linked to policy selection.

The relationships[6] suggested by the present study can be visualized as follows:

Figure 2

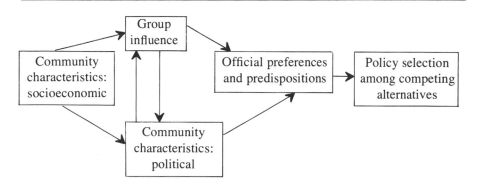

The argument developed here has been that the preferences and predispositions of public officials are the outward manifestation of an underlying set of system characteristics. Bias develops because groups exert influence to establish and maintain relationships that give rise to positional advantages (favorable preferences and predispositions among public officials, who are able to choose a policy direction and manage conflict). Group influence both shapes and is shaped by the political structures and practices of a community. In Atlanta, for example, it appears that business influence helped bring about a reformed and centralized style of politics, and the city's reformed and centralized politics served to maximize business influence and to maintain business unity.

Presumably, group influence and community political characteristics[7] are themselves factors that are related in some patterned way to the socioeconomic characteristics of communities. As those characteristics change, group influence and policy direction may change. But such change is long term, and not an outgrowth of constituency discontent. While the electoral process is not a meaningless exercise, it is also not a guarantor that influence will be widely dispersed. Though no political advantage can be made permanent, power does beget power even in the presence of free and open elections. As a consequence, system bias is not easily altered.

APPENDIXES

NOTES

BIBLIOGRAPHY

INDEX

The Articulation and Specification of
Redevelopment and Relocation Demands

Policy Interest	Substantive Interest Articulated	Actors Who Articulated the Interest and/or Demands in Support of It	Number of Specific Demands in Support of the Policy Interest
CBD renewal: redevelopment	CBD expansion, development of new commercial and civic facilities and luxury apts. in and around CBD, and enhancement of CBD and vicinity through expansion of university and hospital institutions	Business associations and individual businessmen, major newspapers, university and hospital officials, Mayor Ivan Allen, chairman of Citizens Advisory Committee for Urban Renewal (CACUR), and planning officials	18
Neighborhood and residential renewal: neighborhood improvement	Prevention of neighborhood deterioration and upgrading of neighborhood conditions through systematic code enforcement, provision of new community facilities, housing rehabilitation, and replacement of dilapidated housing with new housing	Black and white neighborhood organizations and individuals, neighborhood newspapers, black newspapers, black and white religious organizations, black business and civic organizations, civil rights organizations, Atlanta University social work professors, planning and social service agency officials, CACUR, citizens' committee appointed by county Department of Family and Children's Services, news media, white alderman from East Atlanta, Mayor Ivan Allen	25
Neighborhood and residential renewal: increased supply of low- and moderate-income housing	Use urban renewal and related resources to upgrade and increase supply of standard low- and moderate-income housing	Black neighborhood organizations and individuals, civil rights and black civic, business, and religious organizations, professional organizations, the news media, CACUR, Model Neighborhood Board, Housing Resources Committee, officials in planning and	17

Appendix A—*Continued*

Policy Interest	Substantive Interest Articulated	Actors Who Articulated the Interest and/or Demands in Support of It	Number of Specific Demands in Support of the Policy Interest
		social service agencies, chairman of aldermanic urban renewal committee, federal officials, and Mayor Ivan Allen	
CBD renewal: relocation through selective decentralization	Placement of relocation facilities in a pattern of selective decentralization, that is, away from the CBD but not in Atlanta's affluent Northside	Business associations and individual businessmen, Georgia Baptist Hospital officials, Mayor Hartsfield, the chairman of CACUR, and Housing Authority officials	13
Neighborhood and residential renewal centralized relocation	Provide residential opportunities for low-income blacks close to the CBD with its employment opportunities and other conveniences, and prevent neighborhood disruption for renewal-area residents and institutions	Black and white neighborhood organizations and individuals, black newspapers, black business, political, religious, and civic organizations, city and federal administrative officials, a black alderman, and the chairman of the aldermanic Zoning Committee	15
Neighborhood and residential renewal: relocation through city-wide dispersion	Disperse relocation housing throughout the city, including in particular affluent white areas	Civil rights organizations, black real estate men, black and white neighborhood organizations, chairman of the aldermanic Zoning Committee, CACUR, Housing Resources Committee, planning officials, church-sponsored nonprofit corporation, Metropolitan Atlanta Conference on Equal Opportunity, Georgia State Advisory Committee to U.S. Civil Rights Commission, Sam Massell, as mayoral candidate	7

For all conversion tables in Appendix B, P indicates demands passed through a given stage essentially intact; M indicates demands advanced through a given stage in modified form, with the modification representing more than a token effort on behalf of the original demand; and F indicates demands failed to advance through a given stage even in modified form. Superscript 1 indicates overt conflict present, with an attempt to move forward a demand that was stalled by official inaction; superscript 2 indicates overt conflict present, with an attempt to defeat a proposal that was receiving official consideration; superscript 3 indicates demands conceived as compromises between centralization and decentralization policies and supported by proponents of both policies.

1. The Conversion of CBD Renewal Demands: Redevelopment

Specific Policy Demands	Brought Up for Formal Consideration (Mobilization)	Official Decision Making and Disposition	Imple- mentation
Originating in the Hartsfield Mayoralty			
1. Redevelop Hemphill Avenue	P	F²	
2. Redevelop McDaniel Street	P	F²	
3. Redevelop inner portion of Butler Street for commercial purposes	P¹	P²	P²
4. Redevelop eastern sector of Rawson-Washington project with apartments	P¹	P²	F
5. Provide bond funds for local share of Butler Street and Rawson-Washington projects	P	P	P
6. Designate Buttermilk Bottom for future renewal on high-priority basis	P	P	P
7. Georgia State expansion	P	P	P
8. Redevelop CBD block	F		
9. Redevelop Transportation Plaza	F		
Originating in the Allen Mayoralty			
10. Georgia Tech expansion	P	P²	P
11. Amend Rawson-Washington for stadium reuse	P	P	P
12. Provide bond funds for civic center and urban renewal	P	F²	
13. Provide trimmed bond funds for civic center and urban renewal	P	P²	P
14. Locate civic center in Buttermilk Bottom	P	P	P²

1. The Conversion of CBD Renewal Demands: Redevelopment—*Continued*

Specific Policy Demands	Brought Up for Formal Consideration (Mobilization)	Official Decision Making and Disposition	Imple-mentation
15. Locate Post Office facility on North Avenue	P	F^2	
16. Georgia Baptist Hospital expansion	P	M^2	M^2
17. Georgia Tech no. 2 expansion	P	P	P
18. Further Georgia State expansion	P	F	

2. The Conversion of Demands for Neighborhood Improvement

Specific Policy Demands	Brought Up for Formal Consideration (Mobilization)	Official Decision Making and Disposition	Imple-mentation
Originating in the Hartsfield Mayoralty			
1. Renew Buttermilk Bottom and Vine City to rehouse residents and upgrade surrounding neighborhoods	F^1		
2. Build 500 public-housing units in Buttermilk Bottom	F		
3. Neighborhood conservation for Mechanicsville	F		
4. Neighborhood conservation for Boulevard/Parkway area	F		
5. Rehabilitation in University Center project	P	P	F
6. Rehabilitation in Auburn Avenue section of Butler Street project	P	M	F
7. Designate West End for future neighborhood renewal	P	P	P
8. Renewal for Edgewood	P	F	
9. Neighborhood renewal for northwest neighborhood	F		
10. Build public housing in Poole Creek area	F		
Originating in the Allen Mayoralty			
11. Renew entire West End GNRP as one project	P	P	P^2
12. Renew twelve-acre site centered on Howard High School	P	M	M
13. Renew area in Vine City centered on new school site	F		
14. Neighborhood conservation for Grant Park	F		

2. The Conversion of Demands for Neighborhood Improvement—*Continued*

Specific Policy Demands	Brought Up for Formal Consideration (Mobilization)	Official Decision Making and Disposition	Imple- mentation
15. Renew Bedford-Pine area, to east of civic center	P	P²	M²
16. Improve physical conditions and facilities in Summerhill-Mechanicsville	P¹	P	M
17. Renewal for Vine City	P¹	P²	M²
18. Renewal for Edgewood	P¹	P	M
19. Renewal for Plunkettown	P¹	F	
20. Renewal for Lightning	P¹	F	
21. Expand Vine City NDP project to include area to north	F		
22. Provide new facilities for and improve Browntown	F¹		
23. Conservation program for Kirkwood	F		
24. Include Bass area in NDP	F		
25. Provide bond funds for community facilities and to implement CRP study	F		

3. The Conversion of Demands for an Increased Supply of Low- and Moderate-Income Housing

Specific Policy Demands	Brought Up for Formal Consideration (Mobilization)	Official Decision Making and Disposition	Imple- mentation
Originating in the Hartsfield Mayoralty			
1. Develop 5,500 units of 221 housing	P	M²	M²
2. Redevelop Thomasville at higher density with 221 housing	P	P²	P
3. Redevelop Rockdale at higher density with 221 housing	P	P	F
4. Develop 1,000 units of public housing to meet relocation needs	P	P	M²
5. Establish revolving loan fund for rehabilitation	F		
6. Convene business and civic leaders to initiate and oversee provision of additional land for housing blacks	F		
7. Establish nonprofit corporation to purchase land for housing blacks	P	F	
8. Plan and develop community facilities for new housing projects under 221(d)3 program	F		

3. The Conversion of Demands for an Increased Supply of Low- and Moderate-Income Housing—*Continued*

Specific Policy Demands	Brought Up for Formal Consideration (Mobilization)	Official Decision Making and Disposition	Imple-mentation
9. Establish revolving loan fund for rehabilitation and emergencies	F		
Originating in the Allen Mayoralty			
10. Develop 1,000 units of public housing to meet relocation needs	P	P	P^1
11. Tax abatement for owners who improve substandard properties	F		
12. Develop 1,500 units of public housing to meet relocation needs	P	P	P^2
13. Meet five-year goal of 17,000 low- and moderate-income housing units, including 8,800 public-housing units	P^1	P	M^2
14. Establish housing development corporation with city funding or establish packaging unit for non-profit housing in the Housing Authority	F		
15. Use Federally Assisted Code Enforcement Program	F		
16. Use 221(h) program for rehabilitation	M	M	F
17. Provide tax exemption for nonprofit-sponsored housing	F		

4. The Conversion of CBD Renewal Demands: Relocation through Selective Decentralization

Specific Policy Demands	Brought Up for Formal Consideration (Mobilization)	Official Decision Making and Disposition	Imple-mentation
Originating in the Hartsfield Mayoralty			
1. Build 221 housing in selected sections of the city	P	M^2	M^2
2. Redevelop Thomasville with 221 housing	P	P^2	P
3. Redevelop Rockdale with 221 housing	P	P	F
4. Build public housing in West-side Atlanta	P	P^2	P
5. Build public housing on Egleston			

4. The Conversion of CBD Renewal Demands: Relocation through Selective Decentralization—*Continued*

Specific Policy Demands	Brought Up for Formal Consideration (Mobilization)	Official Decision Making and Disposition	Imple-mentation
site as alternative to Buttermilk Bottom site[3]	M	F[2]	
6. Convene business and civic leaders to initiate and oversee provision of land for housing blacks in outlying areas	F		
7. Establish nonprofit corporation to purchase outlying land sites for housing blacks	P	F	
8. Build public housing planned for Egleston on outlying site and/or distribute among existing projects	P	P[2]	P
Originating in the Allen Mayoralty			
9. Locate public housing in the west sector of Rawson-Washington rather than in Buttermilk Bottom or in the area south of the CBD[3]	M	M	M
10. Relocate C. W. Hill Elementary School outside Buttermilk Bottom	P	P[2]	P
11. Suspend Bedford-Pine redevelopment until residents could be relocated in an outlying area	P	F[2]	
12. Build public housing in outlying areas of Westside, Southside, and East Atlanta	P	M[2]	M[2]
13. Build public housing in suburbs	P	F[2]	

5. The Conversion of Demands for Centralized Relocation

Specific Policy Demands	Brought Up for Formal Consideration (Mobilization)	Official Decision Making and Disposition	Imple-mentation
Originating in the Hartsfield Mayoralty			
1. Redevelop Butler Street, Rawson-Washington, and University Center projects with low- and moderate-income housing	F[1]		
2. Build public housing in Buttermilk Bottom	F		
3. Build public housing on Egleston site as alternative to outlying site[3]	M	F[2]	

5. The Conversion of Demands for Centralized Relocation—*Continued*

Specific Policy Demands	Brought Up for Formal Consideration (Mobilization)	Official Decision Making and Disposition	Imple-mentation
4. As partial substitute for Egleston site build public housing for elderly in outer section of Butler Street	P	P	P
5. Build 221(d)3 housing in outer section of Butler Street project	P	P	P
6. Provide public housing in Transportation Plaza	F		
Originating in the Allen Mayoralty			
7. Build public housing south of CBD or delay Buttermilk Bottom redevelopment	F		
8. Provide public housing in expanded Howard High School project	F		
9. Build public housing in the west sector of Rawson-Washington[3]	M	M	M[1]
10. Keep C. W. Hill Elementary School in Buttermilk Bottom area	P	M[2]	M[1]
11. Build replacement units for Bedford-Pine in number and price to rehouse residents	P[1]	P[2]	M[1]
12. Build replacement units for the Model Neighborhood area, Vine City, and Edgewood in number and price to rehouse residents	P[1]	P	F
13. Improve housing and other facilities in Lightning until permanent housing is built in Lightning or other close-in areas	F		
14. Keep Little Friendship Baptist Church in Bedford-Pine project	F		
15. Redevelop Vernon Place/Fort Street area to rehouse residents	F[1]		

6. The Conversion of Demands for Relocation through City-wide Dispersion

Specific Policy Demands	Brought Up for Formal Consideration (Mobilization)	Official Decision Making and Disposition	Imple-mentation
Originating in the Hartsfield Mayoralty			
1. Build 221 housing in Southwest Atlanta	F		

Specific Policy Demands	Brought Up for Formal Consideration (Mobilization)	Official Decision Making and Disposition	Imple-mentation
2. Designate a Southwest Atlanta site for public housing	F		
3. Designate a Northside Atlanta site for public housing	F		
4. Distribute 221 housing equally among the city's eight wards	F[1]		
Originating in the Allen Mayoralty			
5. Build public housing in Northside Atlanta, on the Lenox site in particular	F		
6. Locate no additional public housing in Westside Atlanta until a substantial number of units are developed in and distributed among other areas of the city	M[1]	M[2]	M
7. Package rezoning	P	F	

6. The Conversion of Demands for Relocation through City-wide Dispersion—*Continued*

Chapter 1

1. Most of the displacement and relocation occurred during the ten-year period from 1956 to 1966. Nearly 67,000 persons were displaced by some form of governmental activity during this time period: an estimated 24,202 for expressway construction and 17,064 by urban renewal. Details are given in the Community Renewal Program study by Eric Hill Associates, "City of Atlanta, Georgia, Report on the Relocation of Individuals, Families and Businesses: Atlanta Community Improvement Program" (September 1966).

2. Atlanta was one of six cities studied by the Commission on the Cities in the '70's. In its report, the commission found that the residents of poor neighborhoods were not only pessimistic about, but openly hostile to, public institutions and programs (Commission on the Cities in the '70's, "The State of the Cities" [Washington, D.C.: National Urban Coalition, 1971], p. 8).

3. See, for example, Roger Montgomery, "Notes on Instant Urban Renewal," *Transaction* 9 (September 1967): 9–12.

4. See, for example, Peter Marris, "A Report on Urban Renewal in the United States," in *The Environment of the Metropolis*, ed. Leonard J. Duhl (New York: Basic Books, 1963), pp. 113–34.

5. The New Haven studies of community power seem to have been especially concerned with Mayor Lee's leadership skills. See Robert A. Dahl, *Who Governs?* (New Haven: Yale University Press, 1961), p. 6 and passim; and Raymond E. Wolfinger, "Nondecisions and the Study of Local Politics," *American Political Science Review* 65 (December 1971): 1065–67.

6. See, especially, Harold Kaplan, *Urban Renewal Politics* (New York: Columbia University Press, 1963); and Jeanne R. Lowe, *Cities in a Race with Time* (New York: Random House, 1967), pp. 45–109.

7. Dahl, *Who Governs?*, p. 84; and William R. Keech, *The Impact of Negro Voting* (Chicago: Rand McNally & Co., 1968), pp. 99–103.

8. See, for example, the discussion of "outlooks" in *International Encyclopedia of the Social Sciences*, 2d ed., s.v. "Ideology," by Edward Shils.

9. See Richard E. Dawson and James A. Robinson, "Inter-Party Competition, Economic Variables, and Welfare Policies in the American States," *Journal of Politics* 25 (May 1963): 265–89; Thomas R. Dye, *Politics, Economics and the Public* (Chicago: Rand McNally & Co., 1966); Brett W. Hawkins, *Politics and Urban Policies* (Indianapolis: Bobbs-Merrill Co., 1971); Chester B. Rogers, "Environment, System and Output: The Consideration of a Model," *Social Forces* 48 (September 1969): 72–87; and Thomas R. Dye, "Governmental Structure, Urban Environment and Educational Policy," *Midwest Journal of Political Science* 11 (August 1967): 353–80.

10. Note, however, the comment by Philip B. Coulter, "Comparative Community Politics and Public Policy," *Polity* 3 (Fall 1970): 28.

11. See the argument developed by Stuart H. Rakoff and Guenther F. Schaefer, "Politics, Policy, and Political Science: Theoretical Alternatives," *Politics and Society* 1 (November 1970): 56–58.

12. For studies conducted at the community level, see Robert L. Lineberry and Edmund P. Fowler, "Reformism and Public Policies in American Cities," *American Political Science Review* 61 (September 1967): 701–16; and James W. Clarke, "Environment, Process, and Policy: A Reconsideration," *American Political Science Review* 63 (December 1969): 1172–82.

13. Floyd Hunter, *Community Power Structure* (Chapel Hill: University of North Carolina Press, 1953).

14. Robert S. Lynd and Helen M. Lynd, *Middletown* (New York: Harcourt, Brace & Co., 1929); Robert S. Lynd and Helen M. Lynd, *Middletown in Transition* (New York: Harcourt, Brace & Co., 1937).

15. Pluralism has various meanings and many referents. The next chapter will specify what is meant by pluralism in the present study. It is used here to refer to a school of thought about community power, a school of thought marked out by the early works of

Robert Dahl, *Who Governs?*; Wallace S. Sayre and Herbert Kaufman, *Governing New York City* (New York: W. W. Norton & Co. for the Russell Sage Foundation, 1965); and Edward C. Banfield, *Political Influence* (New York: Free Press, 1961).

16. In the eyes of some, the pluralists failed to differentiate sufficiently between writers such as C. Wright Mills and Floyd Hunter, and, as a result, attacked a straw man. Hunter, for example, found "pyramids of power" rather than a single hierarchy, found not a ruling class but a central core of leadership that was unconcerned with some issues, and found instead of an unchanging cadre of commanders a structure in which leadership varied somewhat from issue to issue.

17. See, especially, Peter Bachrach and Morton S. Baratz, *Power and Poverty* (New York: Oxford University Press, 1970).

18. See, for example, Michael Lipsky, *Protest in City Politics* (Chicago: Rand McNally & Co., 1970).

19. Michael Parenti, "Power and Pluralism: A View from the Bottom," *Journal of Politics* 32 (August 1970): 501–30.

20. However, an important recent work is that of J. David Greenstone and Paul E. Peterson, *Race and Authority in Urban Politics* (New York: Russell Sage Foundation, 1973).

Chapter 2

1. Many writers are associated with the pluralist view of community power, and no attempt will be made to catalog them all here. I have associated pluralism most closely with Dahl because his treatment of community power has been the most consciously theoretical and because his work has been justifiably the most widely discussed and analyzed. In the discussion that follows, it should be understood that some elements of pluralism (that leadership tends to be specialized, for example) are assumed to be unchallenged "givens" of community politics. What is being questioned here is the open and flexible nature of local politics, which pluralist writers have insisted is prevalent among American communities.

2. Dahl, *Who Governs?*, p. 91. See also Robert A. Dahl and Charles E. Lindblom, *Politics, Economics, and Welfare* (New York: Harper & Brothers, 1953), p. 309.

3. Dahl, *Who Governs?*, p. 164.

4. Banfield, *Political Influence*, p. 290.

5. Aaron Wildavsky, *Leadership in a Small Town* (Totowa, N.J.: Bedminster Press, 1964), pp. 359–60.

6. Ibid., p. 360. It should be remembered that pluralist theory, as first developed in Robert A. Dahl's *A Preface to Democratic Theory* (Chicago: University of Chicago Press, 1956), was concerned mainly with the relationships between majority power and minority power, not with how conflict is resolved when two intense (concerned and active) minorities are involved. The later pluralist works are clear, however, on the positions that (1) influence is exercised by those who are concerned and active, and (2) American politics is largely a matter of compromise and mutual accommodation.

7. See the very enlightening analysis of Edwin Hoffman Rhyne, "Political Parties and Decision Making in Three Southern Counties," *American Political Science Review* 52 (December 1958): 1091–1107.

8. Cf. Walter Dean Burnham, *Critical Elections and the Mainsprings of American Politics* (New York: W. W. Norton & Co., 1970), p. 27.

9. See, for example, Matthew A. Crenson, *The Un-Politics of Air Pollution* (Baltimore: Johns Hopkins Press, 1971), pp. 141–47.

10. E. E. Schattschneider, *The Semi-Sovereign People* (New York: Holt, Rinehart & Winston, 1960), pp. 64–65.

11. See Nelson W. Polsby, *Community Power and Political Theory* (New Haven: Yale University Press, 1963), pp. 128–30. Policy questions vary, of course, in complexity. Those, such as fluoridation, which can be reduced to a yes or no referendum issue, are obviously more susceptible to popular control. Cf. the discussion of "fragile decisions" by Terry N. Clark, "Community Structure, Decision-Making, Budget Expenditures, and

Urban Renewal in 51 American Communities," *American Sociological Review* 33 (August 1968): 588.

12. Oliver P. Williams and Charles R. Adrian, *Four Cities* (Philadelphia: University of Pennsylvania Press, 1963), pp. 251–52.

13. See, for example, Dahl, *Who Governs?*, pp. 90–91, 305–10.

14. The quoted phrase appears in Richard M. Merelman's description of a pluralist system, "On the Neo-Elitist Critique of Community Power," *American Political Science Review* 62 (June 1968): 451.

15. The quoted phrase is from Bachrach and Baratz, *Power and Poverty*, p. 43. Wolfinger takes explicit exception to this Bachrach and Baratz view in "Nondecisions," pp. 1072–75.

16. See, for example, Dahl, *Preface to Democratic Theory*, p. 135.

17. Dahl gave some recognition to the importance of predisposition, but related it primarily to style of leadership and not to policy direction. See *Who Governs?*, p. 308. The concern in the present study is not with style of leadership, but with predilections regarding group interests and policy choices. The assumption made here is that some group and policy predilections are rewarded and reinforced, others are not.

18. Positional advantage is a concept through which the general idea of "mobilization of bias" can be made manageable for research purposes. On "mobilization of bias," see Schattschneider, *Semi-Sovereign People*, pp. 72–73; and Bachrach and Baratz, *Power and Poverty*, p. 11.

19. Cf. Polsby, *Community Power*, pp. 95–96.

20. Robert A. Dahl, "A Critique of the Ruling Elite Model," *American Political Science Review* 52 (June 1958): 467.

21. Merelman, "Neo-Elitist Critique," p. 457.

22. See, especially, Bachrach and Baratz, *Power and Poverty*, pp. 39–46; and Parenti, "Power and Pluralism," pp. 501–30.

23. The diagram presented here is an adaptation of material presented by Rakoff and Schaefer, "Politics, Policy and Political Science," pp. 61–68; and Bachrach and Baratz, *Power and Poverty*, pp. 52–63.

24. Appendix A describes the interests articulated and Appendix B contains the specific demands identified in the land use-related aspects of Atlanta's urban renewal program.

25. On the tendency of decision-making studies to overlook the importance of implementation, see James W. Fesler, "The Case Method in Political Science," in *Essays on the Case Method in Public Administration*, ed. Edwin A. Bock (New York: International Institute of Administrative Sciences, 1962), especially pp. 73–75; and Lipsky, *Protest in City Politics*, pp. 175–81, 198–202.

26. Cf. Heinz Eulau and Kenneth Pruitt, *Labyrinths of Democracy* (Indianapolis: Bobbs-Merrill Co., 1973), p. 465. Confusion has resulted from the failure of some writers to differentiate between a decision, as defined here, and an issue, which may involve a number of particular decisions. Dahl, for example, lists "redeveloping the Oak Street area" as a decision (*Who Governs?*, p. 333).

27. As used in the present study, "overt conflict" refers to situations in which community actors (1) attempted successfully or unsuccessfully to wield sanctions, (2) threatened to wield sanctions, or (3) mobilized support in a manner that constituted a show of strength and therefore an implied threat to wield sanctions.

This definition of "overt conflict" is based on the pluralist view that controversy provides the best setting for the analysis of power because the researcher needs circumstances in which one party is actively resisting another or in which two actors are deploying their resources in opposition to one another ("forceful conflict").

See Dahl, "Critique of the Ruling Elite Model," pp. 466–69; Robert A. Dahl, "The Analysis of Influence in Local Communities," in *Urban Planning and Social Policy*, ed. Bernard J. Frieden and Robert Morris (New York: Basic Books, 1968), pp. 227–28; Banfield, *Political Influence*, p. 9; Wildavsky, *Leadership in a Small Town*, p. 8; and Merelman, "Neo-Elitist Critique," pp. 453, 457.

Chapter 3

1. For an overview of recent developments in Atlanta, see Neal Peirce, *The Deep South States of America* (New York: W. W. Norton & Co., 1974), pp. 243–45, 261–87.

2. City of Atlanta, Department of Planning, Central Area Study Committee, "Central Atlanta: Opportunities and Responses," 1971.

3. The 1960 unemployment rate was only 3.6 percent and had risen only slightly to 4.0 percent by 1970.

4. The exact proportion, according to census figures, was 51 percent.

5. Diversified-Manufacturing cities are those in which employment in manufacturing is greater than it is in retail trade, but less than 50 percent of aggregate employment. For a discussion of the classification system and for city data, see International City Managers' Association, *The Municipal Year Book, 1963* (Chicago: International City Managers' Association, 1963), pp. 85–117.

6. In 1970, Atlanta was maintaining its position as a place with a sizable population that was both mobile and middle class. Median school years completed had risen to 11.5, while white-collar employment had reached the 50 percent mark. Recent migrants had increased to 19 percent.

7. Reports on housing conditions are not comparable from one census to the next. However, it might be noted that owner-occupancy had declined by 1970 to 41 percent.

8. Income figures for 1970 are not directly comparable to those for 1960. Atlanta, however, seemed to follow national trends. The proportion below the 1970 poverty level was only 14 percent.

9. Edward C. Banfield and James Q. Wilson, *City Politics* (Cambridge, Mass.: Harvard University Press, 1963).

10. But see the views expressed by Robert H. Salisbury, "Urban Politics: The New Convergence of Power," *Journal of Politics* 26 (November 1964): 775–97.

11. In the early 1950s, a major governmental reorganization took place. It was part of the "Plan of Development" discussed by Floyd Hunter, *Community Power Structure*, pp. 214–19. See also the articles by Lynwood M. Holland, "Atlanta Pioneers in Merger," *National Municipal Review* 41 (April 1952): 182–86; and M. Clyde Hughes, "Annexation and Reallocation of Functions," *Public Management* 34 (February 1952): 26–30. Governmental practices subsequent to that time are described and discussed in the Community Renewal Program study done for the city by the Public Administration Service, "Report on Administrative-Legal Studies" (Chicago: Public Administration Service, June 1967).

12. Two new aldermanic seats were added for the terms of office beginning in January 1970.

13. Banfield and Wilson, *City Politics*, pp. 35–37.

14. There are several relevant studies. See C. A. Bacote, "The Negro in Atlanta Politics," *Phylon* 16 (1955): 333–50; Jack Walker, "Negro Voting in Atlanta, 1953–1961," *Phylon* 24 (Winter 1963): 379–87; Edward C. Banfield, *Big City Politics* (New York: Random House, 1965), pp. 18–36; M. Kent Jennings, *Community Influentials* (New York: Free Press of Glencoe, 1964), pp. 130–54; M. Kent Jennings and Harmon Zeigler, "Class, Party, and Race in Four Types of Elections: The Case of Atlanta," *Journal of Politics* 28 (May 1966): 391–407; Pat Watters and Reese Cleghorn, *Climbing Jacob's Ladder* (New York: Harcourt, Brace & World, 1967), pp. 78–86; Ivan Allen, Jr., with Paul Hemphill, *Mayor: Notes on the Sixties* (New York: Simon & Schuster, 1971); Harry Holloway, *The Politics of the Southern Negro* (New York: Random House, 1969), pp. 188–228; Charles S. Rooks, *The Atlanta Election of 1969* (Atlanta: Voter Education Project, 1970); and Numan V. Bartley, *From Thurmond to Wallace* (Baltimore: Johns Hopkins Press, 1970), pp. 35–56.

15. In 1961, there was both a first primary and a run-off. The run-off was between Allen and Maddox as the highest vote-getters in the primary. Significantly, Allen, who was not the only racially moderate candidate in the first primary, sought to make the contest a showdown between himself as the coalition spokesman and Maddox as an apologist for white supremacy (Allen with Hemphill, *Mayor*, pp. 52–55).

16. The break was only temporary. Once in office, Massell worked closely with the business community, particularly in the promotion of Atlanta's mass transit system.

17. Some observers might argue that the coalition has not disappeared but has simply reemerged in altered form with middle-class blacks in a much stronger position. There are, in fact, strong indications that old modes of cooperation have retained much of their vitality in the 1970s. However, as a pattern of electoral cleavage, coalition politics has declined. On the modes of cooperation see Bill Schemmel, "Atlanta's 'Power Structure' Faces Life," *New South* 27 (Spring 1972): 62–68; and Fred Powledge, "Profiles: A New Politics in Atlanta," *New Yorker*, 31 December 1973, pp. 28–40.

18. As used here, the "business community" refers to those large and medium-sized businesses that acted as a collective force in the city's politics on the basis of interests they perceived as shared.

19. Hunter, *Community Power Structure*, p. 217. See also the testimony by C. A. Bacote in U.S. Commission on Civil Rights, *Hearings before the United States Commission on Civil Rights: Housing, Atlanta, Georgia, April 10, 1959* (Washington, D.C.: Government Printing Office, 1959), pp. 576–93 (hereafter cited as *Hearings: Atlanta*).

20. Over the twenty-year period studied, there have been from the five commissioners a total of 100 "commission years," 94 of which were served by white members and 6 by a black member. (A second black member, the minister of a large church, was appointed to the commission at the end of the twenty-year period.) Occupationally, service was divided in this way:

Occupation	"Commission Years"	Number of Individuals
Realtors	36	2
Bankers	24	5
Lawyers	20	1
Teachers and professors	14	1
Savings and loan officials	6	1

The lawyer member was affiliated with a firm that had close ties with one of the banks.

21. Business representation has predominated not only on the Housing Authority and the CACUR, but also on other boards and commissions tangentially related to renewal policy; the Community Council Board, the Planning Board, and the Recreation Authority are the most important examples.

22. Allen's own account of his recruitment for the mayoral race and the campaign he waged subsequently may be found in Allen with Hemphill, *Mayor*, pp. 31–63.

23. Ibid., p. 30.

24. It is no coincidence that, even on issues involving city programs, black state legislators, elected on a partisan ballot in single-member districts, have been more prominent defenders of neighborhood interests than have members of the Board of Aldermen. Moreover, when new directions in renewal policy were pressed forward, protests and other direct-action tactics—not the electoral process—were the means chosen.

25. See Allen with Hemphill, *Mayor*, p. 55; and Banfield, *Big City Politics*, p. 76.

26. See Schattschneider on the tendency for dominant conflicts to subordinate and even blot out lesser conflicts (*Semi-Sovereign People*, pp. 62–77). Schattschneider observes that "conflicts compete with each other" (p. 65).

27. See the general comments by Banfield and Wilson on "the trend of city politics," *City Politics*, pp. 330–31.

28. The point is not the "last hurrah" view that the New Deal eliminated the need for machine politics, but the more incisive view of William Foote Whyte about the impact of the depression and New Deal on political relationships (*Street Corner Society*, enl. ed. [Chicago: University of Chicago Press, 1955], pp. 194–252).

29. Note the comments by H. D. Price, review of *Who Governs?* in *Yale Law Journal* 71 (July 1962): 1594–96.

30. The CAIA underwent two name changes during the time period covered by the present study. The first was simply a shortening to the Central Atlanta Association; the second involved the absorption of a "satellite" organization, the Uptown Association, and

the adoption of a new name—Central Atlanta Progress, Inc. To simplify the reader's task, I have used the designation "CAIA" throughout.

31. For an explanation of status and welfare aims, see James Q. Wilson, *Negro Politics* (New York: Free Press, 1960), p. 185.

Chapter 4

1. For additional background material on race and land use in Atlanta, see Nathan Glazer and Davis McEntire, eds., *Studies in Housing and Minority Groups* (Berkeley and Los Angeles: University of California Press, 1960), pp. 14–51; and Karl E. Taeuber and Alma F. Taeuber, *Negroes in Cities* (Chicago: Aldine Publishing Co., 1965), passim.

2. Residential segregation steadily increased in Atlanta, as it did in most southern cities. See Taeuber and Taeuber, *Negroes in Cities*, p. 40.

3. Metropolitan Planning Commission, *Up Ahead* (Atlanta: Metropolitan Planning Commission, 1952), p. 60.

4. Ibid., p. 88.

5. Ibid., p. 57.

6. See the testimony in *Hearings: Atlanta*, pp. 441–88.

7. Glazer and McEntire, *Housing and Minority Groups*, p. 21.

8. There is no comprehensive and up-to-date review of the urban renewal legislation. The early legislative history is covered well by Ashley A. Foard and Holbert Fefferman, "Federal Urban Renewal Legislation," *Law and Contemporary Problems* 25 (Autumn 1960): 635–86. Also, a good concise history up to 1968 may be found in the U.S. National Commission on Urban Problems, *Building the American City* (Washington, D.C.: Government Printing Office, 1968), pp. 152–79. The symposium, "Citizen Participation in Urban Renewal," contains a good legal summary for the period ending with the 1965 Housing and Urban Development Act. The various city case studies are also well done—see *Columbia Law Review* 66 (March 1966): 485–607. Good general discussions of urban renewal include Charles Abrams, *The City Is the Frontier* (New York: Harper & Row, 1965); Scott Greer, *Urban Renewal and American Cities* (Indianapolis: Bobbs-Merrill Co., 1965); Lowe, *Cities in a Race with Time*; and Lawrence M. Friedman, *Government and Slum Housing* (Chicago: Rand McNally & Co., 1968).

9. Research consisted of open-ended interviews and an examination of documents, reports, minutes, memoranda, correspondence, newsletters, and newspaper files. Also, the files of several individuals and organizations were made available to me. Field research was conducted during a period extending from 1967 to 1970. A total of 128 persons were interviewed. The persons interviewed fell into the following categories: federal officials, 10; local officials, 47; neighborhood actors, 36; city-wide black leaders, 8; white business and professional actors, 25; and newspaper reporters, 2. Of the 128 interviewees, 59 were black and 79 were white.

10. Two of the most penetrating studies of community politics have had the advantage of including a longtime scope: Dahl's *Who Governs?* and the study by Roscoe C. Martin et al., *Decisions in Syracuse* (Bloomington: Indiana University Press, 1961).

Chapter 5

1. Harold Fleming, then director of the Southern Regional Council, quoted in Douglass Cater, "Atlanta: Smart Politics and Good Race Relations," *Reporter*, 11 July 1957, p. 18.

2. The CAIA, as explained earlier, was an organization of businesses concerned mainly with the central business district. Members included the major financial institutions, the utilities, the large department stores, the major newspaper, commercial real estate firms, and other businesses with a stake in the economic fate of the CBD. Similar organizations have been formed in other large cities. See Banfield and Wilson, *City Politics*, pp. 261–72; and Salisbury, "Urban Politics," pp. 785–86.

3. Interviews were obtained on a not-for-attribution basis. Moreover, most of the written material that was consulted is available only in Atlanta. I have, therefore, chosen not to use extensive footnoting in the presentation of the narrative account of Atlanta's urban renewal program. However, most of the material herein comes from newspapers,

government documents, and other sources that are accessible to the general public. The partial reliance on confidential materials and the absence of extensive footnotes to strictly Atlanta materials should not be taken as an indication that urban renewal has been shrouded in secrecy. The evolution of Atlanta's renewal program, on the contrary, is very much a part of the public record, and, in its main features, could be traced without difficulty by any reasonably curious and diligent person located in Atlanta.

4. *Atlanta Daily World*, 23 March 1950.

5. *CA Newsletter* (the newsletter of CAIA), 15 November 1956.

6. Contents of letter from M. B. Satterfield to Bruce Wedge approved at a meeting of the Urban Renewal Policy Committee, Minutes, 21 August 1958.

7. Ibid.

8. The bond issue is discussed by Jennings, *Community Influentials*, pp. 114–29.

9. *Atlanta Constitution*, 12 April 1958.

10. Mayor Hartsfield to Alderman Douglas, 11 June 1958.

11. *Atlanta Constitution*, 17 July 1958.

12. The matter did not become a major issue in part because it was quieted with the reassurance that the Board of Aldermen would have to approve all projects and project boundaries.

13. Housing Act of 1949, sec. 105(c), Public Law 171, 81st Cong.

14. U.S. Housing and Home Finance Agency, *Urban Renewal Handbook* (1957), chap. 10, sec. 1.

15. The formal, written statement of the Localities Committee was reprinted in *Hearings: Atlanta*, pp. 563–68.

16. *Atlanta Constitution*, 8 April 1958.

17. Ibid.

18. The city was required to have a relocation *service* for all displacees but it did not have to show that there were vacant units for displacees from programs other than urban renewal programs. The Housing Authority was thus ready at one point to drop the 221 program from its relocation plan altogether.

19. *Atlanta Constitution/Atlanta Journal* clipping file, no exact date, 1957.

20. The resulting controversy is treated in some detail by Jennings, *Community Influentials*, pp. 140–52.

21. *Atlanta Journal*, 18 December 1959.

22. *Atlanta Constitution*, 21 February 1960.

23. Ibid., 2 March 1960.

24. The successful challenger of the incumbent vice-mayor was Sam Massell, who remained in close political contact with the black community and succeeded Ivan Allen as mayor of Atlanta. Significantly, the decision by blacks to oppose the incumbent vice-mayor in the 1961 election was not based on general unhappiness with the urban renewal program, but rather on the vice-mayor's failure to go along with the coalition on the Egleston rezoning issue.

25. *Atlanta Journal*, 9 March 1960.

26. Glazer and McEntire, eds., *Housing and Minority Groups*, p. 32. See also the testimony by the president of the Atlanta Real Estate Board, Arthur Burdett, Jr., in *Hearings: Atlanta*, pp. 535–36; and Samuel L. Adams, "Blueprint for Segregation: A Survey of Atlanta Housing," *New South* 22 (Spring 1967): 73–84.

27. *Hearings: Atlanta*, p. 523.

28. Ibid., pp. 542, 547.

29. CACUR, Minutes, meeting of 5 January 1959.

30. The quoted phrase is from a resolution presented to the Urban Renewal Policy Committee, Minutes, 4 June 1959. See also the testimony by Arthur Burdett, Jr., president of the Atlanta Real Estate Board, in *Hearings: Atlanta*, p. 537.

31. See, for example, the series in the *Atlanta Journal*, 18 May–1 June 1959.

32. *Atlanta Constitution*, 17 October 1958.

33. The reader should be aware that none of the housing projects was completed quickly. Bowen Homes, the 650 units at the Field Road site, was not open for occupancy until 1964. The housing for the elderly was completed in 1965, and the Perry Homes extension was not finished until 1969.

34. CACUR, Minutes, meeting of 13 July 1961.

35. *CA Newsletter*, 3 February 1966. CAIA also argued that Georgia State expansion would upgrade surrounding areas (*CA Newsletter*, 21 April 1960; 9 February 1961; 8 March 1962; and 21 June 1962).

36. Realtors themselves did not have homogeneous interests. Officials in larger firms that handled commercial property were generally less anxious about public housing than officials in the smaller firms that handled residential property.

37. On the Census Bureau's measure of the effective rate of property taxation, Atlanta ranked 96th out of 120 cities over 100,000 in population. Even among the 32 southern cities over 100,000 Atlanta ranks below the median (18th) in the effective property tax rate. See U.S. Department of Commerce, Bureau of the Census, *Census of Governments*, 1967, vol. 2, *Taxable Property Value*, pp. 150–56, table 21.

Chapter 6

1. The Atlanta renewal experience suggests that caution is in order in analyzing communities in terms of a dominant ethos or an "ecology of issues." While the open phases of policy formation tended to be treated in a "public-regarding" manner—that is, proposals were framed and justified in terms of community-wide interests, the closed and behind-the-scenes phases of policy formation involved a number of "private-regarding" operations—that is, coalitions were built and support was mobilized by making particularistic appeals. In Atlanta, the black community especially was treated as an aggregation of particular interests whose support could be secured by special opportunities to gain recognition and advance their material well-being.

2. During the time period under consideration, the membership of the five-man Housing Authority Commission was divided occupationally as follows: one banker, two realtors, one university professor, and one lawyer (a member of a legal firm with close ties to one of the banks). Racially, the commission was all white.

3. On the Urban League, particularly, see Jennings, *Community Influentials*, pp. 111–14.

4. Jack L. Walker, "Protest and Negotiation: A Case Study of Negro Leadership in Atlanta, Georgia," *Midwest Journal of Political Science* 7 (May 1963): 99–124.

5. George Nesbitt to Sid Jagger, 22 April 1958.

6. See the account of the project in James W. English, *Handyman of the Lord* (New York: Meredith Press, 1967), pp. 110 61.

Chapter 7

1. The now-classic study of protest as a political resource for have-not groups is Lipsky's *Protest in City Politics*.

2. Wildavsky, *Leadership in a Small Town*, p. 337.

3. Cf. Fesler, "Case Method in Political Science," pp. 73–75; and Lipsky, *Protest in City Politics*, pp. 175–81.

4. The Neighborhood Development Program (NDP) has been less publicized than other Great Society programs, but NDP is particularly important here because it is a direct part of urban renewal. In brief, it is a revised version of urban renewal in which the planning process is merged with stage-by-stage execution, and in which some form of neighborhood participation is required.

5. The Demonstration Cities and Metropolitan Development Act of 1966 contained a new provision on urban renewal: "The redevelopment of the urban renewal area, unless such redevelopment is predominantly for nonresidential uses, will provide a substantial number of units of standard housing of low and moderate cost and result in marked progress in serving the poor and disadvantaged people living in slum and blighted areas" (Sec. 703(a), Public Law 89–754). The Housing and Urban Development Act of 1968 modified the provision further to require that a "majority of the housing units provided in each community's total of such approved urban renewal projects as will be redeveloped for predominantly residential uses and which receive Federal recognition after the date of enactment of the Housing and Urban Development Act of 1968 shall be standard housing units for low and moderate income families or individuals: *Provided*, That the units for

each community's total of such approved urban renewal projects which are for low-income families or individuals shall constitute at least 20 per centum of the units in such projects, except that the Secretary may waive the requirement of this proviso in any community to the extent that units for low-income families and individuals are not needed'' (Sec. 512, Public Law 90–448).

Administratively, the Department of Housing and Urban Development established new program goals and priorities. First, the department declared that it would ''give priority consideration to projects which contribute to conserving and increasing the existing housing supply for low and moderate-income families.'' The department declared further that it would ''give priority consideration to projects which attack critical slum and blighted areas—those areas of physical decay, high tensions, and great social need, and in which the locality is prepared to utilize all available resources—Federal, State, and local in improving conditions in the slum and blighted areas'' (U.S. Department of Housing and Urban Development, *Urban Renewal Handbook* [1968], chap. 1, sec. 1).

6. The quoted phrase is from remarks by the chairman of the Urban Renewal Committee of the Chamber of Commerce, CACUR, Minutes, meeting of 18 September 1962.

7. The Urban Renewal Department was a small administrative unit in City Hall. Its function was to handle portions of the relocation program and to enforce the housing code. While the department did become involved in some preliminary urban renewal planning, project planning and execution were under the jurisdiction of the Housing Authority.

8. *Atlanta Constitution*, 29 August 1962.

9. *CA Newsletter*, 13 June 1963.

10. See Banfield, *Big City Politics*, p. 32.

11. *CA Newsletter Supplement*, 22 August 1963.

12. Ibid.

13. Memorandum from Richard Forbes, 23 January 1961.

14. See note 7 above.

15. Malcolm Jones to Mayor Allen, 23 February 1962.

16. Ibid. Ordinarily, displacement of low-income blacks is thought to increase the likelihood that blacks will move into adjacent white areas, but in this instance the rationale for clearance appeared to be that the low-income population should be relocated while property values in the Uptown area were still moderately high and stable.

17. Malcolm Jones to members of the Urban Renewal Committee, 9 October 1963.

18. Malcolm Jones to Alderman Everett Millican, 17 February 1962.

19. ''Early Land Acquisition'' is a procedure whereby a site can be acquired for redevelopment before the entire project area has been officially brought into the execution phase of urban renewal.

20. Malcolm Jones to members of the Urban Renewal Committee, 9 October 1963.

21. The land for the stadium itself was already vacant, but parking facilities entailed additional clearance.

22. Because a General Neighborhood Renewal Plan is drawn up for an area that is too large or complex for a single project, execution is supposed to occur in phases.

23. The project was constructed in the western fringe of the city, quite far from the CBD; as a partial consequence, only 13 percent of the relocatees from Buttermilk Bottom accepted public housing.

24. Some observers believe that Auburn Avenue businessmen and church leaders used the PTA as a front through which to express their own opposition to extensive clearance in the area. However, no substantial evidence surfaced that would call into question the sequence of events reported above.

25. Statement presented by Jesse Hill, Jr., chairman of the All Citizens Registration Committee [of the Atlanta Negro Voters League] on behalf of the C. W. Hill PTA and citizens of the community, 8 March 1965.

26. Ibid.

27. Ibid.

28. Jesse Hill, Jr., to Bruce Wedge, regional director of Urban Renewal, 11 March 1965.

29. Ibid.

30. Ibid.

31. *Atlanta Constitution*, 7 April 1965.

32. *Atlanta Journal*, 13 April 1965.

33. Ibid.

34. Ibid.

35 *Atlanta Journal*, 1 May 1965.

36. In December 1965 black leaders threatened to reopen the whole issue if the Board of Aldermen failed to reject a construction contract not guaranteeing that the school would be ready in September 1966.

37. *Atlanta Constitution*, 6 December 1965.

38. J. D. Grier et al., "Resolution," n.d. The numbered material is summarized and paraphrased, not quoted. The resolution was made at a meeting held by the U-Rescue group in December 1965.

39. The street was widened on the Buttermilk Bottom side, as proposed.

40. Urban Renewal Policy Committee, Minutes, meeting of 4 March 1966.

41. Ibid.

42. Subsequently, at the city's initiative, the number was increased to 450.

43. Technically, part of the land request was not for Georgia Baptist, but for a hospital center of which Georgia Baptist would be only a part.

44. *Atlanta Constitution*, 11 March 1965.

Chapter 8

1. See chapter 7, note 5.

2. Community Council of the Atlanta Area, "Interim Report Number 1: Social Blight and Its Causes" (Atlanta: February 1966), p. 4.

3. Ibid.

4. *Atlanta Constitution*, 25 July–3 August 1965.

5. Ibid., 25 July 1965.

6. Ibid., 26 July 1965.

7. Ibid., 29 July 1965.

8. Ibid.

9. *Atlanta Constitution*, 28 July 1965.

10. Ibid., 29 July 1965.

11. Ibid.; see also *Atlanta Constitution*, 3 August 1965.

12. Aside from the five neighborhoods given preliminary attention, renewal activity recently undertaken at that time included (1) the beginning of the execution phase for the Georgia Tech project, (2) the final stages of planning for West End before beginning project execution, and (3) formal planning for the Bedford-Pine project.

13. *Atlanta Constitution*, 29 July 1965.

14. CACUR, Minutes, meeting of 16 September 1965.

15. CACUR, Minutes, meeting of 7 October 1965.

16. Ibid.

17. Ibid.

18. *Atlanta Constitution*, 1 February 1966.

19. *Atlanta Journal*, 1 February 1966.

20. Ibid.

21. *Atlanta Journal*, 2 February 1966.

22. *Atlanta Constitution*, 3 February 1966.

23. Ibid.

24. *Atlanta Journal*, 5 February 1966.

25. *Atlanta Constitution*, 5 February 1966.

26. Ibid.

27. *Atlanta Journal*, 4 February 1966.

28. Ibid., 26 February 1966.

29. Ibid., 18 March 1966.

30. Community Council of the Atlanta Area, "Interim Report Number 1," p. 17.

31. CACUR, Minutes, meeting of 31 March 1966.

32. *Atlanta Constitution*, 7 September 1966.

33. The quoted phrase may be found in Reese Cleghorn, "Allen of Atlanta Collides with Black Power and Racism," *New York Times Magazine*, 16 October 1966, p. 137.

34. Council on Human Relations of Greater Atlanta, statement, n.d. [circa September 1966]. The council also prepared a statement for the members of the board of the Atlanta Housing Authority, 20 September 1966.

35. This "finding" need not have awaited civil disorder, however. Block meetings and other samplings of neighborhood sentiment at the time that the Community Action Program was being planned had already pinpointed grievances. Written evidence of discontent was thus fully available in the files of the Community Council (the city's quasi-public social planning agency) well before any outbreak of civil disorder occurred.

36. The relocation report showed that nearly 21,000 families were displaced by governmental action in the period from January 1956 to July 1966. The report also indicated that public housing authorized in 1958 did not become available until 1964 and that the supply of private housing was being reduced during this period of extensive displacement (Eric Hill Associates, "Report on Relocation," p. 104). The relocation report presented the following figures:

Estimates of Gross Rental Ranges

	Under $55 Per Month		$55 to $79 Per Month	
	1959	1965	1959	1965
Number of rental units	26,139	11,567	29,555	25,617

37. Ibid., p. xi.

38. Ibid.

39. The quotations are from a discussion of the conference in: City of Atlanta, City Planning Department and the Housing Resources Committee, "A Review of Atlanta's Housing Program: Its Problems and Prospects" (Atlanta: October 1967), p. 5.

Chapter 9

1. Reprinted in Allen with Hemphill, *Mayor*, p. 236.

2. *Atlanta Journal*, 3 February 1967.

3. Ibid., 2 February 1967.

4. *Atlanta Constitution*, 29 March 1967.

5. An account of the planning stage is contained in the report to the U.S. Department of Housing and Urban Development, *The Model Cities Program*, by Marshall Kaplan, Sheldon P. Gans, and Howard M. Kahn (Washington, D.C.: Government Printing Office, 1969), pp. 10–34.

6. City officials stated publicly that this policy applied to Vine City (*Atlanta Journal*, 30 January 1967).

7. The specific charge to the steering committee was "to meet with all the various groups within the Nash-Bans area and develop a citizen participation organization that will be acceptable to all residents in the area" (Helen Meyers to Collier Gladin, 5 May 1967). See also HRC, Minutes, meeting of 5 May 1967.

8. *Atlanta Journal*, 7 June 1967.

9. Ibid.

10. Dan Sweat to Collier Gladin, 9 June 1967.

11. The threat of demonstrations came in a letter from Jesse O. Thomas to Mayor Ivan Allen, Jr., 3 March 1968.

12. The specific statement about "no authority" was made in a letter from city planner Collier Gladin to Jesse O. Thomas, 13 November 1967.

13. See the discussion in chapter 7 above.

14. Mayor Allen to John Brown et al., 26 March 1969.

15. The school site was included in the NDP in order to maximize noncash credits and lower the city's costs of participating in the urban renewal program. Noncash credits are a way in which localities can use their expenditures on project area facilities for matching purposes to cover their one-third share of net renewal costs.

16. In fact, the planning and redevelopment emphasis in City Hall was shifting from neighborhoods back to the CBD. Recent planning, including for some types of redevelopment, has been tied in with the mass transit system and with transportation problems generally (City of Atlanta, Department of Planning, Central Area Study Committee, "Central Atlanta," a study funded by the U.S. Department of Transportation).

17. The city had built a new school in the Edgewood area (which provided the noncash credits), and thus had to make no additional expenditures to undertake renewal activity for the area.

18. City of Atlanta, "Application to the Department of Housing and Urban Development for a Grant to Plan a Comprehensive City Demonstration Program," 10 March 1967, pp. 33–34.

19. "The Physical Environment," p. 7. These remarks were made at the Atlanta Goals Conference, session 2, in 1966.

20. Ibid., pp. 10–11. Summerhill is one of the communities included in the Model Neighborhood area. Kirkwood is a neighborhood in East Atlanta that underwent racial transition in the 1960s. See Map. 8.1.

21. Ibid., p. 2. Emphasis in original.

22. Intergovernmental difficulties in the development of low- and moderate-income housing in Atlanta are discussed in U.S. Department of Housing and Urban Development, *Achieving More Effective Delivery of HUD Local Assistance Programs*, vol. 2, *Six Field Analyses*, by National Academy of Public Administration (Springfield, Va.: Clearinghouse for Scientific and Technical Information [PB 187–786], 1969), appendix A.

23. Urban Renewal Policy Committee, Minutes, meeting of 12 May 1967.

24. This was the point on which the mayor proved most responsive, subsequently selecting a black director and two blacks to fill the two appointed positions on the Model Cities Executive Board.

25. Formal complaint against the City of Atlanta and the Atlanta Housing Authority for discriminatory practices, violation of Title VI of the 1964 Civil Rights Law, and violation of announced policies of the U.S. Department of Housing and Urban Development, filed by the NAACP, Atlanta branch, 22 May 1967.

26. City of Atlanta, City Planning Department, "Northwest-Browntown Area: A Neighborhood Study" (Atlanta: October 1967), p. 26.

27. Resolution adopted on 10 April 1968.

28. Resolution adopted on 7 June 1968.

29. All quoted phrases are from ibid., which was on file with HRC.

30. HRC, Minutes, meeting of 12 December 1968.

31. Ibid., meeting of 8 May 1969.

32. Mayor Allen to Cecil Alexander, 3 April 1969. See also HRC, Minutes, meeting of 8 May 1969.

33. City of Atlanta, City Planning Department and Housing Resources Committee, "Atlanta's Housing Program," p. 76.

34. It should be noted that suburban opposition had stalled all efforts to build public housing outside of the city in 1970 when the present narrative closes. However, a subsequent federal court order opened up housing sites in *both* the suburbs and Northside Atlanta.

35. The Community Relations Commission, for example, had only the power to hold hearings. One writer assessed the commission and related city activities in this way: "The Atlanta programs, with their emphasis on handling complaints from ghetto neighborhoods would seem to be more palliative than corrective" (James A. Bayton, *Tension in the Cities* [Philadelphia: Chilton Book Co., 1969], p. 194).

Chapter 10

1. Georgia State Advisory Committee to the United States Commission on Civil

Rights, *Toward Equal Opportunity in Housing in Atlanta, Georgia* (n.p.: Georgia State Advisory Committee, 1968), p. 6.

2. *Atlanta Constitution*, 27 November 1968.

3. Ibid. See also Urban Renewal Policy Committee, Minutes, meeting of 26 November 1968.

4. Mildred West et al. vs. Housing Authority of the City of Atlanta et al., in the U.S. District Court for the Northern District of Georgia, Atlanta Division, Civil Action no. 13570, Complaint for Injunctive and Declaratory Relief, filed by Robert B. Newman, 10 March 1970, p. 5.

5. Ibid., p. 9. The quoted phrase is from the city Workable Program submission.

6. The meeting is reported in *Atlanta Constitution*, 18 March 1970.

7. "List of Demands for Immediate Action by the Housing Authority." The demands were submitted at the meeting of 17 March 1970.

8. Ibid.

9. Ibid.

10. The number of temporary units remained at 60 until a new wave of large-scale clearance was begun in the 1970s after the close of the present narrative. By the summer of 1973, when the city had reached the point of disposing of a 78-acre tract for residential reuse, the Planning and Development Committee recommended that rebuilding be oriented toward middle-income (that is, "non-subsidized") housing. On an adjacent tract at that time, the Housing Authority had newly completed or had in the planning stage 283 public housing units for the elderly and 168 units for families. Thus public housing was being built in the numbers originally agreed on, although not on the schedule or with the relocation arrangements agreed on; but the plans to build 221(d)3 housing were being scotched in favor of a new policy of maximizing "housing possibilities for all income levels" (*Atlanta Constitution*, 28 June 1973).

11. See Mancur Olson, Jr., *The Logic of Collective Action* (1965; reprint ed., New York: Schocken Books, 1968), pp. 125–67. On the problems of neighborhood organization, see the excellent study by John H. Mollenkopf, "On the Causes and Consequences of Neighborhood Political Mobilization" (Paper presented at the Annual Meeting of the American Political Science Association, New Orleans, La., 4–8 September 1973).

12. The CAIA was the principal backer of the idea put forth in 1973 that redevelopment in the area should include middle-income housing.

Chapter 11

1. Frances F. Piven and Richard A. Cloward, *Regulating the Poor* (New York: Random House, Pantheon Books, 1971), p. 338.

2. See, for example, Lipsky, *Protest in City Politics*.

3. See the observations in the report of the Commission on the Cities in the '70's, "The State of the Cities," pp. 8–9.

4. This writer would argue that the Atlanta business community was not an innately cohesive group (there were unmistakable signs of interest diversity); its cohesion came from a favorable set of circumstances and from the conscious efforts of city officials to promote unity and to counter divisive tendencies. Almost certainly, there are other circumstances in other cities that make business groups less cohesive and therefore less influential.

5. One of the questions for the future, of course, is whether or not the presence of a black majority and the election of black officials will alter the prevailing system bias. Very likely they will. Significantly, Mayor Jackson's first several months in office have occasioned charges that he is variously politicizing city government, engaging in a "power grab," conducting an antiwhite administration, "grandstanding," and trying to be mayor to only "a segment of Atlanta." The attack on Jackson through the news media comes from the stance that the city was in the past led by persons who were civic-minded and politically neutral, but that under Jackson self-serving and factional considerations have become dominant. For the flavor of the opposition to Jackson see the *Atlanta Constitution*, 10 September 1974; ibid., 21 September 1974; *Atlanta Journal*, 27 December 1974; and the series, "A City in Crisis," *Atlanta Constitution*, 23–30 March 1975.

From the perspective developed here, Mayor Jackson is in the process of modifying a prevailing bias, and in the process he has disturbed what had been some settled relationships. Efforts such as his to bring about change are more recognizably political than are efforts to maintain the status quo. Yet, even if change is in the offing for Atlanta, we do not know how much change will occur or what form it will take. Political relationships based on a black majority might alter the old bias without necessarily elevating the fortunes of neighborhood and low-income groups.

6. Dahl, *Who Governs?*, p. 309.

7. Ibid., p. 310.

8. Wildavsky, *Leadership in a Small Town*, p. 359.

9. Polsby, *Community Power*, pp. 118, 132. For a full discussion of the concept of disjointed incrementalism, see David Braybrook and Charles E. Lindblom, *A Strategy of Decision* (New York: Free Press of Glencoe, 1963), pp. 81–131. But see also the comments on nondecision making by Crenson, *Un-Politics of Air Pollution*, pp. 178–79.

10. Dahl, *Who Governs?*, p. 204.

11. See Banfield, *Political Influence*, pp. 250, 270–76; and Dahl, *Who Governs?*, pp. 75, 93–94, 310.

Chapter 12

1. The general argument is that of Murray Edelman, *The Symbolic Uses of Politics* (Urbana: University of Illinois Press, 1964).

2. Sayre and Kaufman, *Governing New York City*, p. 716.

3. Polsby, *Community Power*, p. 135.

4. Dahl, *Who Governs?*, p. 201.

5. Banfield, *Political Influence*, p. 288.

6. A comparison of Atlanta's urban renewal program with Baltimore's program shows some striking differences. Atlanta, for example, has been much more inclined to use total clearance and also more likely to convert land from a residential to a nonresidential use. See Clarence N. Stone and Robert K. Whelan, "Urban Renewal Policy and City Politics: Urban Renewal in Atlanta and Baltimore," in *Proceedings of the Georgia Political Science Association* (Athens, Georgia: University of Georgia, Institute of Government, 1972), pp. 173–213. On Atlanta's low tax rate, see chapter 5, note 37, above.

7. See, for example, the arguments discussed by William G. Grigsby, "A General Strategy for Urban Renewal," in *Urban Renewal*, ed. James Q. Wilson (Cambridge, Mass.: M. I. T. Press, 1966), p. 661; Jerome Rothenberg, *Economic Evaluation of Urban Renewal* (Washington, D.C.: Brookings Institution, 1967), pp. 27, 70–78, 85–96, 234; and Greer, *Urban Renewal and American Cities*, pp. 31–34.

8. Edward C. Banfield, *The Unheavenly City* (Boston: Little, Brown & Co., 1970), p. 62.

9. The quoted phrase is from Edelman, *Symbolic Uses of Politics*, p. 8. The Edelman theory would appear to be much more appropriate for the *status* aims of *blacks* in Atlanta than for the *welfare* aims of *neighborhood groups*.

10. Lipsky, *Protest in City Politics*, p. 202.

11. On the campaign and election see Allen with Hemphill, *Mayor*, pp. 219–36; Bartley, *From Thurmond to Wallace*, pp. 96–101; and Rooks, "The Atlanta Election of 1969." By all accounts, Massell made peace with the business community shortly after he assumed office, and he worked closely with the business community in promoting perhaps the major policy measure of his mayoralty, Atlanta's mass transit system. Renewal policy was not a matter of high priority with Massell.

12. A thorough analysis of the 1973 campaign has been done by Robert K. Whelan and Michael W. McKinney, "Black-White Coalition Politics and the Atlanta Mayoralty Election of 1973" (Paper presented at the Annual Meeting of the Georgia Political Science Association, Athens, Ga., 1–2 February 1974).

13. *Washington Post*, 10 October 1971.

14. *Atlanta Constitution*, 28 June 1973.

15. Ibid., 13 December 1973.

Chapter 13

1. The initial criteria for including a policy interest for examination was that the interest be articulated by more than one actor in the community and that it show continuity beyond one year. In grouping demands, the broadest possible categories were used. Ideological opposition to federally subsidized low-income housing in redevelopment and relocation gave rise to a few demands that are not included in the tabular presentation below because they represent a narrowly based (and, to some extent, time-bound) policy position and can be discussed adequately as opposition to other policy interests. A few other isolated demands could be identified, but were not included in the analysis since they were isolated. The two policy alternatives discussed below thus represent almost all of the visible demands for urban renewal action related to land use, and they represent a clearly recurring cleavage of interest in the community.

2. If only those demands reaching the stage of official decision making are tabulated, the results are as follows:

Policy Alternative	Total Number of Demands	Number and Percentage Encountering Opposition
CBD renewal (business-supported)	28	19 (68%)
Residential and neighborhood renewal (nonbusiness-supported)	30	12 (40%)

3. Dahl, *Who Governs?*, p. 84.

4. Demands do not differ from decisions in this regard. The weighting problem is basically unsolvable. While there is a common sense appeal to suggestions like those of Nelson Polsby's that decisions be ranked in accordance with criteria such as the number of people affected and the amount of resources distributed, there are inherent difficulties with these criteria. Specifically, a partially formed proposal that receives strong official backing may be expanded into a large program whereas a similarly undeveloped proposal that lacks official backing may be kept on a small-scale level. Thus the number of people affected or the amount of money allocated is itself a heavily influenced matter and not a neutrally engendered object. Further, size of budget and scope of impact may be more easily estimated for a policy area such as urban renewal (which may be what Polsby had in mind, anyway) than for a decision or even a demand. Also see the comments by Frey, "Issues and Nonissues," 1082–88.

5. See Dwaine Marvick, *Political Decision-Makers* (n.p: Free Press of Glencoe, 1961), p. 15; Dahl, *Who Governs?*, p. 91; Merelman, "Neo-Elitist Critique," pp. 459–60; and Dahl and Lindblom, *Politics, Economics, and Welfare*, pp. 309, 333–34.

6. A particularly insightful analysis is presented by Charles H. Levine and Clifford Kaufman, "Urban Conflict as a Constraint on Mayoral Leadership: Lessons from Gary and Cleveland," *American Politics Quarterly* 2 (January 1974): 78–106.

7. Banfield, *Political Influence*, p. 276.

8. The phrase is Dahl's, "Critique of the Ruling Elite Model," p. 467.

9. Wolfinger, "Nondecisions," p. 1067.

10. Dahl, *Who Governs?*, pp. 137, 309–10; Polsby, *Community Power*, pp. 128, 130–31; Wildavsky, *Leadership in a Small Town*, pp. 277, 343–45; Wolfinger, "Nondecisions," p. 1067; and Banfield, *Political Influence*, pp. 240, 252, 270.

11. Wildavsky, *Leadership in a Small Town*, p. 345.

12. Polsby, *Community Power*, p. 137.

13. Banfield, *Political Influence*, p. 253.

14. Wildavsky, *Leadership in a Small Town*, p. 332.

15. See Merelman, "Neo-Elitist Critique," p. 457. It might be argued that not all conflict outcomes are important, only the outcomes of key issues. Presumably, if power relations do not seem to correspond with outcomes at a given time, the researcher could look for key issues in an earlier time period. However, such a research process begins to

smack of "infinite regression" against which pluralists have argued so persuasively (Polsby, *Community Power*, pp. 34, 50–51).

16. Jennings and Zeigler, "Class, Party, and Race," pp. 401–3.

17. Cf. Frey, "Issues and Nonissues," p. 1094.

18. The comment was made partly in reference to Georgia Baptist Hospital and its financial capacity to acquire land. The tactic imputed to the hospital was to buy out one lot owner in a block and then use that as a way to convince others that they could not hold out forever and should therefore sell while they could receive a good price. The hospital, incidentally, conducted these transactions through a black real estate company.

Chapter 14

1. John C. Harsanyi, "The Measurement of Social Power, Opportunity Costs, and the Theory of Two Person Bargaining Games," *Behavioral Science* 7 (January 1962), p. 69.

2. Anthony Downs, *Urban Problems and Prospects* (Chicago: Markham Publishing Co., 1970), p. 38.

3. On the latter point, see Dahl's discussion of "the new men" (*Who Governs?*, pp. 52–62).

4. It is tempting to conclude that a two-party system is especially open and adaptable on a continuing basis. See, for example, Theodore J. Lowi, *At the Pleasure of the Mayor* (New York: Free Press of Glencoe, 1964), pp. 23, 197–99. But contrast Rhyne's view of two-party politics at the community level, "Political Parties and Decision Making," pp. 1105–7.

5. Burnham, *Critical Elections*, p. 136.

6. Obviously, the model could be made more complex; feedback loops, for example, could be included. But the purpose of the model here is only to highlight a set of relationships through which the demand conversion phase of policy formation can be related to community context.

7. Community political characteristics, it should be emphasized, are not to be equated with formal structure. The two are related, of course, but the relationships are too complex to use formal structure as a reliable indicator of political characteristics. Atlanta's "weak mayor" form, for example, masks a centralized style of politics. Not to be overlooked, also, is the possibility that a given community, perhaps because of differences in the groups involved, might have contrasting styles of politics for different policy areas. Law enforcement might, for example, be administered in an unreformed manner while in the same city education or redevelopment might be conducted in a reform style.

Bibliographical Note

Urban renewal has always required hearings and extensive documentation because it is federally assisted, it calls for large expenditures of money, and it involves sensitive race-relations issues. The written record is thus an important, but not the sole, source of materials on Atlanta's urban renewal experience. The following bibliography lists some of the major references, documents, and reports, but a wealth of other materials was used. These can be categorized as follows: (1) newspapers, (2) interviews, and (3) miscellaneous written materials that include minutes, official reports, documents, newsletters, petitions and statements by citizen groups, letters, and memoranda.

Three newspapers were used for an ongoing account of significant events. The two large-circulation dailies, the *Atlanta Constitution* (morning) and the *Atlanta Journal* (afternoon), are jointly owned and co-publish a Sunday issue. The *Atlanta Daily World* is a small-circulation paper but it is, as the name indicates, a daily paper; it is black-owned. The *Constitution* and the *Journal* very generously allowed me to use their clipping file. In addition, the Atlanta Public Library and the Atlanta Housing Authority also maintain clipping files, which were available to me.

Open-ended interviews were conducted with 128 persons (whose background characteristics are described in chapter 4, note 9). Most interviews were thirty minutes to an hour in length, though many ran for a longer time. Several persons were interviewed two or more times, and some supplemented their oral comments with written materials from their personal files. All interviews were conducted on a not-for-attribution basis.

The miscellaneous written materials were available from a variety of sources. These included official minutes of aldermanic committees, the Urban Renewal Policy Committee, the Citizens Advisory Committee for Urban Renewal (CACUR), and the Housing Resources Committee (HRC). The central and regional offices of the U.S. Department of Housing and Urban Development allowed me complete use of their libraries and urban renewal files. At the city level, the files of the Department of Planning and of CACUR were fully open and particularly valuable sources of a variety of materials. Supplementary materials were obtained from the Atlanta Housing Authority and the Community Council of the Atlanta Area. The latter was an especially valuable source of information on neighborhoods and neighborhood groups. Two members of HRC gave me complete access to their personal files on the committee. The actions and objectives of the business community were traced largely through the newsletters of the Central Atlanta Improvement Association (CAIA) and the reports of the Uptown Association and the Urban Renewal Committee of the Atlanta Chamber of Commerce.

Books and Articles

Aberbach, Joel D., and Walker, Jack L. *Race in the City: Political Trust and Public Policy in the New Urban System*. Boston: Little, Brown & Co., 1973.

Abrams, Charles. *The City Is the Frontier*. New York: Harper & Row, 1965.

Adams, Samuel L. "Blueprint for Segregation: A Survey of Atlanta Housing." *New South* 22 (Spring 1967): 73–84.

Agger, Robert; Goldrich, Daniel; and Swanson, Bert E. *The Rulers and the Ruled: Political Power and Impotence in American Communities*. New York: John Wiley & Sons, 1964.

Alford, Robert R., with the collaboration of Scoble, Harry M. *Bureaucracy and Participation: Political Cultures in Four Wisconsin Cities*. Chicago: Rand McNally & Co., 1969.

Allen, Ivan, Jr., with Hemphill, Paul. *Mayor: Notes on the Sixties*. New York: Simon & Schuster, 1971.

Bachrach, Peter, and Baratz, Morton S. *Power and Poverty: Theory and Practice*. New York: Oxford University Press, 1970.

Bacote, C. A. "The Negro in Atlanta Politics." *Phylon* 16 (1955): 333–50.

Banfield, Edward C. *Big City Politics*. New York: Random House, 1965.

————. *Political Influence*. New York: Free Press of Glencoe, 1961.

————. *The Unheavenly City: The Nature and Future of Our Urban Crisis*. Boston: Little, Brown & Co., 1970.

Banfield, Edward C., and Wilson, James Q. *City Politics*. Cambridge, Mass.: Harvard University Press, 1963.

Bartley, Numan V. "Atlanta Elections and Georgia Political Trends." *New South* 25 (Winter 1970): 22–30.

————. *From Thurmond to Wallace: Political Tendencies in Georgia, 1948–1968*. Baltimore: Johns Hopkins Press, 1970.

Bayton, James A. *Tension in the Cities: Three Programs for Survival*. Philadelphia: Chilton Book Co., 1969.

Bellush, Jewel, and David, Stephen M. *Race and Politics in New York City: Five Studies in Policy-Making*. New York: Praeger Publishers, 1971.

Bellush, Jewel, and Hausknecht, Murray. *Urban Renewal: People, Politics and Planning*. Garden City, N.Y.: Doubleday & Co., Anchor Books, 1967.

Bloomberg, Warner, Jr., and Schmandt, Henry J., eds. *Power, Poverty, and Urban Policy*. Urban Affairs Annual Reviews, vol. 2. Beverly Hills, Calif.: Sage Publications, 1968.

Braybrooke, David, and Lindblom, Charles E. *A Strategy of Decision: Policy Evaluation as a Social Process*. New York: Free Press of Glencoe, 1963.

Brugmann, Bruce, and Sletteland, Greggar, eds. *The Ultimate Highrise: San Francisco's Mad Rush toward the Sky*. San Francisco: San Francisco Bay Guardian Books, 1971.

Burnham, Walter Dean. *Critical Elections and the Mainsprings of American Politics*. New York: W. W. Norton & Co., 1970.

Carmichael, Stokely, and Hamilton, Charles V. *Black Power: The Politics of Liberation in America*. New York: Random House, Vintage Books, 1967.

Cater, Douglass. "Atlanta: Smart Politics and Good Race Relations." *Reporter*, 11 July 1957, pp. 18–21.

Champlin, John R. "On the Study of Power." *Politics and Society* 1 (November 1970): 91–111.

"Citizen Participation in Urban Renewal." *Columbia Law Review* 66 (March 1966): 485–607.

Clark, Terry N. "Community Structure, Decision-Making, Budget Expenditures, and Urban Renewal in 51 American Communities." *American Sociological Review* 33 (August 1968): 576–93.

————, ed. *Community Structure and Decision-Making: Comparative Analyses*. San Francisco: Chandler Publishing Co., 1968.

Clarke, James W. "Environment, Process and Policy: A Reconsideration." *American Political Science Review* 63 (December 1969): 1172–82.

Cleghorn, Reese. "Allen of Atlanta Collides with Black Power and Racism." *New York Times Magazine*, 16 October 1966, pp. 32 ff.

Cobb, Roger W., and Elder, Charles D. "The Politics of Agenda Building." *Journal of Politics* 33 (November 1961): 892–915.

Connolly, William E., ed. *The Bias of Pluralism*. New York: Atherton Press, 1969.

Conway, M. Margaret, and Feigert, Frank B. *Political Analysis: An Introduction*. Boston: Allyn & Bacon, 1972.

Coulter, Philip B. "Comparative Community Politics and Public Policy." *Polity* 3 (Fall 1970): 22–43.

Crain, Robert L. *The Politics of School Desegregation: Comparative Case Studies of Community Structure and Policy-Making*. Chicago: Aldine Publishing Co., 1968.

Crain, Robert L.; Katz, Elihu; and Rosenthal, Donald B. *The Politics of Community Conflict*. Indianapolis: Bobbs-Merrill Co., 1969.

Crenson, Matthew A. *The Un-Politics of Air Pollution: A Study of Non-Decisionmaking in the Cities*. Baltimore: Johns Hopkins Press, 1971.

Dahl, Robert A. "The Analysis of Influence in Local Communities." In *Urban Planning and Social Policy*, edited by Bernard J. Frieden and Robert Morris. New York: Basic Books, 1968.

_____. "A Critique of the Ruling Elite Model." *American Political Science Review* 52 (June 1958): 463–69.

_____. *Pluralist Democracy in the United States: Conflict and Consent*. Chicago: Rand McNally & Co., 1967.

_____. *A Preface to Democratic Theory*. Chicago: University of Chicago Press, 1956.

_____. *Who Governs?: Democracy and Power in an American City*. New Haven: Yale University Press, 1961.

Dahl, Robert A., and Lindblom, Charles E. *Politics, Economics, and Welfare: Planning and Politico-Economic Systems Resolved into Basic Social Processes*. New York: Harper & Brothers, 1953.

Daland, Robert T. *Dixie City: A Portrait of Political Leadership*. Birmingham: University of Alabama, Bureau of Public Administration, 1956.

D'Antonio, William V., and Form, William H. *Influentials in Two Border Cities: A Study in Community Decision-Making*. Notre Dame, Ind.: University of Notre Dame Press, 1965.

Davies, J. Clarence, III. *Neighborhood Groups and Urban Renewal*. New York: Columbia University Press, 1966.

Davis, Morris, and Weinbaum, Marvin G. *Metropolitan Decision Processes: An Analysis of Case Studies*. Chicago: Rand McNally & Co., 1969.

Dawson, Richard E., and Robinson, James A. "Inter-Party Competition, Economic Variables, and Welfare Policies in the American States." *Journal of Politics* 25 (May 1963): 265–89.

Doig, Jameson W., and Danielson, Michael N. "Politics and Urban Development: The Case of the New York Region." *International Journal of Comparative Sociology* 7 (March 1966): 76–95.

Downs, Anthony. *Urban Problems and Prospects*. Chicago: Markham Publishing Co., 1970.

Dye, Thomas R. "Community Power Studies." In *Political Science Annual: An International Review*, edited by James A. Robinson, vol. 2. Indianapolis: Bobbs-Merrill Co., 1970.

_____. "Governmental Structure, Urban Environment and Educational Policy." *Midwest Journal of Political Science* 11 (August 1967): 353–80.

————. *Politics, Economics, and the Public: Policy Outcomes in the American States*. Chicago: Rand McNally & Co., 1966.

Edelman, Murray. *The Symbolic Uses of Politics*. Urbana: University of Illinois Press, 1964.

Edgar, Richard E. *Urban Power and Social Welfare: Corporate Influence in an American City*. Beverly Hills, Calif.: Sage Publications, 1970.

English, James W. *Handyman of the Lord: The Life and Ministry of the Reverend William Holmes Borders*. New York: Meredith Press, 1967.

Eulau, Heinz, and Eyestone, Robert. "Policy Maps of City Councils and Policy Outcomes." *American Political Science Review* 62 (March 1968): 124–44.

Eulau, Heinz, and Pruitt, Kenneth. *Labyrinths of Democracy: Adaptations, Linkages, Representation, and Policies in Urban Politics*. Indianapolis: Bobbs-Merrill Co., 1973.

Fainstein, Norman I., and Fainstein, Susan S. *Urban Political Movements: The Search for Power by Minority Groups in American Cities*. Englewood Cliffs, N.J.: Prentice-Hall, 1974.

Fesler, James W. "The Case Method in Political Science." In *Essays on the Case Method in Public Administration*, edited by Edwin A. Bock. New York: International Institute of Administrative Sciences, 1962.

Flaming, Karl H.; Paleu, J. John; Ringlien, Grant; and Taylor, Corneff. "Black Powerlessness in Policy-Making Positions." *Sociological Quarterly* 13 (Winter 1972): 126–33.

Foard, Ashley A., and Fefferman, Holbert. "Federal Urban Renewal Legislation." *Law and Contemporary Problems* 25 (Autumn 1960): 635–86.

Fox, Douglas M. "Methods within Methods." *Western Political Quarterly* 24 (March 1971): 5–11.

Frey, Frederick W. "Comment: On Issues and Nonissues in the Study of Power." *American Political Science Review* 65 (December 1971): 1081–1101.

Friedman, Lawrence M. *Government and Slum Housing. A Century of Frustration*. Chicago: Rand McNally & Co., 1968.

Glazer, Nathan, and McEntire, Davis, eds. *Studies in Housing and Minority Groups*. Berkeley and Los Angeles: University of California Press, 1960.

Greenstone, J. David, and Peterson, Paul E. *Race and Authority in Urban Politics: Community Participation and the War on Poverty*. New York: Russell Sage Foundation, 1973.

Greer, Scott. *Urban Renewal and American Cities*. Indianapolis: Bobbs-Merrill Co., 1965.

Grigsby, William G. "A General Strategy for Urban Renewal." In *Urban Renewal: The Record and the Controversy*, edited by James Q. Wilson. Cambridge, Mass.: M. I. T. Press, 1966.

Hahn, Harlan, ed. *People and Politics in Urban Society*. Urban Affairs Annual Reviews, vol. 6. Beverly Hills, Calif.: Sage Publications, 1972.

Hamilton, Charles V. "Blacks and the Crisis in Political Participation." *Public Interest*, no. 34 (Winter 1974): 188–210.

————. "Conflict, Race and System-Transformation in the United States." *Journal of International Affairs* 23 (1969): 106–18.

Harsanyi, John C. "Measurement of Social Power, Opportunity Costs, and the Theory of Two-Person Bargaining Games." *Behavioral Science* 7 (January 1962): 67–80.

Hartman, Chester. *Yerba Buena: Land Grab and Community Resistance in San Francisco*. San Francisco: Glide Publications, 1974.

Hawkins, Brett W. *Politics and Urban Policies*. Indianapolis: Bobbs-Merrill Co., 1971.

Hawley, Willis D., and Svara, James H. *The Study of Community Power: A Bibliographic Review*. Santa Barbara, Calif.: ABC-Clio, 1972.

Hawley, Willis D., and Wirt, Frederick M., eds. *The Search for Community Power*. Englewood Cliffs, N.J.: Prentice-Hall, 1968.

Hayes, Edward C. *Power Structure and Urban Policy: Who Rules in Oakland*. New York: McGraw-Hill Book Co., 1972.

"Hector Black: White Power in Black Atlanta." *Look*, 13 December 1966, pp. 137–40.

Herson, Lawrence J. R. "In the Footsteps of Community Power." *American Political Science Review* 55 (December 1961): 817–30.

Holland, Lynwood M. "Atlanta Pioneers in Merger." *National Municipal Review* 41 (April 1952): 182–86.

Holloway, Harry. *The Politics of the Southern Negro: From Exclusion to Big City Organization*. New York: Random House, 1969.

"Housing and Minority Groups." *Phylon* 19 (Spring 1958).

Huber, Joan, and Form, William H. *Income and Ideology: An Analysis of the American Political Formula*. New York: Free Press, 1973.

Hughes, M. Clyde. "Annexation and Reallocation of Functions." *Public Management* 34 (February 1952): 26–30.

Hunter, Floyd. *Community Power Structure: A Study of Decision Makers*. Chapel Hill: University of North Carolina Press, 1953.

Hutcheson, John D., Jr., and Steggert, Frank X. *Organized Citizen Participation in Urban Areas*. Studies in Urban Change, no. 1. Atlanta: Emory University, Center for Research in Social Change, n.d.

International City Managers' Association. *The Municipal Year Book, 1963*. Chicago: International City Managers' Association, 1963.

International Encyclopedia of the Social Sciences. 2d ed. S.v. "Ideology," by Edward Shils.

Ivey, John E., Jr.; Demerath, Nicholas J.; and Breland, Woodrow W. *Building Atlanta's Future*. Chapel Hill: University of North Carolina Press, 1948.

Jennings, M. Kent. *Community Influentials: The Elites of Atlanta*. New York: Free Press of Glencoe, 1964.

Jennings, M. Kent, and Zeigler, Harmon. "Class, Party, and Race in Four Types of Elections: The Case of Atlanta." *Journal of Politics* 28 (May 1966): 391–407.

Kaplan, Harold. *Urban Renewal Politics: Slum Clearance in Newark*. New York: Columbia University Press, 1963.

Keech, William R. *The Impact of Negro Voting: The Role of the Vote in the Quest for Equality*. Chicago: Rand McNally & Co., 1968.

Keynes, Edward, and Ricci, David, eds. *Political Power, Community and Democracy*. Chicago: Rand McNally & Co., 1970.

Kirby, David J.; Harris, T. Robert; and Crain, Robert L. With a chapter by Christine H. Rossell. *Political Strategies in Northern School Desegregation*. Lexington, Mass.: D. C. Heath & Co., Lexington Books, 1973.

Kotter, John P., and Lawrence, Paul R. *Mayors in Action: Five Approaches to Urban Governance*. New York: John Wiley & Sons, 1974.

Ladd, Everett Carll, Jr. *Ideology in America: Change and Response in a City, a Suburb, and a Small Town*. New York: W. W. Norton & Co., 1969.

Levine, Charles H., and Kaufman, Clifford. "Urban Conflict as a Constraint on Mayoral Leadership: Lessons from Gary and Cleveland." *American Politics Quarterly* 2 (January 1974): 78–106.

Lindblom, Charles E. *The Intelligence of Democracy: Decision Making through Mutual Adjustment*. New York: Free Press, 1965.

Lineberry, Robert L., and Fowler, Edmund P. "Reformism and Public Policies in American Cities." *American Political Science Review* 61 (September 1967): 701–16.

Lipsky, Michael. *Protest in City Politics: Rent Strikes, Housing and the Power of the Poor*. Chicago: Rand McNally & Co., 1970.

Long, Norton. "The Local Community as an Ecology of Games." *American Journal of Sociology* 64 (November 1958): 251–61.

Lowe, Jeanne R. *Cities in a Race with Time: Progress and Poverty in America's Renewing Cities*. New York: Random House, 1967.

Lowi, Theodore J. *At the Pleasure of the Mayor: Patronage and Power in New York City*. New York: Free Press of Glencoe, 1964.

Lowry, Ritchie P. *Who's Running This Town?: Community Leadership and Social Change*. New York: Harper & Row, 1965.

Lynd, Robert S., and Lynd, Helen M. *Middletown: A Study in Contemporary American Culture*. New York: Harcourt, Brace & Co., 1929.

————. *Middletown in Transition: A Study in Cultural Conflicts*. New York: Harcourt, Brace & Co., 1937.

McFarland, Andrew S. *Power and Leadership in Pluralist Systems*. Stanford: Stanford University Press, 1969.

McGill, Ralph. "You'd Think He Owns Atlanta." *Saturday Evening Post*, 31 October 1953.

Marris, Peter. "A Report on Urban Renewal in the United States." In *The Environment of the Metropolis*, edited by Leonard J. Duhl. New York: Basic Books, 1963.

Martin, Roscoe C.; Munger, Frank J.; Burkhead, Jesse; Birkhead, Guthrie S.; Herman, Harold; Kagi, Herbert M.; Welch, Lewis P.; and Wingfield, Clyde J. *Decisions in Syracuse*. Bloomington: Indiana University Press, 1961.

Marvick, Dwaine. *Political Decision-makers*. N.p.: Free Press of Glencoe, 1961.

Merelman, Richard M. "On the Neo-Elitist Critique of Community Power." *American Political Science Review* 62 (June 1968): 451–60.

Montgomery, Robert. "Notes on Instant Urban Renewal." *Trans-action* 9 (September 1967): 9–12.

Mowitz, Robert J., and Wright, Deil S. *Profile of a Metropolis: A Case Book*. Detroit: Wayne State University Press, 1962.

Murin, William J. *Mass Transit Policy Planning: An Incremental Approach*. Lexington, Mass.: D. C. Heath & Co., Lexington Books, 1971.

Murphy, Russell D. *Political Entrepreneurs and Urban Poverty: The Strategies of Policy Innovation in New Haven's Model Anti-Poverty Project*. Lexington, Mass.: D. C. Heath & Co., Lexington Books, 1971.

Olson, Mancur, Jr. *The Logic of Collective Action: Public Goods and the Theory of Groups*. 1965. Reprint. New York: Schocken Books, 1968.

Parenti, Michael. "The Possibilities for Political Change." *Politics and Society* 1 (November 1970): 79–90.

———. "Power and Pluralism: A View from the Bottom." *Journal of Politics* 32 (August 1970): 501–30.

Peirce, Neal R. *The Deep South States of America: People, Politics, and Power in the Seven Deep South States*. New York: W. W. Norton & Co., 1974.

Piven, Frances Fox, and Cloward, Richard A. *Regulating the Poor: The Foundations of Public Welfare*. New York: Random House, Pantheon Books, 1971.

Polsby, Nelson W. *Community Power and Political Theory*. New Haven: Yale University Press, 1963.

Powledge, Fred. "Profiles: A New Politics in Atlanta." *New Yorker*, 31 December 1973, pp. 28–40.

Presthus, Robert. *Men at the Top: A Study in Community Power*. New York: Oxford University Press, 1964.

Prewitt, Kenneth. "Political Ambitions, Volunteerism, and Electoral Accountability." *American Political Science Review* 64 (March 1970): 5–17.

Price, Hugh Douglas. Review of *Who Governs?*, by Robert A. Dahl. *Yale Law Journal* 71 (July 1962): 1589–96.

Rakoff, Stuart H., and Schaefer, Guenther F. "Politics, Policy, and Political Science: Theoretical Alternatives." *Politics and Society* 1 (November 1970): 51–77.

Rhyne, Edwin Hoffman. "Political Parties and Decision Making in Three Southern Counties." *American Political Science Review* 52 (December 1958): 1091–1107.

Ricci, David. *Community Power and Democratic Theory: The Logic of Political Analysis*. New York: Random House, 1971.

Rogers, Chester B. "Environment, System and Output: The Consideration of a Model." *Social Forces* 48 (September 1969): 72–87.

Rooks, Charles S. *The Atlanta Election of 1969*. Atlanta: Voter Education Project, 1970.

Rossi, Peter H. "Power and Community Structure." *Midwest Journal of Political Science* 4 (November 1960): 390–401.

Rossi, Peter H., and Dentler, Robert A. *The Politics of Urban Renewal: The Chicago Findings*. New York: Free Press of Glencoe, 1961.

Rothenberg, Jerome. *Economic Evaluation of Urban Renewal: Conceptual Foundations of Benefit-Cost Analysis*. Washington, D.C.: Brookings Institution, 1967.

Salisbury, Robert H. "Urban Politics: The New Convergence of Power." *Journal of Politics* 26 (November 1964): 775–97.

Savitch, Harold V. "Powerlessness in an Urban Ghetto." *Polity* 5 (Fall 1972): 19–56.

Sayre, Wallace, and Kaufman, Herbert. *Governing New York City: Politics in the Metropolis*. 1960. Reprint. New York: W. W. Norton & Co. for the Russell Sage Foundation, 1965.

Schattschneider, E. E. *The Semi-Sovereign People: A Realist's View of Democracy in America*. New York: Holt, Rinehart & Winston, 1960.

Schemmel, Bill. "Atlanta's 'Power Structure' Faces Life." *New South* 27 (Spring 1972): 62–68.

Scoble, Harry. "Leadership Hierarchies and Political Issues in a New England

Town.'' In *Community Political Systems*, edited by Morris Janowitz. Glencoe, Ill.: Free Press, 1961.

Scott, Austin. ''The New Mayor Atlanta Style.'' *Washington Post*, 27 January 1974.

Sitton, Claude. ''Atlanta Example: Good Sense and Dignity.'' *New York Times Magazine*, 6 May 1962, pp. 22 ff.

Spector, Samuel Ira. *Municipal and County Zoning in a Changing Urban Environment*. Research Paper no. 53. Atlanta: Georgia State University, School of Business Administration, Bureau of Business and Economic Research, 1970.

Stinchcombe, Jean L. *Reform and Reaction: City Politics in Toledo*. Belmont, Calif.: Wadsworth Publishing Co., 1968.

Stone, Chuck. *Black Political Power in America*, Rev. ed. New York: Dell Publishing Co., Delta Book, 1970.

Stone, Clarence N., and Whelan, Robert K. ''Urban Renewal Policy and City Politics: Urban Renewal in Atlanta and Baltimore.'' In *Proceedings of the Georgia Political Science Association*. Athens, Ga.: University of Georgia, Institute of Government, 1972.

Taeuber, Karl E., and Taeuber, Alma F. *Negroes in Cities: Residential Segregation and Neighborhood Change*. Chicago: Aldine Publishing Co., 1965.

Terrell, Robert L. ''Black Awareness versus Negro Traditions: Atlanta University Center.'' *New South* 24 (Winter 1969): 29–40.

Verba, Sidney, and Nie, Norman H. *Participation in America: Political Democracy and Social Equality*. New York: Harper & Row, 1972.

Vidich, Arthur J., and Bensman, Joseph. *Small Town in Mass Society: Class, Power and Religion in a Rural Community*. Princeton: Princeton University Press, 1958.

Walker, Jack L. ''Negro Voting in Atlanta, 1953–1961.'' *Phylon* 24 (Winter 1963): 379–87.

———. ''Protest and Negotiation: A Case Study of Negro Leadership in Atlanta, Georgia.'' *Midwest Journal of Political Science* 7 (May 1963): 99–124.

Walter, Benjamin. ''On the Logical Analysis of Power Attribution Procedures.'' *Journal of Politics* 26 (November 1964): 850–66.

Watters, Pat, and Cleghorn, Reese. *Climbing Jacob's Ladder: The Arrival of Negroes in Southern Politics*. New York: Harcourt, Brace & World, 1967.

Whyte, William Foote. *Street Corner Society: The Social Structure of an Italian Slum*. 1943. Enl. ed. Chicago: University of Chicago Press, 1955.

Wildavsky, Aaron. *Leadership in a Small Town*. Totowa, N.J.: Bedminster Press, 1964.

Williams, Oliver P., and Adrian, Charles R. *Four Cities: A Study in Comparative Policy Making*. Philadelphia: University of Pennsylvania Press, 1963.

Wilson, James Q. *Negro Politics: The Search for Leadership*. New York: Free Press, 1960.

———, ed. *Urban Renewal: The Record and the Controversy*. Cambridge, Mass.: M. I. T. Press, 1966.

Wirt, Frederick M. ''Alioto and the Politics of Hyperpluralism.'' *Trans-action* 7 (April 1970): 46–55.

Wolfinger, Raymond E. ''Nondecisions and the Study of Local Politics.'' *American Political Science Review* 65 (December 1971): 1063–80.

Wolman, Harold W., and Thomas, Norman C. ''Black Interests, Black Groups, and Black Influence in the Federal Policy Process." *Journal of Politics* 32 (November 1970): 875–97.

Documents, Reports, Papers

City of Atlanta. "Application to the Department of Housing and Urban Development for a Grant to Plan a Comprehensive City Demonstration Program." Atlanta: March 1967.

City of Atlanta, City Planning Department. "Nash-Bans Discussion Report no. 1." Atlanta: January 1968.

———. "Northwest-Browntown Area: A Neighborhood Study." Atlanta: October 1967.

City of Atlanta, City Planning Department and Housing Resources Committee. "A Review of Atlanta's Housing Program: Its Problems and Prospects." Atlanta: October 1967.

City of Atlanta, Department of City Planning. *Shall We Rebuild Again?* Atlanta: Department of City Planning, 1959.

City of Atlanta, Department of Planning, Central Area Study Policy Committee. "Central Atlanta: Opportunities and Responses." Atlanta: 1971.

Candeub, Fleissig and Associates. "Equal Opportunity in Housing: Community Improvement Program, City of Atlanta, Georgia, Supplementary Report on Negro Housing Needs and Resources." Atlanta: November 1967.

———. "Final Report, City of Atlanta, Georgia, Equal Opportunity in Housing: Atlanta Community Improvement Program." Atlanta: December 1966, amended June 1967.

———. "Program for Improvement Action: Technical Report: Community Improvement Program, City of Atlanta." Atlanta: July 1967.

Commission on the Cities in the '70's. "The State of the Cities." Washington, D.C.: National Urban Coalition, 1971.

Community Council of the Atlanta Area. "Final Report, City of Atlanta, Georgia, Social Report on Neighborhood Analysis, Atlanta Community Improvement Program." Atlanta: [July 1967].

———. "Interim Report Number 1: Social Blight and Its Causes." [Atlanta]: February 1966.

Eric Hill Associates. "City of Atlanta, Georgia, Report on the Relocation of Individuals, Families and Businesses: Atlanta Community Improvement Program." Atlanta: September 1966.

———. "City of Atlanta, Georgia, Relocation Study Supplement: Atlanta Community Improvement Program." Atlanta: March 1967.

Georgia State Advisory Committee to the U.S. Commission on Civil Rights. *Toward Equal Opportunity in Housing in Atlanta, Georgia*. N.p.: Georgia State Advisory Committee, 1968.

Jones, Mack H. "A Frame of Reference for Black Politics." Paper presented at the Annual Meeting of the Southern Political Science Association, Miami, Fla., 6–8 November 1969.

Metropolitan Planning Commission. *Now, for Tomorrow*. Atlanta: Metropolitan Planning Commission, 1954.

———. *Up Ahead*. Atlanta: Metropolitan Planning Commission, 1952.

Mollenkopf, John H. "On the Causes and Consequences of Neighborhood Political Mobilization." Paper presented at the Annual Meeting of the American Political Science Association, New Orleans, La., 4–8 September 1973.

Public Administration Service. "Report on Administrative-Legal Studies." Chicago: Public Administration Service, June 1967.

Stone, Clarence N. "Overt and Latent Issues in the Urban Renewal Program of Atlanta: A Response to the Pluralist Critique of Non-Decisionmaking." Paper presented at the Annual Meeting of the American Political Science Association, New York, N.Y., 2–5 September 1969.

Tyler, Robert Scott. "Atlanta's West End: A Study of Neighborhood Participation in Urban Renewal." M.A. thesis, Emory University, 1969.

U.S. Commission on Civil Rights. *Hearings before the United States Commission on Civil Rights: Housing, Atlanta, Georgia, April 10, 1959*. Washington, D.C.: Government Printing Office, 1959.

U.S. Congress. House. Committee on Banking and Currency. *Basic Laws and Authorities on Housing and Urban Development*, 91st Cong., 2d sess., 1970.

U.S. Department of Commerce. Bureau of the Census. *Census of Governments, 1967*. Vol. 2, *Taxable Property Value*.

U.S. Department of Housing and Urban Development. *Achieving More Effective Delivery of HUD Local Assistance Programs*. Vol. 2, *Six Field Analyses*, by National Academy of Public Administration. Springfield, Va.: Clearinghouse for Scientific and Technical Information [PB 187 786], 1969.

––––––. *The Model Cities Program*, by Marshall Kaplan, Sheldon P. Gans, and Howard M. Kahn. Washington, D.C.: Government Printing Office, 1969.

––––––. *Urban Renewal Handbook*. 1968.

U.S. Housing and Home Finance Agency. "Program for Community Improvement: Workable Program." 1957.

––––––. *Urban Renewal Handbook*. 1957.

––––––. "Workable Program for Community Improvement." 1962.

U.S. National Commission on Urban Problems. *Building the American City*. Washington, D.C.: Government Printing Office, 1968.

––––––. *Hearings before the National Commission on Urban Problems*, vol. 3. Washington, D.C.: Government Printing Office, 1967.

Uptown Association of Atlanta. "Uptown Ideas." Atlanta: January 1962.

Whelan, Robert K., and McKinney, Michael W. "Black-White Coalition Politics and the Atlanta Mayoralty Election of 1973." Paper presented at the Annual Meeting of the Georgia Political Science Association, Athens, Ga., 1–2 February 1974.